THE ELFISH GENE

Also by the Author

Girlfriend 44
Infidelity for First-Time Fathers
Lucky Dog

THE
ELFISH
GENE

Dungeons, Dragons
and Growing Up Strange

Mark Barrowcliffe

SOHO

First published in the United Kingdom by Macmillan, an imprint of
Pan Macmillan Ltd

Copyright © Mark Barrowcliffe 2007

Published in the United States in 2008 by
Soho Press, Inc.
853 Broadway
New York, NY 10003

Library of Congress Cataloging-in-Publication Data

Barrowcliffe, Mark.
The elfish gene : dungeons, dragons and growing up
strange / Mark Barrowcliffe.
p. cm.
ISBN 978-1-56947-522-5
1. Barrowcliffe, Mark—Childhood and youth. 2. Authors,
English—21st Century—Biography. 3. Teenage boys—
England—Coventry. 4. Dungeons and dragons (Game)—Social
aspects—Humor. I. Title.
PR6052.A7263Z46 2008
823'.914—dc22
2008012471

10 9 8 7 6 5 4 3 2 1

To Tabitha

Avoid this.

CONTENTS

1. An Unhealthy Interest   1

2. The Last Sunshine   5

3. Come to Mordor, It's Nicer Than Where You Live   12

4. Lord of the Ring Binders   26

5. The Land of Shadow   36

6. A Journey in the Dark   53

7. Being Andy Porter   69

8. Pale Exile   82

9. A Conspiracy Unmasked   87

10. A Light in the West   92

11. A Suburban Dragon   101

12. The Gathering of the Clouds   111

13. An Unexpected Party   122

14. Out, Daemon, Out!   135

15. Vigils   146

16. Pilgrimages   151

17. Moonchild   168

18. The Sorcerer's Apprentice   176

19. In the Cave of the Svartmoot   185

20. Time of the Hawklords   194

21. Character Assassination   202

22. The End of Days   215

23. Girls and Other Non-human Creatures   225

24. A Short Cut to Mushrooms   231

25. The Worlds Collide   239

26. The Breaking of the Fellowship   247

27. Dabbling with Reality   252

28. The Shadow of the Past   259

29. The Lost Boys   265

30. Homeward Bound   276

'When Dick Gibson was a little boy, he was not Dick Gibson.'

STANLEY ELKIN
The Dick Gibson Show, 1971

The names of wargamers in this book have been changed to protect their identities. If there ever was a real Andy Porter or Sean Gardener, for instance, in Coventry at that time then they are not the ones portrayed here. Similarly, all teachers, parents and other adults featured here have had their names changed. Only on occasions where I specifically say so, or when I identify the author of a work, are the names real.

An Unhealthy
Interest

An elf cloak is designed to render its user invisible.

Worn in the Coventry shopping precinct when the City soccer team is playing at home, however, it has rather the opposite effect.

What follows explains why, on 24 October 1981, I was thrown into a fountain by soccer hooligans and how I eventually came to wish they'd done it years earlier.

You may consider that you wasted your youth. Perhaps you spent it shooting pool in some smoky hall, locked in your bedroom playing the guitar or just partying hard when you should have been studying.

That is not a waste. That is not even the beginning of a waste. I'll show you a waste. When others were developing the ability to win a few bucks hustling in a local bar, to lead a singalong at a barbecue or just to speak to the opposite sex, what I got for my endeavours was a wizard with a frost wand.

Yes, I spent my youth playing Dungeons and Dragons.

Even though the game was at its height played by millions of boys and two girls around the world, most people today have a hazy idea of what it is. They might know it involves shaking a lot of funny-shaped dice, they might know that players act out the roles of warriors, wizards and priests seeking treasure and adventure in a fantasy kingdom, they may have some recollection of scares involving Satanism and the occult. One fact, however, will be clear in their minds—that everyone who ever played the game more than once was a nerd.

That's all you really need to know to read this book. By the time you've finished you might still have no idea of how to calculate whether an elf kills an orc or whether rolling dice propels you into the arms of Lucifer, but you will, I promise, know your nerds.

I'd like to say the nerd thing is a misconception, but I can't. I should know; I was a total nerd. I probably still am a total nerd, and so was everyone I ever played with—vicious nerds, shy nerds, egotistical nerds, semi-psychotic nerds, but all nerds to a boy. There were no girls, not even nerdy ones.

From what I know of women—which, given the fact I went to a single-sex school, had only brothers and spent my entire youth locked in fart-filled rooms with boys, isn't much—they can also be obsessed. They tend to focus on people, though—pop stars or film stars, boyfriends or even horses, which they treat like people. The image of a schoolgirl obsession is that of a febrile focus on a relationship—a crush.

Men's obsessions are about relationships too, but everything about their culture and upbringing stops them recognizing it, so they focus on things—cars, records, sport. I can't imagine a woman picking up a 1977 copy of *The Monster Manual* as I did the other day and actually stroking it, hugging it. I only just stopped myself muttering 'the precious' under my breath. This represents a significant cooling of ardour.

For five years of my life between eleven and sixteen, I never stopped playing D&D, not even to eat. To this day, I eat one-handed. The other was always for a rule book, a fanzine or a fantasy novel. After that I played less frequently—maybe twice a week—until I was twenty. Today, other than for research for this book, I don't play at all. The legacy of the game, however, is still etched on my personality.

During the time I was playing, the nerds were my whole world.

They were the people I learned to relate to while others were out talking to girls, getting sun tans, having various kinds of fun and even being bored—in short, growing up.

I knew far more about the wants and needs of a golden dragon than I ever did a girl. I was never bored, either. I was always waiting for the next game with a sense of intense anticipation, like most boys do when approaching a first date.

When I was at the gaming table I felt like I was plugged into the power grid, at an absolute peak of excitement and attention. I thought that anything that didn't give you that level of stimulation wasn't worth doing, which was a bit of a problem a few years later when it came to going to work. From what I've heard of other obsessions and addictions, they're similar, and people experience similar levels of difficulty getting over them. The details may differ, but at the root it's the same thing; an obsession is a way for damaged people to damage themselves more.

I've tried to overcome the influence my D&D years had on me and I hope I've made some progress. I have a wife I love and friends I try to treat as equals and not as competitors. Getting there's been a struggle, though. Even now I sometimes don't really feel like an adult, more a recovering adolescent.

It's likely I may have spent years as a social liability without the game; I think I'm probably a natural at it. However, it's one thing to have the talent to be a dope; it's another to put in the practice. That's exactly what I was doing when I was playing D&D.

Though the forces that acted on me while I was a boy were particular to me, they were products of a wider male culture which helps, if that's the right word, men form their identities. D&D was more than a craze; it was a phenomenon, spawning films, cartoon series, toys, novels and, finally—its own undoing— computer games. An estimated 20 million boys worldwide have played the game and spent over £1 billion on its products. Anything that popular with young males clearly speaks to them on a deep level and says something about them. What it says is the subject of this book.

I hope to provide an answer for anyone who has ever looked at a man and thought, 'Why is he such a wanker?'

For many boys who grew up in the seventies and eighties, our peer group and education constituted a sort of wanker factory. This is the story of the operation of its most efficient department.

The
Last Sunshine

Everyone plays roles in life, though they're not always the ones they'd choose.

For a brief, blazing summer in 1976, though, I had that luxury and I chose to be cool.

On the loose and on my own, I turned down my tape recorder in case my mum heard David Bowie's 'Lady from Another Grinning Soul' mention breasts; I wore a baggy sweater with the sleeves too long no matter what the heat, and I tore up my Green Flash sneakers on my Woolworth's Flyer skateboard.

Before setting off for the day I put on a pair of octagonal sunglasses I'd bought from a gift shop at a zoo and a large badge that my dad had got from work: 'Polish a floor and put a rug on it? You might as well set a man trap!' I found this extremely funny and imagined my nan saving time on the polishing in her cleaning job by putting down a huge, spiked, spring-loaded clam.

Now I can see that, even by the standards of the time, I looked like an idiot. However, when you're an oldest son and unobserved, there's no one to tell you you're wrong, and I felt pretty good about myself. The seven weeks of the summer holiday are enough to forget the inhibitions that school requires of you.

Down the road I'd bunk into the playground of my old junior school and meet up with my friend Dill Grigson. Dill was a shy kid who was careful to keep his clothes within social norms, something that was more difficult then than it is now.

At the time I'm writing, kids can wear a Nike tracksuit, swish trainers and a baseball cap and fit in. In the mid-seventies there weren't the same brand names, just a general style of clothing, a feel that you'd interpret for yourself by buying your clothes from catalogues and market stalls. It was easy to get it wrong, as I proved. Dill got it right, with his mild flares, big-collared shirt and centre-parted haircut, though he never commented on what I wore. I'd hang around with him, discussing the wrestling, keeping one eye out for the hard lads from the public housing projects, another to see if the gorgeous Karen Maclachlan had been sent to the shops for cigarettes by her mum.

I remember Karen with her white-blonde hair. She was so delicate and fine-featured she seemed to me to have stepped out of some story—Tinkerbell floating by with a packet of Embassy cigarettes. If I saw her on the horizon I'd put the board to the floor, hold on to my glasses and totter down to the path that led back to her house.

The last time we met sticks in my mind very clearly. It was my final stab at a normal life.

'What you doing?' I said, rolling up to her and stopping, which was lucky. I elected to remain on my skateboard as I always found dismounting from the thing very tricky. Staying on seemed the safe option, particularly as it made me look taller, almost Karen's height.

'Getting fags,' she said. She flicked back her hair—twice, in case I'd missed it the first time. I hadn't missed it the first time.

'Oh, yeah? I'm skateboarding. Wanna see a trick?'

'Go on, then.'

'Got a bad ankle, but I'll show you next time.'

'OK.' She flicked her hair again.

I wanted to ask her for a kiss, but I didn't know how. From what I'd gleaned at school, that sort of thing only went on at youth clubs. Karen attended one, but I hadn't ever summoned up the courage to go to it.

The idea of having to play table tennis, or some other sport at which I was invariably rubbish, in front of other boys and, more horrifically, girls made me hotter than even my sweater did on that boiling day. Anyway, I knew very well that anyone who ever walked through the door of a youth club was instantly beaten to death, and by fifteen-year-olds, too. Worse than being picked on by bigger boys, though, I might get picked on by a tough smaller boy. Worse than that, I might get picked on by a weedy smaller boy. That had happened before. I felt a shiver of shame even thinking about it. Fighting just wasn't my thing.

Several of these tough boys lived near Karen, and it was a nightmare of mine that she'd be impressed by their gum-chewing, bus-stop-defacing, insouciant disregard for authority and start going out with them.

Karen and I stood looking at each other, me wobbling slightly in an effort to keep my balance. I knew you were meant to kiss girls, but there was something else that you were meant to do first, and I didn't know what it was. I had no tricks to impress her with, no amazing collection of soccer cards or bubblegum stickers; I couldn't even put my hand under my arm and make a quacking noise, which I knew Stewart MacMahon, who lived next door to her, could because that's all he'd done for one whole lesson when I'd been trying to hear Miss Raybley tell us about Richard III. That was it.

'Richard the third,' I said, 'gave battle in vain.'

She continued looking at me without expression.

'It's an ace way of remembering the order of the colours of the rainbow,' I said, 'Red . . .' I couldn't remember what colour began with T. Turquoise. 'Red, turquoise, green, blue, indigo, violet.' I paused for effect. 'Little tip,' I said, touching my nose and pointing my finger at her. My scout master Skip did that and I thought it looked very grown-up, wrong though I clearly was.

Karen nodded.

'I better get back with my mum's cigs.'

'See ya,' I said.

'See ya.'

I waited until she had turned away and then went for a two-footed dismount, taking them off one at a time being a bit difficult for me. It was slightly surprising to find myself on two feet and with the board next to me. Emboldened by this success, I swept it up from the floor in an extravagant arc with a loud 'Easy!' Karen didn't take a backwards glance.

I walked back to Dill. It's difficult to skateboard uphill, and, having hopped off without incident, I didn't want to push my luck. As I made my way up the path I kicked the board in front of me, hoping that would disguise the twist I have on my left leg when I walk, should Karen turn around.

'Who's that?' said Dill.

'Karen,' I said. 'She's my girlfriend.'

'You should pull in your belly when you talk to her,' said Dill, swelling himself up like the Incredible Hulk. 'Girls like the look of it.'

'How do you know that?'

'My brother told me. Little tip.' He touched his nose and pointed at me. He went to the same scouts as me. 'It's especially important at Cov Baths. What you look like in trunks is essential for girls.' Dill had learned the word 'essential' from his brother the week before and was using it as often as he could in an effort to appear mature.

Cov was Coventry, city of my birth and upbringing, of big wide roads, factories, concrete and the sixties municipal aesthetic. The historic centre of the city had been flattened in World War II, and it had been rebuilt as an experiment in modern living. The experiment had failed. Within a couple of years of going up, the tower blocks and pedestrianized shopping complex had come to resemble a giant, run-down multi-storey car park. This is the city where The Specials wrote 'Ghost Town.'

Dill and I lived in the suburbs, away from the desolate city centre but near to the roaring A45 and the Whoberley projects, all two-up two-down houses, thin walls, pebble dashing and large, half-empty car parks. A thick feeling of apathy lay on the entire area. The estate wasn't yet ten years old, and already it looked shabby but not what you'd call deprived. It was as if it had given inner-city deprivation a go but decided that, in the end, it couldn't be bothered with it.

I pulled in my belly as an experiment. I didn't have much of a belly to pull in but I thought I'd try Dill's tip. His older brother was a marvellous source of information on anything about life.

It was then I realized I'd made a terrible mistake. It wasn't 'Richard the Third gave battle in vain' like I'd said; it was Richard of York. Red, orange, yellow, green, blue, indigo, violet. She was going to think I was a complete dunce.

I just wasn't making it with girls. The future, I decided, would be different. I would discover what it was you did between just talking to a girl and kissing her. How you bring up the subject of kissing, for instance? I would perfect a special girl-impressing trick. I had it in my mind that I could start carrying around this magic cup I'd got with a conjuring set for my birthday. You put a small ball in, put the lid on the cup and then, 'Hey Presto!', took the lid off to show it transformed into a larger ball.

Dill, who was more in touch with sex and reality than me, had suggested the best approach to girls was to get them to come back to your house when your mum and dad were out. You then turned up the fire really hot so they would have to take off all their clothes. I'd been filled with the erotic possibilities of this idea until I realized that, in the hour and a half from when I got back from school to when my mum got in it would be difficult to get Karen into my house, boil her half to death and strip her naked, while hoping my brothers would be out playing.

Also, and this had killed the fantasy entirely, my mum would study the gas bill, notice the heavy fuel consumption and demand an explanation. It was a non-starter.

The other obstacle before us, as Dill and I were painfully aware, was that we were both yet to hit puberty. Dill used to talk about it as if it were winning the lottery, being given the keys to the city and taking Olympic gold all at the same time. I was still unsure exactly what would happen. My only experience of sex, other than lots of speculative conversations with Dill, was hearing Spec Clarke in the school library read out bits of the saucy novels she'd pinched from her mum. I could stand the embarrassment up to 'he caressed her smooth breasts beneath the light cheesecloth of her blouse,' but when we got to 'he touched her wetness,' I had to shoot beneath the desk in case a teacher came in.

I was *that* close to normality, touching it really, doing the things normal kids do and feeling what they feel.

If I'd continued my interest in Karen then I might have been saved. I think girls really do help boys mature; they at least get them focused on someone else, teach them to think about other people and what happens if you don't. Under different circumstances maybe I would have summoned the courage to go to the youth club. I might have come up with the idea that asking the girl about herself and then saying, 'Will you kiss me?' is a good start if you want to kiss a girl.

Maybe I'd have ditched my glasses and taken the respect for being Karen's boyfriend. I could have bought a pair of spoon shoes to finish the damage to my feet that platform heels had started and travelled the road of fashion from punk to Rude Boy to dressing like a grown-up. I could have learned to like soccer and forged friendships at school from my knowledge of Coventry City, won admiration by showing people a player's autograph. There was a chance I could have been happy on a Sunday in the mall, satisfied with the things you should be satisfied with— family, home, a job.

It never happened. The slow progress, the learning to fit in with a peer group, the conforming to fashions in order to camouflage your weaknesses and, weirdly, to have more freedom to be yourself: that never came.

I had a dream when I was twelve that in some way I would be magically transformed. I would become a good fighter, able to beat up the likes of MacMahon, who ruined lessons; I'd have a beautiful girlfriend like the elfin Karen; I'd find friends who respected intelligence and wanted to learn things; I'd be in an environment where people told each other facts and read books and were proud of it.

Disaster befell me and it came true.

The mundane world, the world—and I'm going to let my teenage self have a word here—YOU ALL LIVE IN, would never be enough for me again.

I didn't know it then, but that was the last I'd ever see of Karen. On the Monday the school term began, and by the Tuesday the dark forces would take me. Family, friends, girls, food, everything would become as bright images receding into a void as I slipped into a shadow world from which I have never truly emerged. I would discover Dungeons and Dragons.

The thing is that, had I known my fate, I wouldn't have run away. I would have run towards it.

Come to Mordor,
It's Nicer Than Where You Live

I knew the second year at secondary school was going to be difficult from the end of the first gym class, when I saw my classmate Dale Cortt standing in the showers swinging his monster cock beneath his luxuriant bush and singing 'Yes, Sir, I Can Boogie.' Over the summer, he'd been given a whole new sexuality to play with. I'd only got a magic set.

I'd been born in July—ten months after the oldest boys in my class—and so would have nearly a year longer to wait before I could boogie too, provided I was an early developer. No one tells you this when you're that age, though, and you view your unbroken voice as a symptom of some inner moral weakness. The sprouting of my classmates made PE a trial. I'd been stuck at the back of the field when I was competing against little boys. Against these bursting adolescents I was lucky to finish a cross-country on the same day.

I had a black-and-white view of the world back then. If you're bad at sport then you're bound to be good at the academic side of things. If you were good at sport you were bad behind a desk. This appeared to be a received wisdom at school. However, it seemed the brains I had were scant reward for how awful I was when it came to games. I mean, I was OK at the pen work, destined for the de-gooned top classes when the pupils were split according to academic ability in the fourth year, but, given my appalling ability at sport, I felt I deserved to be marked for greatness intellectually by way of compensation.

There was an advert a few years ago featuring the basketball player Michael Jordan and the film-maker Spike Lee. Jordan goes through his paces, flipping and turning before spiralling in the air to slam the ball into the net with breathtaking ease. The legend of the ad was: 'This you cannot do.' For me they could have shown a boy kicking a ball five yards accurately to another boy or hitting a ball with a bat. That I could not do.

Sport as a spur for fantasies was denied to me. I couldn't dream of being a top soccer player, of netting the winner with a second to spare in the cup final or of dancing past the Welsh pack on the way to a scintillating score. By the age of nine I'd worked out that simply wasn't going to happen.

I think this is a healthy thing. Part of growing up is coming to terms with the person you are. The other part, of course, is coping with it well—or effectively at least.

That's where the school wargames club stepped in. There, pupils took part in table-top gaming, using model soldiers, dice, measuring tape and a set of rules to recreate famous battles and see if they could do any better than the original generals. Through my first year it provided me with a competitive activity that didn't require me to run, jump or throw anything—other than dice. I did get a bit of a bruise when I reacted extravagantly to the annihilation of my French cavalry after they'd charged the British guns at Waterloo, fell off a stool and banged my elbow, but apart from that I got on OK.

The club, too, was free of the sort of kid who cheeked the teacher and called you a spod for answering questions in class. Wargames were immediately something I could call my own, an arcane system, the knowledge of which set me apart from others and made me feel good about myself.

Being able to handle a huge table of figures that tells you the effects of cannonballs against different types of target at different ranges feels like being very clever. Also—and this is crucial to any sport—there's a lot of gear.

There was something vaguely Masonic about my approach to gaming. I had a number of items that showed my easy familiarity with my craft—an old armoured car first-aid box to contain the figures, a map tube for the dice, charts I'd covered in see-through plastic, badly cut-out pieces of cardboard that showed the shape of a cannon blast. There was a pleasure in taking part in an activity that others didn't understand, of being an initiate in a social order that I'd convinced myself was more important than the one I found in the day-to-day life of the school. This is one of the chief appeals of a hobby: you enter a world where intensity of interest can guarantee you social position. Talent doesn't have to come into it.

I could say to a newcomer, 'You don't know what grapeshot is? This is grapeshot!' I'd hold up a triangular piece of paper that represented a cannon firing musket balls as a cone in two dimensions. Let's face it, it wasn't grapeshot. It was a triangular piece of paper.

It was in this first year that my imaginative life began to take a shape that was, back then, out of the ordinary. In the mid-1970s 'fantasy'—which is what we called swords and sorcery literature—was still largely the preserve of hippies and nowhere as near part of the mainstream as in these Buffy-filled days.

Many of my daydreams fell within conventional culture. I'd bought the *Victor*, a WWII adventure comic for boys, and gone playing with Dill as we pretended to be Commandos hosing down German pill boxes with machine guns, and I'd been keen on Spiderman, the wise-cracking superhero who's transformed from the weedy Peter Parker. The one that really took me, though, was Ursula K. Le Guin's *A Wizard of Earthsea*, which I read three times in the one year. This was not yet an obsession, just a keen interest.

Le Guin's story is a sort of early, darker *Harry Potter*, where an orphaned boy is discovered to have magical powers. He's destined to be a great magician but makes a terrible mistake, summoning a spirit from the kingdom of death which will stalk him for ever.

There were lots of reasons I liked this book. It has obvious appeal for the mildly put-upon schoolboy, as bullies are vanquished and apparent weaknesses are shown as enormous strengths. For me, though, it was the idea of the magical power that held particular appeal. There's nothing about the wizard's abilities that relates to the normal world, no way of assessing them or testing them in a classroom.

I thought it very likely I might have this sort of untestable power myself. It was kind of logical—no good at sport, alrightish at my studies, there must have been some field in which I excelled. Magic had to be it.

It's difficult for adults to picture just what a grip these fantasies can take on a child. There's occasionally a reminder as a kid throws himself off a roof pretending to be Batman, but mostly the interior life of children goes unnoticed.

When I say I thought I could be a wizard, that's exactly true. I really did believe I had latent magical powers, and, with enough concentration and fiddling my fingers into strange patterns, I might suddenly find how to unlock the magic inside me.

I wouldn't call this a delusion, more a very strong suspicion. I'd weighed all the evidence, and that was the likely conclusion—so much so that I had to stop myself trying to turn Matt Bradon into a fly when he was jumping up and down on the desk in French saying, 'Miss, what are mammary glands?' to the big-breasted Miss Mundsley. I feared that, if I succeeded, I might not be able to turn him back. It was important, I knew, to use my powers wisely.

There's nothing that you'd have to call a psychoanalyst in for here. At the bottom line my growing interest in fantasy was just an expression of a very common feeling—'there's got to be something better than this,' an easy one to have in the drab Midlands of the 1970s. I couldn't see it, though. My world was very small, and I couldn't imagine making things better incrementally, only a total escape.

There was another appeal to the character of the wizard over other forms of fantasy. When he's transformed, your average super-hero is pretty much invulnerable. You know he's not going to cop it in *Spiderman* 3, or there won't be a *Spiderman* 24. In *A Wizard of Earthsea*, the main character is threatened even when he's at the height of his power; in fact it's the demonstration of his power that unleashes the demon that will eventually threaten his undoing.

It was easy to feel vulnerable at my school, the all-boys Woodlands Comprehensive, Colditz to its pupils—a huge 1950s complex of glass and steel resembling the factories many of the lads were destined for.

It was preparing us for a world of discipline and deference which, even then, had ceased to exist. My nephew attends the school today, and, if I tell him about the punishment regime—and I think regime is the right word—he simply does not believe me.

It is a matter of absolute fact, however, that caning offences included running—anywhere, including the playgrounds—putting your hood up if it was raining (the only item of headgear acceptable being a school cap) and wearing gloves in winter. The head hadn't had them when he was a child in Yorkshire; so he didn't see why we needed them in the semi-tropical paradise of the industrial Midlands. The fact that the odd pupil might have his hands welded to a bicycle by cold was a small price to pay if we weren't to grow up soft.

When I first saw the images of prisoner abuse from the Abu Ghraib prison in Iraq, the first thing I thought was that it was just like school. This is not hyperbole.

The photo that grabbed my attention showed an Iraqi standing on a bucket with a bag over his head and clasping two wires. He'd been told that he had a powerful electric current flowing through him and that, if he dropped the wires or stepped off the bucket, he'd be fried. Apart from one detail that's exactly the punishment that Mr Arden the science master used to hand out to unruly pupils.

There was a board full of dials and gauges on the wall in the sixth-form lab. He'd run the wires out of the back of this, give them to the child, stand him on a bucket and flick a switch. The gauges would spring into life and Mr Arden would return to his class while the boy sweated away the rest of the seventy-minute lesson in fear of his life. Mr Arden never, to my knowledge, put a bag on anyone's head, but I bet he wished he'd thought of it. He's dead now, so we can't ask him.

These things seemed normal to us, though—slightly comic but certainly not disturbing. Mr Arden was a popular and effective teacher, inspiring even, as was Mr Stort, who would make you choose your punishment from implements ranging from a cane to a rubber hose. One teacher, a Mr Lofty Lee, responded to a crying boy who said he'd been punched by a mystery assailant in a line by caning the whole class, including the boy who said he'd been punched, just in case he'd been lying. This sort of stuff seemed unremarkable. Perhaps that was why there seemed to be so many weirdos about at my school.

On the night I discovered D&D, I was at the wargames club fighting the battle of Stalingrad. I was competing against a fourth-year, Kevin Gerling, who was being the Nazis.

Gerling was always the Nazis, for the very good reason that Gerling was a Nazi. This isn't some trendy lefty insult for someone whose politics are a little bit conservative. It's an accurate and impartial description. In fact, it was Gerling's description. At fourteen years old he believed in the extermination of the Jews, thought the overwhelmingly white school should address its 'race problem' and had proposed, in a letter to the headmaster, that the older pupils should be allowed to wear SS insignia 'to encourage respect.'

The headmaster had responded, as he did to almost any pupil who came to his attention, by caning him—not for the suggestion but because Kevin had his top button undone when he was summoned to explain himself.

'Console yourself, you'd have got a lot worse if you'd turned up like that in front of Himmler,' said the head to the sobbing youth.

In 1976 the lost art form of belittling children was enjoying its final, florid expression, teachers egged on by the sarcastic example of John Cleese in *Fawlty Towers*.

The classrooms rang with sentences such as 'Wrong again, Goldmann, oh why didn't your parents have you crucified?' and 'You are as ugly as you are dim, Richardson. Your life is without hope. I presume the only thing that has prevented you from committing suicide is that you couldn't write the note.' This sort of thing is as much part of the period as 'Dancing Queen' and *The Muppet Show*. Things were rougher then.

The battle Kev and I were fighting wasn't, historically, strictly that accurate. For a start Stalingrad itself, even today, looks very little like a shoebox, which is what was standing in for the city. Secondly, there is nothing in the documents of the battle to suggest that either side was assisted by dragons, trolls, wizards or a giant rubber slug.

During the previous year Phil Dowis, a touchy-feely fifth-former, had brought along his Mythical Earth collection of painted figurines, and we'd battled with these under a set of rules he'd got from *Military Modelling* magazine—Wizards and Warfare.

The first time I'd seen him pull a dragon from its box the creature had almost seemed to glow. Under the influence of *A Wizard of Earthsea* I'd developed a sharp thirst for fantasy that I was having difficulty quenching. Marvel Comics did Dr Strange, which was great, but most of the books I got from the library didn't seem to give me the hit of that first experience. Only Alan Garner's *The Weirdstone of Brisingamen* had come close. In my pocket I carried a glass pebble I'd found that I suspected might be just such a Weirdstone.

Phil's fascination with wargames had been a brief one, just enough to distract him from his General Certificate of Education exam revision and frustrate his desire to enter further education. Then angling had taken his interest. I'd gone with him twice, though he'd seemed more interested in wrestling by the river-bank than catching fish. Phil's mum caught him sitting on top of me when she returned to pick us up and, when she gave me a lift back to my house, kindly suggested I should find someone my own age to play with. I was eleven and Phil was sixteen.

Our abrupt parting had left me with some of his figures, and I added them to my own to make a reasonably sized army. However, a Roman craze was sweeping the wargames club at the time, leaving me as the only boy interested in fighting wargames with monsters and Kev the only one who consistently wanted to revisit World War II in hope, I suspect, of a different outcome.

Two odd ones out don't necessarily make a pair, and we spent most of the game arguing about rules. On the night in question it was about whether a King Tiger tank could shoot down a dragon. I remember Kevin, in an accent heavy with B-movie Bavarianism, leaning over the table and saying, 'For you, dragon, ze var ist over,' but that's got to be my mind playing tricks on me. There again, it might not be, as Gerling often did play a sort of comic Nazi. A few years later, when he reached the sixth form and the schoolboys started organizing their own discos, he would occasionally enliven an evening by asking the DJ to play a record he'd bought with him. So in between Dr Hook and Boney M the revellers would be treated to 'Am Adolph Hitler Platz' or the 'Horst Wessel Lied' with its catchy German refrain, *'Already millions are looking to the swastika full of hope / The day of freedom and bread is dawning,'* while Gerling stomped about the floor with a stiff right arm. It was no competition for John Travolta.

'Gerling, Barrowcliffe, *raus!*' said a voice at the side of the wargames table. 'There's something you should see going on next door.'

This was Lee Hatherley, another fourth-year who spoke with an inexplicably posh accent. He and his friend Dennis Walters had voices that would be considered fruity in the Household Cavalry's officers' mess, but, as far as I knew, their dads worked at factories, just like mine.

Lee was a curious child. He ran a share club for other fourth-years and would stand ostentatiously reading the *Financial Times* while other boys stuck their heads into the soccer magazines. He appeared to regard far right politics as very alluring but simultaneously very funny. Gerling was open and evangelical in his Nazism; whereas Lee seemed to regard it as a sexy little secret he shared with his friends in coded references and the odd hidden salute. As far as I recall he described himself as a Conservative but certainly expressed admiration for the jackboot brigade and was fond of peppering his conversation with '*schnell,*' '*raus,*' and '*Juden.*'

'Does a dragon or does a dragon not get affected by puny tank shell fire?' I said to Lee, exasperated, as if I was asking him to say if black was black or, as Gerling contended, was in fact white.

'You'd better come and ask Porter,' he said.

'Who's Porter?'

'Someone who would know!' said Lee raising his eyebrows.

When I walked into the next classroom, I couldn't believe what I was seeing. A group of about six fourth-years was sitting around a teacher's desk. The boys clearly did not have permission to be there. That could quite easily result in a caning for the lot of them, confiscation of whatever they held dear—shoes if nothing else was available—and tar and feathering in front of an angry mob if the headmaster's hype was to be believed.

Even more unbelievably, one of them was actually sitting in the teacher's chair. At Woodlands this was the sort of thing that they'd invent a new punishment for, keelhauling on the rowing boat on the school pond, maybe.

I studied the boy in the chair. No one looks like this any more. He had the sort of haircut that would today be considered child abuse, a great lank cowl in the shape of an inkcap mushroom, abruptly sliced off pudding-bowl style above the collar to comply with school rules. It was dark and rod straight, and it all seemed the same length, even at the front. I suppose the nearest well-known style it approached was that of a Beatles moptop, but one done by feel rather than sight.

For the time, though, it wasn't that unusual. Most of us in the 1970s had haircuts that would be thought utterly mental by present standards. Strangely, the *outré* cuts—the spikes and the Mohawks—appear most normal today. It's the nice boys' styles—the centre partings and the flicks—that look truly weird.

From beneath this subversion of the very idea of a haircut protruded a large set square of a nose, and below the nose was a collision of lanky limbs, a sort of cubist take on the schoolboy figure. He reminded me of a praying mantis squatting above the table waiting for something to trigger him into life.

Then something did. He consulted an exercise book. On the back of it was written 'The Mines of Karlaak, a dungeon by A. Porter' in large, ornate tombstone writing above an illustration of a skull.

'Goblins, fifteen of them now, bursting from a trap door at your feet, what do you do?'

He sounded animated, as if, if he didn't get an answer immediately, something terrible might happen.

On the table were four humanoid figurines—a wizard, a warrior and two I didn't recognize. They were all incredibly skilfully painted, much better than the daubs I managed, and they appeared to be on a piece of graph paper upon which was drawn a representation of a passageway with some doors leading off it. The graph paper was surrounded by other blank sheets that obscured the rest of the map.

The amazing thing to me was that the boys didn't respond as if they were wargaming. They responded as if they themselves were being attacked by goblins, shouting out, 'I fire my crossbow!' or saying they threw flaming flasks of oil. It was as if they were voicing a radio play rather than playing a game. Porter didn't appear to be playing it, more narrating to the players, telling them that they had found a magic sword or that a gorgon, snakes writhing in its hair, had leaped from behind a door.

The table was a frenzy of rolling funny-shaped dice and measuring. Bits of paper were taken away, revealing more of the maze as the figurines were pushed through it, and more monsters were plopped onto the board until it seemed that the figures had a scrum of beasts behind them as they fled across the paper.

At one point Porter rolled a dice and said that a goblin had sunk an arrow into Hatherley's character and killed him. Hatherley slumped forward in his chair, head in his hands. He looked like he was going to cry, or even as if he himself had been shot.

When one of the boys cried, 'Sleep spell!' and all the monsters were knocked over, I could contain it no more. A 'wow!' escaped me.

Everyone turned to me, with hard, evaluating stares. I felt I had to say something that would put me on a level with them, to show them I was part of their world.

'I want to know!' I said, over-loudly, 'if a dragon could swallow a tank shell that was fired at it.'

Porter raised a brow.

'It could tear it from the air and send it back with interest,' he said, illustrating his words by making a rending motion with his hands. 'Andy Porter, dungeonmaster. It sounds like you'd better take a seat.'

I did, and over the next hour I was transported to another world. This was a home-made version of D&D that Porter had put together from reading reports about the game in the press, an act requiring a lot of invention and effort. It was like nothing I'd experienced. Instead of commanding an army, like in a wargame, you controlled just one person, known as your character. You found out everything about them—their strength, IQ, magical ability, by rolling dice and recording the results on a piece of paper known as a character sheet.

I called my character Ralponto the Necromancer and sat trying to look hollow-cheeked, as if there might be a monster from the kingdom of death after me. They call games like this RPGs, role-playing games, but it didn't feel like I was playing a role; it felt like me in those mines.

Early on in the game I was told I had a huge door in front of me. I said I'd give it a push. Porter smirked, reached into his bag and took out a large green figure. I didn't recognize it at all.

'What's that?' I said, 'is it a mara from the *Weirdstone of Brisingamen?*'

'It's a hill troll, as anyone can see,' said Porter, 'from *The Lord of the Rings*, and it's about to turn you into its breakfast; so I'd pick up that dice smartish if you don't want to be served up with the troll cornflakes before the next round.'

I shook. These boys were older than me, and I clearly had a lot to learn.

'What's *Lord of the Rings?*'

'Only the best book ever written,' said Hatherley, 'perhaps you haven't heard of it. It's for adults.'

'Is it fantasy?'

'It's *the* fantasy,' said Porter, shaking a dice. 'The troll hits you, you're dead.'

I drew up another character and entered the dungeon again, but not before I'd written down '*The Lord of the Rings*' on the back of my hand.

The game went on, and I seethed with interest. You have a greater capacity for excitement at that age, and I didn't have the wit to contain it. I shrieked and screamed, shouted and moaned, sounding more like I was on a bucking bronco than playing a game. The fourth-years displayed a lot of enthusiasm themselves, and though I caught a couple wincing at my antics, I didn't care. I was completely immersed as I'd never been in a book or in a film. I *was* Ralponto, and it was as if I could add power to his spells by waving my arms myself and calling out invocations to 'the mighty powers' as I threw my dice.

By the end of the session I was on to Ralponto IX. In fact, I was throwing to see what the characteristics of Ralponto X were before Ralponto IX had even been crushed by a rock fall. Porter didn't even have to look in his book to know it was there, so great was my mistake in taking the left passageway rather than the right.

Ralponto IX died. Importantly, though, before he did I'd got hold of a fireball wand and flamed a giant spider. It felt fantastic, totally different to the wargames I'd played before.

If you compared gaming to soccer, playing wargames would be like watching Pele or, at its best, managing Brazil. Dungeons and Dragons was like being Pele. In fact, it was probably better than being Pele. Pele must be quite used to being Pele. It couldn't have been much of a surprise to him when he left four players for dead and rifled one home from the corner flag. If you or I could have stepped into his consciousness, though, and experienced the game through his eyes but still retain our spectator's distance, we'd marvel at how graceful we felt, how powerful and how quick. Even warming up, you'd probably look down at your own feet and say, 'Look, I can keep the ball up with my heels! It's amazing!'

Saying, 'I point the wand at the spider,' and hearing Porter tell me that a great ball of fire had shot from the end to burn the creature to a crisp gave me exactly that feeling—elation and surprise.

'So what do you call this?' I said, as the figures were packed away.

'It's my fantasy game,' said Porter. 'It's based on a very sophisticated game from America—Dungeons and Dragons. It's much better than mine.'

'Gosh, will you be playing that soon?' I said.

'I wish,' said Porter. 'I can't afford it.'

'Will you be playing this, then? This is great.'

'Yeah,' said Porter 'but I think we'll try to limit the numbers in future. It's kind of a fourth-year thing.'

I hardly heard what he was saying, I was so excited. I could virtually feel the fireball wand still in my hand.

'Hang on a minute,' I said, 'how much is this D&D?'

'It's £6.30,' said Porter, like a Ferrari salesman being asked if they do finance by a road sweeper.

'Oh, I've got that. I've still got some money from my birthday,' I said.

'Really?' said Porter. 'Well, hang on a minute. I'll get you the address.'

He rummaged in his bag and took out a sheet of paper that had been torn from *Battle* magazine, the competitor to *Military Modelling*.

'Right,' I said, 'I'll send off for it tonight.'

'Great,' said Porter, with a smile, 'I'll see you here next week, then.'

'Someone should cut out your tongue,' said Walters. 'If this school had a man of the right political will in charge you'd be executed as a defective.'

I didn't care, though. I could do magic, and somewhere on the sandy floor of the Mines of Karlaak, there was the smoking husk of a giant spider to prove it.

That night I insisted my dad run me down to the library, where I took out a copy of *The Lord of the Rings*. To me it was like a book of spells: the dark cover, the strange-looking runes. I imagined the librarian nodding sagely as she stamped my card, as if to say, 'This one has come to his knowledge young.' I really felt like I was stepping into the adult world at last.

'Do you want chips?' said my dad as we returned to the car.

I did. I didn't know that, within a week, the only thing I'd really want was the Lembas bread of the elves.

Lord of the
Ring Binders

I'd spent the two weeks waiting for the books to arrive on the edge of ecstasy, bursting with ideas of the delights that awaited me once I got my hands on them. *The Lord of the Rings* had consumed me, and I couldn't wait to actually enter that world properly myself, to feel the cold blue sword Sting in my hands and the weight of a Mithril coat on my shoulders just as I'd felt the hum of the fireball wand as it let fly at the spider. Porter's game was good, but he had filled me up with promise of the delights in store when the real thing arrived.

For days I'd been waiting at the door for the post. On one occasion, tormented beyond endurance as only a few bills hit the floor in front of me, I'd gone out and stopped the postman on the way back down the path to ask him to check there was absolutely nothing for me. Finally, in the first post of a Thursday morning, the rules were pushed through my letterbox. I'd been sitting on the stairs behind the door and nearly caught them as they fell.

It's said that taking heroin is like a million screaming orgasms. Opening the package that contained D&D wasn't quite like that—more like a million screaming Christmases, all at once.

I felt a tingle like hunger as I tore away the packaging to reveal a white box about 9 inches by 6 inches and an inch deep. On the box lid was a poorly drawn picture of a wizard casting a spell on some orcs. Never mind, to me this just added to its authenticity.

It looked like the sort of thing that had been scratched out in a book of incantations by a sorcerer as he stood looking into a bubbling cauldron.

There were three books in the set, and I wanted to read them all simultaneously. I could hardly start one for wanting to look at the other. They were a sort of tan colour, as if yellowed by age, and bore strange, and bad, illustrations of dragons and warriors. This, I thought, as I opened the first volume, *Men and Magic*, was the first day of a new life. I had never felt so utterly fulfilled as I looked inside it and my eye fell upon the enticing words: 'Inquiries regarding rules should be accompanied by a stamped returned envelope and sent to Tactical Studies Rules, POB 756, Lake Geneva, Wisconsin.' Good lord! I could actually contact the demi-gods who wrote these rules, as soon as I had read them and had something to enquire about. It was eight in the morning; I was due at school, but I took out a pad and pen and wrote down 'Inquiries,' copying the spelling, ready to get a list together. I imagined them reading my letter and saying: 'Hmm, we've rarely had such intelligent inquiries. Nor so many. Here is a true believer.' I wondered if there would be some prize for the most 'inquiries' received.

I read the introduction. Anyone unfamiliar with wargaming, I believe, would have had a hard time understanding exactly what E. Gary Gygax, D&D's originator and editor, was on about in this first section. In fact, the whole first set of rules is full of holes and assumes that whoever is reading them has a solid wargaming background. I lapped it up, though, feeling glad that terms such as 'campaign' and 'characters' were familiar, separating me from the herd to whom such terms would mean nothing. Clearly, this was a game for superior sorts. Gygax expressly pointed out that people with no imagination wouldn't like it. It was for those whose imaginations knew no bounds. 'Strike a light, that's me!' I thought.

Most interestingly of all, the game promised a world 'where the fantastic is fact and magic really works.' I couldn't wait to enter it, but it was 8.20, and I had to cycle in to school. Life felt very unfair. It was the longest day of my life up to that point as I groaned through the boredom of English, the irrelevance of maths, the cosmic joke of gym.

When 3.30 came I made it to the cycle racks like a Le Mans driver to his car, at a kind of zooming walk that couldn't be said to be running and so would call down no delaying punishment on my head. My dad had taken me to Coventry Cycling Club and put me in for a couple of time trials in an effort to interest me in physical exercise. I'd done predictably poorly. If someone had a stopwatch on me as I cycled the two and a half miles back from school to my door that evening they'd have marked me out as a future Tour de France winner.

I spent the evening consuming the books, and, by the time I'd finished, I had no enquiries or inquiries. Reading between the lines, I realized that the invitation to submit them was probably a ruse to detect thick people who shouldn't be playing the game and to exclude them from further purchases.

The world I was entering was like that of a computer game before they had computers. In it you assumed an identity of a person in a magical land. This identity was known as your character. His or her abilities were determined according to the roll of three dice. You found out how strong you were, how intelligent, how wise, how nimble, how hardy and how charismatic. These statistics were recorded on a piece of paper known as a character sheet and formed the basis for the first choices you'd make in the game—whether to be a warrior, a priest or a wizard.

Immediately I came to the obvious conclusion that I was a D&D character and would very likely be called upon to go adventuring at any moment. Accordingly, I drew up a character sheet for myself in addition to the others I'd already punched unevenly and stored in my binder. This is what it looked like.

Character Name: Mark Barrowcliffe, aka the Sorcerer Prince of Angharna.

Strength—8. I'd always thought of myself as weak and, considering that the heaviest thing I lifted during my childhood was a dice, then I was probably right.

Intelligence—17. I modestly moved myself off the maximum score of 18 because, I had to concede, there were areas of schoolwork where I wasn't that strong. Geography sprang to mind. And any other subject that required a lot of neatness and colouring in. I was near the top of the class in most subjects, and, I concluded, the only reason I wasn't further up was a combination of bad handwriting and not being asked the right questions. Bugger it, I put it up to 18.

Wisdom—14. That's right, I gave myself a score of 'well above average,' which in itself said all you needed to know about my wisdom right there. This from the boy who couldn't even understand that leaping about, screaming and wailing in a high-pitched voice was not the way to endear himself to boys two years older than him.

Dexterity—8. A tough one. I was clumsy, I knew, but there again I was probably quite good at dodging, spear-throwing, acrobatics and a whole host of other things I hadn't tried. In fact, it was Sod's Law that the only things I had tried—walking down the street without tripping over, not breaking anything I touched, cycling without crashing into oncoming vehicles—I was bad at. A few months previously I'd had a head-on collision with a car on my bike. I was turning right and looking over my shoulder at the time, wondering what I'd have for tea. I'd planted my head into the bonnet of the car, and my backside had gone through its windscreen. I'd somersaulted through the air and landed on my feet. I was entirely unhurt, although the car was badly damaged. This confirmed two opinions in me—one, that my dexterity emerged when it needed to—I landed on my feet—and two, that I had high 'constitution' and 'hit' points—higher than a Chrysler Alpine anyway.

Constitution—17. As proved by what I was beginning to think of as my victory over the car. Plus I walked the dog to my nan's every day, a fact that caused a friend's older brother to call me a liar. He couldn't envisage anyone walking four miles a day. He was much older than us, so his incredulity proved that I was performing a difficult feat.

Charisma—12, but 16 when I was at school and playing up to my nickname (more of which later). This sustained my illusion that I was a 'loved by all' sort rather than the natural target for bullies that I was. I think the true figures were nearer 5 and 7.

Then there was the question of 'alignment,' your outlook on life. In the early game you chose to have your character follow law, chaos or neutrality. Later on this was refined, and you could be anything from 'lawful good,' sort of an ideal policeman, through 'lawful evil,' more or less like the Nazis, through 'neutrality,' like Buddhism, through 'chaotic good,' a hippy attitude, and 'chaotic evil,' psychopathic. I thought I'd be chaotic, which, at that time, roughly equated to evil. No kid likes to see himself as a goodie-goodie.

Most children spend a wobbly time in their adolescence figuring out who they are. I didn't have to. I'd done it in five minutes, and there it all was, written out on a sheet of paper.

These scores would have allowed me to play any sort of character in the game, apart from a fighter, because I was too weak. I pondered what I should be. When I say I pondered it, my pondering went on for about four years, and I occasionally still ponder today. I came to the conclusion that I would be a magic-user. This was easier with the original rules, because there were fewer choices than in the years that followed.

The type of character you play in D&D is known as the character class. When I began there were three—fighter, cleric, magic-user—warrior, priest or wizard in layman's terms. This expanded down the years through official additions, fanzines and our own inventions to take in scores of different types—from aborigines to witches through thieves, assassins, druids and berserkers.

Each class has its own requirements and abilities. Fighters can use all the weapons and armour and are tough in combat; clerics have a range of spells to heal and protect, though are more limited in a battle; and magic-users are weak, unarmoured and only able to use a dagger. They can grow to be the most powerful figures in the game, however, rising to throw lightning from their fingers or turn a troll into a pebble to put into a pocket.

If you've only an intelligence of 9 you won't make it as magic-user; likewise a strength of 3 won't be much cop for your role as a fighter. Your dexterity of 15, however, means that you'll make a fine thief.

I decided I'd have 6 hit points because of how I'd bounced off the car. Hit points are how D&D calculates if your character lives or dies. Back then all characters had 1–6 hit points (in improved versions of the game fighters were given more, spell-using classes less). A sword did 1–6 damage. In this basic version of the game, if you had 4 hit points and a goblin hit you and shook 3 damage, then you were all right. If it hit you again and did 1 damage you were dead.

It's worth saying a bit here about how the game is actually played.

When it begins you enter, in your mind, an underground maze to battle monsters for treasure and to get the experience to enable you to fight bigger monsters. If you want, you can take on a persona from fantasy literature—Beowulf or Sir Lancelot or Conan. You might even choose some other inspiration—you could play Becky Sharp from *Vanity Fair* or Tony Blair or even your mum or yourself, but most people invent their own characters, and most characters fit into the fantasy world.

Generally the players all enter the dungeon together, in a theoretically cooperative unit known as 'the party.' Ideally this will be a mix of character types, fighters to hold off the monsters, magic-users to zap them, clerics to heal the damaged.

Your success in almost any task, from persuading a barman to give you information to climbing a wall or cutting a hill giant in two, is determined according to throws of a dice. Each monster, like the character you play, is represented statistically, and you discover what dice rolls you need to make to hit it, kill it or subdue it with a spell by consulting a chart. Once you've killed it you will be awarded 'experience points.' When you have enough of these, you 'go up a level,' which means you can learn more spells or become a better fighter. You also become more difficult to kill. Combats are rarely over quickly, and it can take several turns of the game, or 'rounds,' before you kill or are killed. Competitive dice-rolling was one of the key excitements of the early game, although there are modern versions that do away with it completely.

For instance, some referees might determine that, given your charisma score of 17, your chance of getting that barman to tell you the strange rumours surrounding the disappearance of Priestess Marna of the Temple of the Blood Moon is seven out of ten—shake more than 6 on D&D's signature twenty-sided dice (known as 1D20) and you've succeeded. Another might actually require you to play out the role of glad-handing the barman.

The maze—although it could be a city, a country, a house or a temple—is designed by the game referee, the dungeonmaster, or DM, according to the rules. He plays the key role in the game—something between that of umpire and storyteller. He says what his world is like and populates it with treasure and monsters. You don't see the maze, the DM describes it to you as you go along.

To call the DM a referee is a bit misleading. His role is nearer to that of a god. He creates a world, sets challenges for players' characters and rewards or punishes them according to the wisdom of their actions.

Whatever form the setting for the adventure takes, it tends to be known as 'the dungeon.' Sometimes the referee will design a whole world with towns, tombs, caves, wilderness areas, ocean kingdoms, mountains, forests and more. In theory the game could take decades. Unlike, say, Monopoly, it has no one goal. The designer of the game, Gary Gygax, once pointed out that to talk about a 'winner' in D&D is like talking about a winner in real life. If I had to sum D&D up that would be how I'd do it—a game with no winners but lots of losers.

Anything you can do in reality you can do in D&D, only more

so. The aim is the personal advancement of your character: to learn more spells, be a more efficient fighter, own more treasure and go on ever-more dangerous adventures. That's the most basic level. When it gets more sophisticated the aim can be to be a participant in a good story, to be really true to your role. For instance, some players may continue sending their gnome thief on more and more adventures for more gold and glory. Others may decide that he had quite enough adventure the last time he was nearly skinned alive by trolls and that he'll go out of his way to avoid it. That sets a challenge for the dungeonmaster in coming up with ways to force him into tight spots: kidnapping his children, receiving instructions from his guild, that sort of thing. This works best in the series of linked adventures known as a 'campaign'—where the characters always inhabit the same world designed and run by the same person from adventure to adventure.

When D&D is played it sounds like a series of questions and answers.

'There is a room ahead of you twenty feet square. In it stands an ogre—eight feet tall, humanoid, massively muscled and wielding a mace. Behind him is a chest. It's open and overflowing with gold pieces. What do you do?' The person who's asking the questions is the dungeonmaster. Mostly he'll be a harrowed-looking youth with a god complex.

'We rush the ogre and attack him,' you say, keen to test your warrior in battle.

'We should try to speak to him,' says another player.

'Too late, I've rushed him,' you say.

'Hard luck,' says the dungeonmaster, 'there's a covered pit full of tiny poisoned spikes between you and him. Shake 1D20 to see if you avoid it. Oh dear, 4. You fall in. Now shake more than 16 or you're poisoned and will die in three rounds.' The dungeonmaster then watches you roll the dice with an expression on his face like a cat toying with a spider. You shake a 9 and your character starts to die.

'I told you we should have spoken to him. Why didn't you

listen to me?' says the other player, who is clearly honing skills he will one day use on his wife.

'I, Andaris Andaron, priest of wise Osiris, cast Cure Poison,' says yet another spotty youth. In fact, there's no point saying 'spotty' here. It's easier to point out when one of the youths isn't spotty. Unless I specifically say otherwise, assume that they are.

The dungeonmaster consults a chart in the rules, rolls a dice and announces that the cure is successful. Your warrior is cut, bruised and in a pit, but he will live to fight another day. But there's still the ogre to take care of. Luckily your mate Dave is playing an elf. He says he draws his bow and looses an arrow across the pit. The ogre is armour class 5—about the equivalent of a human in chainmail owing to his tough hide. Dave roles a 20! Critical hit. Another role and another chart. The ogre falls to the floor with an arrow in his eye. Great, the magic-user still hasn't discharged any of his spells so he's ready with his sleep spell for the ten orcs that are running in behind you. They won't be so difficult to kill once they've gone bye-byes.

This is the game's most basic form. At more advanced levels you engage in politics, marry, build cities, things you might have a chance of eventually doing in real life, were you not wasting every waking hour thinking about a game.

For the time that you're playing—and, in some cases, for a lot of the time you are not—you act out the personality of an elf, a dwarf or a lizard man. Some will talk as if they've walked out of a rather hammy version of *The Lord of the Rings*, as above; some will just say, 'I cast Cure Poison.' Each boy gets into his role according to his taste, peer group expectations and embarrassment threshold.

One of the misconceptions held about D&D is that it involves casting spells or summoning devils. This is akin to looking at Ralph Fiennes playing a Nazi concentration camp commander and demanding that he be tried for war crimes. D&D is a game, and players are no more summoning devils than children playing cowboys are shooting people. Which isn't to say, of course, that some of the children playing cowboys won't go on to shoot people, just that the vast majority of them won't. However, when the game is working properly, it certainly feels like you're casting spells or fighting people for real, and the emotions conjured up can seem deep ones.

Very rarely, in my experience, do people refer to each other by their character's names while playing the game. They don't say, 'I cast my "cure light wounds" spell on Jerablah the Iridescent,' they say 'I cast my "cure light wounds" spell on Billy.' People are identified very strongly with their characters, and they identify very strongly with them. This is where it differs from a computer game. You can't just reboot if your character is killed. In D&D if the character dies, he's dead, which usually, but not always, is a serious threat to his future. Losing a character, that you've had for some time, maybe years, can be a major emotional experience. At fourteen years old it can be the first real grief you've known in your life. It's like having an imaginary friend but one you get to actually look at, that other people will discuss as if they're real and may even attempt to kill.

This, as I read the rules for the third time with my torch under the bedclothes, was the world I was entering. More worryingly, it was entering me.

The
Land of Shadow

A month after the rules had arrived, I was someone else. Some people come to their addictions slowly. I fell for D&D at my first hit.

Within a day of the white box dropping through my door Porter had borrowed the books to design a dungeon, and we were off—gaming as much as we could, lost in a world of barrow wights, vampires, manticoras and gargoyles, rings of X-ray vision, girdles of giant strength and mirrors of life-trapping. I couldn't get enough of this stuff and ached for the half-term when we would be able to game all day, every day, despite the fact that my characters were regularly killed—by monsters or by the treachery of other players.

There's nothing in the rules of D&D to prevent player-on-player attack—my magic-user can freeze your fighter solid if he chooses—they only advise against it. Accordingly, my characters were often slaughtered by the fourth-years as an outlet for their irritation with me. I told myself that it was just a matter of learning the game, that I'd work out how to come out of a dungeon alive eventually. In fact, it was a matter of learning about life, but I couldn't see that at the time.

Two weeks before half-term, disaster struck. To my horror, my mum insisted I accept Dill's parents' invitation to go on holiday with them. They'd found a cheap deal to spend a week in

Llandudno in October. To this day I still can't imagine just how cheap it must have been to make that an attractive prospect.

For readers who might not have a clear picture of what Llandudno (pronounced Clandudno with a throat-clearing Welsh *Cl* at the start) is like, it's actually very hard to bring across the level of depression it was capable of inspiring back then. The whole town had the air of an unpopular person's party, attended only by a couple of bare acquaintances who are shuffling their feet, wondering when it might be polite to leave. It's a Victorian seaside resort in North Wales built around the arms of a broad bay—the Little Orme and the Great Orme. In the 1970s it had a feel of long-standing decay, that there had been nothing new in the town since it was built in the nineteenth century. Outside of its brief summer it laboured under a heavy sky of the sort that seemed to have been imported from the old Eastern Bloc, one of those that had drained the will of invaders for centuries.

Add to this the Welsh cold—a cold that seems to affect your soul as much as your flesh—and the questions: 'What is your normal life like that this represents entertainment? Where are you coming from that this is an improvement, a *resort?*' spring to mind.

The answer is plain: Coventry. I would have been happy to go had it not been for Dungeons and Dragons.

By the time we went away I was incapable of thinking or talking about anything else but D&D. There was never an inappropriate moment to bring it up or to think about it, and anything at all seemed like an invitation to launch into a monologue on the uses of wyvern poison or how dwarves can detect gold. Half the time I didn't even need the scantest relation between the subject under discussion and D&D. I wasn't just incapable of saying anything that didn't relate to the game, I was incapable of hearing it either.

'Oh, look at those seagulls.'

'I doubt they'd be flying quite so freely were the Nazgul abroad.'

Or:

'Today we're going out to a beekeeping centre then on to a waterfall and coming back for a meal in the pub. What do you think of that, Mark?'

'Green dragons are found in forest and wooded areas. If the dragon can talk there is a ten per cent chance it can use magic. First- and second-level spells only, naturally.'

A week before my Llandudno sentence began our kitchen caught fire. I found this hugely exciting. I imagined a fire elemental had broken free, and while we were waiting for the fire brigade I hung around outside the house trying to cast a 'summon storm' spell by twiddling my fingers at the blaze while my mum stood crying.

Dill had been my best friend, someone I'd known since I was seven. His parents had been very kind to me and had allowed me to come home for lunch with him when I'd been having a miserable time at junior school. I'd fallen out with my friends, and, in a pattern that was to repeat itself throughout my school life, I was being mildly bullied. It was worst at lunchtimes. Dill's mum, the funny and warm Mrs Grigson, took me in, fed me coconut cake and had us in hysterics with stories about her friend getting taken short in an alley and accidentally wiping his behind with a piece of paper that had a lump of coal stuck to it.

I'd felt more comfortable with these people than I did with my own family most of the time. Their house was calm and fun, although very traditionally run. The kitchen and the back room were the province of the women and children, the front of Dill's granddad and dad. It wasn't that you weren't allowed into the front room, just that you instinctively gave the men their space.

A year before I'd have jumped at the chance of a week by the sea with them. That October, though, as I slouched into the back of the Morris Marina, I felt as though I was being deported, a doomed prince torn from his people, hollow-eyed and wan, beginning his exile in the land of dragons, far from the source of power for his terrible sorcery, clutching to him only a few slim tomes of magic smuggled from the ancient library at Kra Laaak. That's not an exaggeration, in fact, as I recall, it's *exactly* what I thought. In one way I'd achieved my ambition of being able to do magic: at least I was in two places at once.

Through D&D I had met fantastic beings, older boys who seemed creatures of impossible glamour, who appeared to know everything and who seemed proud of knowing everything. There was no dancing on the desks in French for them, more listening to Emerson Lake and Palmer's *Pictures at an Exhibition,* saying, 'It's based on a piece of classical music, you know,' and luxuriating in the implied superb discernment that came with renting such a record from the library. They'd discuss the concepts of Einstein and know about things like black holes and supernovas.

To me Dill seemed less like a best mate now and more like a dull jailer.

Llandudno appears in my memory as just a field of grey lines, the shore and the sea on the horizontal, the rails of rain on the roughly vertical, depending on the wind.

Porter still had my Dungeons and Dragons books, but I'd spent the last of my birthday money on some fanzines and magazines. I took them with me and tried to spend all my time reading them in the room in the guesthouse I was sharing with Dill. The Grigsons had to virtually crowbar me out in the mornings to go on the day trips they'd very kindly arranged. I only bucked up when we visited the Great Orme. At least I could pretend we were going to see a great orc.

Dill and I clung on to what little we still had in common. We'd spend the week exchanging violent fantasies, his involving soldiers and the Gurkha Regiment, with whom he seemed to be in love, me explaining the cannibalistic cave-dwelling tendencies of kobold hordes. The rest of the time he would be doing press-ups on the floor and experimenting with aftershave, and I'd have my head stuck in *Strategic Review,* volume 1, issue 1. And, yes, I still do have it.

On the Wednesday his parents had decided they could do

without us for the day, given us some money and pointed us towards the pitch and putt, the rides and the arcades.

'What if we run out of money and get bored?' said Dill.

'When I was your age we didn't get bored,' said his dad from beneath his flat cap. 'Do what we did: make your own amusement, find a bomb pit to play in.' The generation gap was a robust one in the 1970s. Tea hadn't come off rationing until Mr Grigson was in his twenties, and bananas had been brought in to school as objects of wonder and awe. From this viewpoint, you don't have to do much to be decadent.

So we hung around the pier for a bit while I talked about the soul-drinking properties of the sword Stormbringer, as featured in Michael Moorcock's book of the same name, and Dill looked for girls. I hadn't actually read any Moorcock, but I'd heard Andy Porter talking about him and couldn't wait to start once I'd recovered from *The Lord of the Rings*. I'd read it twice already and wasn't sure I was yet ready to offer my loyalty to another book.

Eventually we ran out of cash. Well, Dill did. I was saving my money until the end of the holiday when, Mrs Grigson had said, if I still had enough, I could buy an ornamental sword from one of the souvenir shops. Intriguingly it was in a dark iron, like Stormbringer. I hoped that I could spend my £10 on it, and perhaps it would be the beginning of a strange, dependent relationship in which we would win many battles, the sword devouring souls and feeding their unearthly energy on to me. I thought it very likely that its blood lust could not be slaked on my enemies, and it would possess me, causing me to kill friends and family in a bid to quench its foul thirst. I'd be left a gaunt wreck in a broken tower overlooking the Weeping Wastes, alone with my sorcery and my bitter, bitter, memories. Well, fingers crossed, eh?

It was five o'clock on the seafront, grey, wet and cold, the wind whipping in from the Great Orme and cutting through my thin jacket. I was dressed as near to how I imagined a D&D adventurer would dress as I could get, within the constraints of what was on offer from my mum's club catalogue.

This meant a bum-length brown denim jacket with big lapels, the like of which hadn't been fashionable since 1973, and jeans, because there was, as far as I could see, no other sort of trouser available. Medieval-style hose were in short supply in the Littlewoods catalogue. I wore a T-shirt because Mithril mail tunics were irritatingly unavailable too. I'd also swiped my Dad's Derry boots that he wore on his motorbike during the winter. These were basically insulated Wellingtons, and I wore them because they looked like the sort of thing an elf might sport, despite the fact they were a size or two too big and required two pairs of soccer socks to make them fit. In the seeping chill of the Llandudno autumn they were just about bearable. Still, I had to stop once in a while to take them off and let my feet cool.

Dill was dressed more fashionably—not punk but smoothie. He wore an open-necked shirt, slacks, spoons (wide-fronted shoes) and a sports jacket. He'd made a point of never washing his top lip, in order to give the illusion of a moustache. Dill thought it looked like stubble, but I couldn't see anything. He also wore a St Christopher medallion. I decided it might be worth getting one of those because it looked like a magic amulet. I thought I might try to find one with a jewel in it, though, the sort that might contain an imp.

We were heading back to meet Dill's parents when, at a bus shelter on the road to the guesthouse, we saw two girls. They were fifty yards away. Both Dill and I went to the all-boys Woodlands School; both of us only ever socialized with boys; both of us had only brothers. The only females I'd ever spoken to since leaving junior school had been a minimum of twenty years older than me. I felt my legs stiffen as if even something as straightforward as walking had suddenly become difficult. Actually, given my motor skills, walking had never been straight-forward for me. I was always tripping over something or bumping into something else. Now it seemed impossible. I felt the steam rising from my Derry boots and dearly wanted to take them off. Dill had gone red, though he had followed his brother's advice to pull in his belly. We had to pass these girls if we were going to get back to the guesthouse and have our tea, for which we were starving.

To me, it was exactly the same feeling that I got when seeing a gang of hard kids up the road from me. It wasn't that I feared a battering—though I did—it was the attention I didn't want, to be helpless in the corrosive gaze of people who were, to quote my older, D&D-ing associates, 'inferiors.' I've always been proud to call myself a physical coward, but the similarity in the emotions I experienced faced with the girls to those I felt faced with a gang of boys makes me think there was something more than bodily pain that I was afraid of.

In these situations, of course, you can't turn back. Attention is what you are trying to avoid. Changing your course would only invite it.

I glanced over at Dill. He seemed to be bent double with his back to the girls. I prayed a bus would come and they would go.

It's an odd fact of life that you don't really remember the good times all that well. I have only mental snapshots of birthday parties, skiing, beach holidays, my wedding. The bad times too are just impressions. I can see myself standing at the end of some bed while someone I love is dying, or on the way home from a girlfriend's after I've been dumped, but again, they're just pictures. For full Technicolor, script plus subtitles plus commemorative programme in the memory, though, nothing beats embarrassment. You tend to remember the lines pretty well once you've woken screaming them at midnight a few times.

'What are you doing?' I said.

'Applying a bit of the old magic potion,' said Dill.

'What, of invisibility?' I felt moved to tell him that, if he was pretending to be using a healing potion, he was wasting his time. Healing potions only work after you've been wounded. It's pointless to apply one before an encounter with a monster.

He was splashing something into his hands. I moved round him to see it was a bottle of Hai Karate.

'They'll see you!' I said.

'Not if I pretend I'm being sick,' he said, 'that's why I'm bending over.'

'Why do you want them to think you're being sick?'

'Show I've been drinking, like a proper man.'

'You haven't been drinking.'

'They don't know that.'

Dill stood up and put the bottle back into his pocket. He had so much aftershave on that I could taste it, almost feel it on my hands.

'Right, just walk past casual, like,' he said.

'Hang on,' I said. I couldn't believe my luck. A bus was coming, one of those green Welsh single-deckers that looked like they were from the 1940s.

'We can't pass them while they're getting on the bus,' said Dill, 'we'll look right twats.'

'God, yeah,' I said. I couldn't imagine the complications of nodding and saying 'All right?' if they were getting their change. Imagine if you said it and they didn't see you, or thought you were stupid for talking to them when they were obviously busy. You could shrivel on the spot.

The bus stopped. The girls said something to the driver, but they didn't get on. We heard him shout, 'Bloody kids!'; then the bus pulled off. My hope sank. These girls were clearly just the sort who hung around bus stops, and bitter experience told me that the sort who hung around bus stops were trouble. They'd even cheeked the driver. We were in serious bother.

Then I had an idea. Lee Hatherley had told me that the lower orders only respect one thing—authority.

I would walk past at a magisterial pace, the sort of pace used by an elf lord sweeping into the palace of a vanquished enemy. Dill set off behind me in his perfumed cloud. Vampires can turn themselves into gas, and I imagined Dill as one, floating beside me. Vampires can't go out in the day, though, no matter how Welsh and dull (the day, not the vampire), and their gaseous form would be likely to smell even more rancid than Hai Karate, so I felt a bit stupid for even thinking that.

Still, he reminded me of a character from a horror novel I'd read in which a sorcerer is rotting from the inside after a pact with demons. He's a lecturer at a school, and all the kids wonder why he wears so much perfume and washes so often. Dill was too short to be a sorcerer, though, I thought. In my imagination they were always tall and thin and hollow-eyed (see self, above). Actually, his obsession with the Gurkhas might have been explained by his size. The Gurkhas—recruited from Nepal—are the smallest men in the British army, short but deadly.

We got level with the bus stop, and I had a good hope of passing it unmolested when a voice emerged from the benches.

'It's my birthday today. Do I get a kiss?'

Her accent was thick; to me it sounded like something grinding, a cog come free in the gearbox or a branch being fed into a wood chipper.

I stopped, even though I wanted to keep going, and turned to face a couple of stout Liverpudlians. They were at least two years older than me, but girl years. I was a boy, hovering on the edge of adolescence. To me, these seemed a couple of young women, lipstick, short skirts, blotchy legs and bubble gum. Neither looked anything like the women of my dreams. Those had long hair and resembled the pale maidens on art nouveau posters, which was how I imagined the elves. They certainly didn't chew gum.

Other than the people in the shops on holiday, I'd never spoken to anyone who came from outside my home town in my life before. In fact, I'd hardly spoken to anyone who didn't come from Whoberley or the neighbouring couple of districts. At first I didn't think I'd understood what she said. I found her accent nearly impenetrable.

'What, fair maiden?' I thought this was the best way of steering the conversation in a D&D direction. They would ask me why I was talking like that, and I'd be able to tell them about the Plateau of Rleyh, Porter's latest dungeon.

'It's her birthday. She wants a kiss,' said the other one, enunciating deliberately. 'It's my birthday too. Do I get one?'

'Art thou twins?' I said.

'No,' they both said, in that fourteen-year-old, 'are you mental?,' down-the-nose way.

'Oh, so it's quite a coincidence you twain being whelped on the same day, isn't it?' I said. I think I thought whelping was the same as being born.

The first made a noise, pushed her tongue into the bottom of her lip and, I thought, said 'mong' under her breath.

'She wants a kiss,' said the second one.

I didn't know what to do. Luckily, Dill did.

'Full snog or just lips?' he said, with a polished air, like a rather louche airport employee asking you, 'Window or aisle?' God, I was such a no-hoper. I didn't even know it was important to get that sorted out before you dived in. How many other social snakepits were there for me to fall into? What if this girl wanted to marry me and didn't play Dungeons and Dragons? The whole thing was just such a potential mess.

'Full snog!' said the first one, puckering forward her lips.

This was way too strong for me. I needed to go back a bit. A million obstacles were before me. 'I can't kiss you. I'm too hungry; it's too cold; it's raining; his parents will wonder where we are. We mean no harm. Let us pass.' It crossed my mind to take my money out of my pocket, throw it to the floor as a distraction and then just run for it. I knew that discarding your treasure can cause some monsters to break off their pursuit to examine it. Then I heard my mum's voice in my head: 'You can't kiss her, you don't know where she's been.'

Dill had perfected his belly-pulling-in technique at Coventry Baths. Now, approaching the girl, he was employing it while swinging his arms back and forth, as if summoning up the courage to dive off the high board.

I'd read about dryads—evil elf maidens who dwell in the woods and seduce men to follow them into the trees from where they never emerged, lost for ever in the enchanted forest. These could be public transport dryads, I thought: touch them and you will be lost for ever in the enchanted bus stop. I dismissed the idea. Both had highlighted blonde hair and denim skirts. The girl I was looking for was clothed in crinoline, tripped through fields of swaying grass and probably slept in a bed of swans' wings in a tree.

Dill attached himself to one of their faces and went for it like an anteater trying to get the last termite out of the mound.

There was always hope that there was more to the remaining girl than met the eye. I just didn't want to get stuck with some-one who didn't share my interests. Dill's brother had warned us about 'clingy girls,' and I didn't want one of those interfering with my gaming. Mind you, Dill's brother was only fifteen, and, come to think of it, I'd never seen him standing next to a girl, let alone with one clinging to him.

'Have you,' I said, trying to make the best of a bad job while Dill applied maximum suction, 'ever played Dungeons and Dragons?'

'I've played Doctors and Nurses. I'm quite good at that if you want to give it a go,' she said, clearly showing me her bubblegum.

'It's not like Doctors and Nurses!' I said. 'There's no poofy stuff like that.' I felt hot and angry just having her compare D&D to a kids game involving stethoscopes and hats with red crosses on them. I also felt annoyed that I could remember having just such a stethoscope when I was a kid. Why hadn't I been playing with wizards? What was wrong with me?

The girl just looked at me, one of those 'go on, say something to impress me' stares.

I breathed in, drew myself up tall and examined her down my nose. 'Look. It's the best and most sophisticated wargame ever devised,' I said. I was clearly going to have to start from scratch with her.

The girl clacked on, blowing a bubble and letting it burst all over her face.

Walters, one of the D&Ders, had an expression that I was sure was appropriate here. He always called the school lunch ladies 'slatterns.' This, I was sure, was a slattern.

One of the things you get from D&D is to see yourself as a character in one of its games and other people as monsters you meet. I sketched out the girl in terms of the *Monsters and Treasure* book, part two of the three, as if you even had to ask.

'Slattern. Armour class 9 (light top and denim skirt), hit points 3, habitat: bus stops, weapons: corrosive Liverpudlian voice and scorn. If the slattern scorns you, you must use a twenty-sided dice to make a saving throw. If you shake less than 12 you will be scorned and rooted to the spot until the city tows you away.'

I decided to persevere. If I could run her through the basics of the game then I could get on with telling her about Alf the Elf, my fourth-level fighter/magic-user who had a ring of shadows. You won't find that in the official rules—it was from a fanzine, and I thought she'd be impressed that I was fully up to speed on publications such as *News from Bree, Owl and Weasel* and *Alarums and Excursions.*

'In its most basic form you choose to be a magic-user, a fighter or a cleric, this is your character for the game. You shake dice to see how strong you are or clever or . . .' I couldn't bear to leave any character attribute out, 'or wise or your constitution or your dexterity or charisma. You then go into an underground maze and fight monsters for treasure and experience,' I said.

'You do that round here?'

'I wish. You don't literally go. The dungeonmaster . . .'

'The what?' I could hardly understand what she said. To me she sounded like a big clacking duck.

'The *dungeonmaster!*' I said, as if she was being wilfully difficult. 'He's the referee. But, oh, is he so much more than a referee! He designs, according to a set of rules, a whole world, populates it with monsters and powerful magical treasures. Then . . .' I cut to the chase. I couldn't bear to keep wading through this basic stuff. 'My best character is a fourth-level elven fighter/magic-user. He's got a beautiful wife. Charisma 18, generated on three six-sided dice, the maximum,' I said.

'What's charisma?'

'Put simply,' I said, showing a very precocious talent for being patronizing, 'it's how good-looking you are, it's from 3 to 18, three being a mong, 18 my wife.'

'Your wife?'

'My elf's wife.'

'What's my charisma?' she said.

'About 6, I'd say,' I said, looking at her blotchy legs.

'So I'm nearer to a mong than the elf bird?' she said. I have to say, she picked it up quickly. Perhaps, I thought, there was promise she could learn the game.

'No,' I said, 'no. You're . . .' I didn't want to flatter her too much, and I knew that piss-takes were a top way to get on with anyone from my time with the D&Ders. Something, however, held me back.

'You're quite good-looking.' *In a slightly wonky sort of way*, I was going to add but didn't.

'Oh, that's nice,' said the girl. She clacked a bit more on the gum.

'I have this character who takes many forms,' I said, 'he's an eternal champion.'

This wasn't true, although I'd have liked a character like that. It was more Moorcock, via Porter.

Dill and the girl next to me were making a thick, wet noise with their snogging.

'His forms are Elric of Melniboné, Dorian Hawkmoon, Corum.'

'If you take me in the phone box you can feel my tits,' said the girl.

Oh God, she'd asked. I was still a good day away from puberty, I reckoned. When I say a day, I didn't know exactly but I couldn't believe God would let me wait any longer. I could feel all the social pressure to go and feel her tits but only strange flashes of the desire that would make it enjoyable.

Perhaps she was a bus-stop dryad, or a GPO dryad, and I'd be trapped for ever in an enchanted phone box. Still, it would be better than Llandudno, I thought. Could you charm spell a dryad? Now that was a question. I had to get back and look at the book. I also had to feel this girl's tits, and Dill would think I was a poof if I didn't. I weighed my responsibilities.

She stood up and took my hand. Mine was freezing, but hers seemed hot. She let go.

'Put them in your pockets to warm 'em up before you start anything,' she said, as we walked towards the box, which was opposite our guesthouse.

My head was spinning with desire to read more about dryads, but I decided to just keep talking about normal stuff until we got to the phone box. Then I'd feel the tits and say I had to go and have my tea.

'The eternal champion exists across many levels of the multiverse,' I said, as we walked, 'often killed and reincarnated elsewhere.'

Then a sudden thought troubled me. What if this girl wanted to see my knob, as I understood that girls often did. It hadn't reached a stage where it was suitable for display. The image of Dale Cortt in the showers came back to me.

'Before we start,' I said, 'is there anything else you'd like to know about D&D?'

'Absolutely nothing at all,' said the girl.

I found this very frustrating. 'It's really good,' I said, 'you'd love it if you got to play it. Anyone would.'

'Are your hands warm yet?' she said.

We walked to the end of the street, but before we got to the box I saw someone I knew. Emerging from the Morris Marina was the flat cap of Mr Grigson.

'Dill's just coming and everything's OK,' I said to Mr Grigson, for some reason flapping my arms as if trying to flag down a car in an emergency.

'Been getting up to a bit of hanky panky?' said Mrs Grigson, laughing.

'No,' said the girl, 'we haven't.'

Dill had clearly seen his parents and was virtually running up the street to get away from his girl.

I turned to mine.

'I'm sorry,' I said, 'I don't think it's going to work between us. We are from different milieus.' That was another D&D word.

'Well then,' she said, loud enough for the Grigsons to hear, 'take your milieu and fuck off.' She gave a brief little smile and turned back to her friend.

Suddenly I realized what an idiot I was being. She had tits, and they were there for the taking. They might not be elf tits, they might not be charisma 18 tits, but they were, undeniably, tits, tits you could say you had felt to the other kids in your class. Also, they were tits that were walking away down the street, which removed the main brake on my feeling that I wanted to touch them—the threat of actually having to.

'See you tomorrow?' I shouted after her up the street.

'Fuck off, little boy,' she shouted back.

'Little boy!' A massive sense of injustice swept over me. A little boy does not have the sophistication and skill to develop a fourth-level fighter/magic-user in under a month or to read *The Lord of the Rings* twice. I was more familiar than any little boy could be with the horror that is the Balrog, fire spirit of the subterranean passageways.

'I bet you don't even know what a Balrog is!' I shouted after her, 'QED! QE blinking D!'

QED is what Andy Porter said when concluding any argument. I didn't know what it meant, but it sounded good. The girl just flicked me the vees as she returned to the bus stop.

That night I lay listening to Dill have one off the wrist in the next bed to me. The gift of puberty had arrived for him, and he was not one to leave it in its box.

I lay in bed trying to think of lying with a dryad in a boat of reeds, floating down a river of leaves and stroking her tits. Another fantasy kept butting in, though, a dream of a beefy Liverpudlian girl with blotchy legs and the smell of bubblegum on her breath and me with my hands up her sweater. Then the words 'little boy' came back into my head. I was stewing in humiliation, and I wished I could stop thinking about what her tits might have felt like. Wanting her seemed to make the insult worse.

Dill's aftershave pervaded the room. You were only allowed a bath every other day at the guesthouse, and, even though his mum had made him have a thorough wash, I'd still been able to taste Hai Karate on my chips that evening.

'Dill,' I said.

'Yes.'

'Do you want to talk about orcs?'

'Not really,' he said.

'Have I told you about the Morgul sword that leaves black shards in its victims that work their way to the heart?'

'Yes.'

'Oh.'

'Mark?'

'Yes?'

'I'm not very interested in D&D.'

I felt as though a shard of the Morgul sword had made it to my heart. Up until that point I'd assumed Dill hadn't thought he was clever enough to play the game or was intimidated by the talk of fourth-years, not that he found it boring. My fourth-year friends would not only want to talk about orcs, they would probably be able to tell me things I didn't even know about them. Dill was not a suitable companion for me any more. He wasn't bright enough for me. Just as Gygax had warned, he lacked the imagination to play the game and, by association, to be my friend.

I was one of the high, a spiritual elf; he was one of the low, a Morlock to my Eloi, to use two races from the *Time Machine* dungeon Lee Hatherley had come up with the week before. Boy, did he show some invention thinking of that scenario.

'Dill,' I said.

'Yes.'

'Please don't mention Gurkhas again. I find them dull. And short. I don't believe they're that tough, either. I think you'd find a unit of the Gondor Citadel Guard would see them off pretty quick. Or one half-decent magic-user.'

Another silence.

'Mark.'

'Yes, Dill.'

'I hope you don't mind, but I've been thinking about having sex with yours as well.'

'She's not mine,' I said, turning over on my side.

I have to say, I thought he was showboating with the masturbation after that. I lay in the darkness for a while, the beat of Dill's wanking marking the passage of time, trying to force my imagination to take me away. The more I tried to get back to the river and the dryad, the more I was in the phone box. I found the idea very sexy in parts, but I was never very far from that feeling of burning embarrassment.

In future I'd have to practise harder at having the right fantasies. In all things, I thought, I should strive towards the perfect ideals of the fantasy world where there was no bubble gum, definitely no blotchy legs. There, the women would call you 'my lord' and be impressed by you instead of shouting 'little boy' in front of your mate and his parents.

I'd outgrown Dill, I decided. I didn't want friends who spent their days interested in Gurkhas and girls and the real world. I didn't want real girls, I didn't want real anything. I hadn't since I'd started D&D, and I wouldn't again, for years.

A Journey
in the Dark

I'd prayed that Mr and Mrs Grigson would set off from Llandudno early on the final Saturday so I might be back in time for a game. In those days the games at Andy's house only went on to the early evening, until he had his tea at around six. By tea, I mean the main evening meal. In the seventies you could have determined someone's class very easily just by asking did they take their meals in the order breakfast, lunch and dinner or breakfast, dinner and tea. I had no idea that there were unbelievably posh people out there who called eating at six dinner, or even posher ones who ate at eight. Neither did I know that there was an echelon above even them who described the evening meal as 'supper' and only had dinner on special occasions. Anyway, Andy was having his tea. This meant we all had to be out for five. The reason he needed an hour to prepare was obscure to me. In my house, if you were doing something else you could eat your tea while you were doing it. In Andy's it seemed a formal occasion.

Mrs Grigson had said we would need to leave the guest house by ten, but this wasn't my idea of early. I wanted them to begin the journey at about four in the morning so I could be sure of making it to the game at Porter's house by eleven. In fact, I'd have preferred us to go on the Friday night so I could be absolutely sure of not missing a second.

Ever since the holiday had begun I'd been wanting to go, but I'd learned to take things day by day, hour by hour. It was a technique I'd picked up at school. We had twenty lessons a week. I never allowed myself to consider how many I had left until at least break time on the Monday. Nineteen to go is so much better than twenty—you've started, inroads have been made. However, one lesson to go can feel worse than ten. I found this particularly bad at school because my last lesson on a Friday at this time was PE. It felt like irony, being kept back when it would have been so easy to let me go. Instead I had to stand in a field for an hour, often freezing to death.

That's how I felt on the last night in Llandudno, a big 'why?' burning inside me—why do I have to be here, why can't we leave now? I read the D&D mags I'd brought with me again. I was reading the *Strategic Review* magazine from D&D publishers TSR, all about the illusionist character class and trying to lose myself in the beautiful names of the spells—Prismatic Wall, Phantasmal Force, Audible Glamour, Chromatic Orb. These to me seemed as promising as the old firework names—Incandescent Fountain, Golden Lantern, Silver Rain. The difference was that the spells never went off with a damp fizzle and the sound of your father in the background saying, '50p—a pint and a scotch egg, we could have bought for that.' They only went off in your head, and, if they disappointed, you'd just think about them again until they didn't.

I spent a lot of time wondering what the gleam on +3 armour looked like or the edge on a flaming sword. When I was having these thoughts, though, I wasn't aware I was purely exercising my imagination. To me, I was involved in a deductive process—like when historians say, 'From what we can piece together, we believe the songs of the Vikings would have sounded something like this . . .' I was referring to a world that, in my mind, actually existed and, like my journey home that day or my release from school on a Friday lunchtime, its lack was felt more keenly for its proximity than its distance.

We had plenty of arguments on this basis in the wargames room—whether the acid from a giant ant would be strong enough to corrode through metal bars, for instance, as one enterprising character attempted to remove himself from a cage by this method.

The conversation would become incredibly detailed, with recourse to periodic tables and encyclopaedias. Of course, the only real answer is that the acid of a giant ant can burn through metal if the referee—the dungeonmaster—says it can. It's his world; he designed it, and, if he wants, the ant's sting can contain specific metal-melting compounds or pure water. We didn't see this at the time, though. We thought we could uncover the reality of the situation through argument.

It is sad to note that, even at this distance of years and without having to look it up, I know formic acid (the stuff in your everyday ant) does not combine with metals and is used in tanning and, crucially, wire stripping. It takes off the insulation but leaves the wire untouched. In high concentrations this would make it burn flesh but not the bars of a cage. This is the sort of stuff I was learning while others were concentrating on how to be nice to a girl.

On my last morning in Llandudno I was first in the breakfast room at eight and had finished my ration of two Weetabix, two slices of toast (one pat of butter allowed) and tea by about one minute and thirty-nine seconds past. I'd been hungry throughout the mornings for the entire holiday.

I was looking forward to returning home, where I could take my habitual ration of five Weetabix eaten in three visits with a liberal sprinkling of cornflakes on top. I'd tried to go back for more on the first morning, and the landlady had nearly cut off my hands. Like Mr Grigson, she'd had her formative years during rationing, and the spirit of frugality would not leave her. I know five seems like a lot for breakfast, but I'd got into the habit at junior school, where there was no option to bring sandwiches. Even before I developed a taste for fantasy, the school lunch ladies reminded me of mythical creatures, stocky half-humans you might find toiling beneath the earth. You really don't see women like that any more, looking like Andy Capp's wife with their head-scarves and overalls, formidably sturdy and with the attitude that children need to be punished for what they might do, rather than any actual offence.

One of them, the incredibly named Mrs Hex, had a ladle that seemed every bit as terrifying as the hammer of Thor, the Viking thunder god, and was employed to similar effect. Mrs Hex is one of only two names I've left unchanged in this book, other than my own, simply because I think I must have remembered it wrong. No one can be called that, can they?

It would seem amazing now, but, in England in the 1970s, the lunch lady had full licence, not only to tell children what to do, but to administer ad hoc punishments. I remember being told to clean a floor by Mrs Hex. It had been muddied by children. I was a child; therefore I was responsible. I don't blame her; this sort of reasoning was very common back then.

'Put some elbow grease into it,' she said.

I'd never heard this expression before and enquired, as you might, where the elbow grease was kept. To put things into the language of *The Lord of the Rings,* deep bit the ladle into childish skull. Today, of course, this would be classed as assault. It's not a view I would have liked to put to Mrs Hex. I imagine her saying, 'That's not assault, *this* is assault.' I have to say that my opinion of Mrs Hex was coloured slightly because the first time I had ever seen her she had been standing over an industrial-sized pot of boiling potatoes which, to the childish eye, is indistinguishable from a cauldron.

The look of these fierce women meant that I couldn't bear to put anything they had touched into my mouth, and so I'd have nothing between breakfast and tea, hence my mini-hibernation tactics at breakfast.

In Llandudno my habits were thrown out, and so I spent much of the mornings hungry. This quite pleased me. It was the sort of hunger, I thought, that might be experienced by a ring-bearer on his way to Mount Doom.

'What time are we off?' I hiccupped at Mrs Grigson, a bolus of toast still stuck in my throat.

'Give us a second, kid, I'm only just sitting down,' she said. 'Don't you want one last look at the sea?'

Of course I didn't want to look at the sea. I wanted to gaze upon the sparkling oceans of the Grey Havens or see dragon smoke rising above a stricken galleon off the Isle of Pendor. All that would be visible from Llandudno seafront was the pier and the crazy golf course, things, it seemed, that had been put in place to spite my fantasy.

It was 9.30 before the Marina began to nose east and nearly three o'clock before the Grigsons deposited me at home. I forced a 'thank you' from myself and ran back into the house.

'How was it?' said my mum as I zinged upstairs to fetch the bag with the bulk of my D&D books in it.

'I'm just going out,' I said, still coming in.

I think this moment was the beginning of my adolescence, when my motivations became utterly mysterious to my parents and my parents' simply irrelevant to me. To tell the truth, I think my motivations had been fairly mysterious to them even up to that point.

The rift of understanding between parents and their children had been widening since the 1950s, and in 1976 it looked like a chasm. Even for the more forward-thinking of my mum and dad's generation of the working class, their role models had been their parents. If you read the British literature of the early sixties—*Room at the Top, Saturday Night and Sunday Morning, A Kind of Loving*—you have the sense of people longing for sexual and financial freedoms that the older generation never had but, at the same time, of essentially wanting to be the same people. In *Saturday Night and Sunday Morning* Arthur Seaton settles down and stops his tricks; in *Room at the Top* Joe Lampton sells his soul for the wealthy girl, but he's still in a context his parents would understand—marriage, a good job.

In the seventies, though, something strange happened. Lots of us became aliens. We wanted to be pop stars or actors or other sorts of people we had never met. These weren't the actors and pop stars of today, who go out of their way to emphasize their normality, but unearthly beings who lived at the edge of things. As Marc Bolan, lead singer of the glam rock band T. Rex put it: 'I'm not the boy next door. I never was. That's what makes me successful.' Back then we didn't want to look at our drab selves, all poverty, brown Formica kitchen units and cheese in a tube. On stage and screen, and in front of our bedroom mirrors, we wanted a taste of the exotic. We didn't want to be the boy next door, even those of us who, like me and Bolan, grew up in terraced houses. We became convinced that we were in some way fundamentally strange and saw our strangeness reflected in David Bowie's ill-matched eyes. We didn't want, to quote Joe Lampton, the protagonist of *Room at the Top,* a three-guinea shirt and a girl with a Riviera tan. We boys wanted to live in a capsule, go out with pale moongirls, be bisexual—as long as it didn't involve touching a man—destroy passers-by and die young—as long as it didn't actually involve dying young.

We were growing up a decade after the collapse of the old certainties in the sixties. General state education had increased hugely in quality, there were free grants for further study and we felt that the world was open to us. The trouble was that the prize of a life on easy street looked pretty dull when seen close up. The boy who sat next to me at school wanted to be an accountant. A generation or two before that would have been a wild dream for kids of our background, but to me it seemed like choosing a form of penal servitude.

I, and lots of people like me, didn't want to be ourselves, but we didn't know what we did want to be.

Our mums and dads couldn't understand our taste for the bizarre. They grew up with the memory of the falling bombs clear in their minds. The physical and economic repercussions of World War II were still very much with them, so my parents' generation sought prosperity and stability. Growing up in stability and relative prosperity, we wanted a bit of danger.

I'd like to emphasize the word 'relative' in that last sentence. British rock stars of the seventies were still awestruck when they travelled to the States to find the seats reclined on planes and that ice was served with water. Most people didn't have central heating—the average temperature in a British front room in 1970 was 15 degrees centigrade or 59 degrees Fahrenheit. This is the sort of level at which most people today would require a jacket if they were going out. We had a telly that came with a slot meter that meant you paid for your viewing by putting a coin into its back. Watching an Agatha Christie was always made more exciting by the knowledge that the money might run out before Poirot put his hand on the killer's shoulder.

This wasn't what you'd call poverty, but it certainly bore no resemblance to wealth. Poverty might have given us a purpose, wealth something to do. The problem for us was that, in our youth, nothing happened. At all. We had the Cold War, of course, but that was just nothing happening on a grand scale. The days seemed endless and not in a good way—nowhere to go and nothing to do. Devoid of any real excitement, we sought other outlets, outlets that seemed wilfully perverse to an older generation. They couldn't understand the growing trends of violence and vandalism, but, given the alternatives, it was amazing the whole country wasn't burned to the ground just for the fun of watching the blaze. The kids were off their nuts with boredom.

We had seen other worlds on the stage of *Top of the Pops,* even James Bond. This incredible life was just the other side of the screen, but we couldn't touch it. It was like having a beautiful new car that you could sit in all you liked but never drive. Then a set of magic keys arrived, in the form of D&D. With just some rulebooks and some dice I could start living my fantasy life that second. All I had to do was get to Porter's house.

I stuffed down a couple of liberally salted mayonnaise sandwiches and in seconds was through the door, hammering out past my school to the semi-rural outskirts of the town where Porter lived. I was on my bike or, as I knew it, Shadowfax, the blazing star of the stables of the Rohirim. I feel sure that King Theoden's swiftest mount might have made it up the hill to Andy's house slightly more ably than I did. If a passer-by had been reminded of one of the characters of Middle Earth I don't think it would have been the white rider Gandalf or even noble Legolas the Elf but more Sam Gamgee, the sweating gardener hauling himself up the slope with a bag of provisions.

It was a quarter to four when I arrived at Porter's and knocked on the door. The front room of Andy's house was used as a dining room, and the boys were clearly visible gaming around the table through the leaded glass. There were two boys from my class at school, Dave Fearnly and Pete White, who I'd become friends with since starting gaming, Porter, Hatherley and his brother, Gerling and another fourth-year, the cheery Glebe. I felt I was coming home.

There was an hour to go until they'd have to leave. I felt simultaneously elated to have got there before the game had finished and full of a sort of cosmic bitterness that I'd been forced to miss the preceding five hours. I pushed my bike through the gates that led to Andy's carport and waved at Hatherley through the window. He acknowledged my presence with a sort of half sneer, like I wasn't quite worth a full one, and I waited at the door. After a minute or so no one had come to it, so I rang the bell.

Porter eventually answered.

'Yes?' he said, not quite opening the door as fully as he might have.

'Hail,' I said, without irony, 'are you having a game?'

'It's nearly over,' said Porter.

'Ah, what's happened?' I said.

'It's complicated,' said Andy, with the heavy implication that I wouldn't really understand.

'Ah,' I said. I suppose I had been expecting the sort of welcome

Gandalf the White received hopping up with an extra 10,000 cavalry to lift the siege of Helm's Deep.

Porter stood looking at me for a second.

'Have you still got my D&D books?' I said.

'Yes,' said Andy, 'I suppose you better come in.'

'Great!' I said.

I wanted to lock up my bike but I feared that, if I did, he might
close the door, and I might never get in. I left it up against the
wall.

'Aren't you going to lock that?' said Andy as I came inside.

'No need,' I said, making a twirling motion with my fingers,
'I've put a spell on it.'

Andy didn't greet this with cynicism or derision, which was
surprising because I'd never seen him or any other wargamer do
anything without cynicism or derision. He might have not
believed that I could put a spell on the bike. He might not have
even believed anyone could put a spell on anything, but, like me,
he wanted to believe he lived in a world where spells were possible. If anything, he would criticize the way I cast the spell, not
the casting itself.

Andy's house was to me a fantasy all of its own. Although it
was a modern three-bedroom place that was no bigger than mine,
it seemed as though it was from another and vastly more attractive world.

The décor in my family's house was typical of the aspirational
working class of the day—the gas fire with moulded plastic logs
given a flame effect by a wonky fan moving over a red bulb (normally broken within two weeks of installation), glass animals for
ornaments, a nodding bird that dipped its beak in a glass of water
until the felt came off his nose, a collection of tiny tumblers with
vintage cars on them and a blue carpet with large circles on it that
made very good marble targets or, in later years, demon-
summoning circles for wizard figures. I think the items that
summed up the home best were a set of plastic oranges that was

pinned on the wall at one end of the kitchen and a large false window at the other that depicted an Alpine scene rendered in sticky-backed plastic. The seventies was full of stuff like that—things designed for decoration but somehow doing its opposite—making the room duller and more depressing than if the walls had been left bare.

The world of the suburban schoolboy is a very small one. I think I'd actually seen the insides of about ten different houses in my entire life by the time I was twelve. My mum's and my auntie's houses were furnished in the modern style, my nan's and my great aunt's in an older, more solid taste—they were from the generation that bought its furniture when it got married and, other than the sofas, never really changed it. Beyond this were the houses of friends—pretty much like my mum's and my auntie's—and the chalet we stayed in on holiday.

I believed that the richest people in the country lived in Surbiton—the suburban area of London that was home to the super-posh folk of *The Good Life* sitcom—and in Coventry's new Cannon Park—four-bedroomed houses, the ownership of which was to me as sure a sign of blue blood as any entry in *Debrett's Peerage & Baronetage.*

Andy's house was like nothing I'd seen—it had a sense of history about it. His family were in the Sealed Knot, a society that recreates the battles of the English Civil War. The room in which we played the game contained muskets, uniforms, a drum, swords and stranger items—belts dangling powder charges, helmets and part of a pike. Instead of the plasticky flat-pack furniture that everyone else seemed to have the table was in a dark, carved wood and the glass-fronted cabinets displayed things that seemed to me like archaeological treasures—bottles and boxes, old books.

Only one thing in my experience came close to it. When I was at junior school my mum had a cleaning job at a large house in the posh-ish Earlsdon area of Coventry, the home of the evocatively named Eldritches. I sometimes used to go with her. It had seemed like somewhere from another world—parquet floors, large ferns in pots, deep, dark windows and a harpsichord in a music room. It had felt like an amazingly calm and solid place where a beautiful life was lived and people were concerned with more than the day-to-day round of school or work, meals and TV.

At home my mum used Mr Sheen on the furniture. At Mrs Eldritch's she used beeswax. This seemed like a significant difference to me, like there was something more important about the lives that were lived in that house than the ones that were lived in ours, worth taking more care over. As a young kid, I'd had a very clear understanding that I was only a spectator in that world. At Porter's I felt like a participant.

As if being a D&D nerd wasn't bad enough, I was committing the crime against cool of the century. Given the sort of working-class background that certain sorts love to dine out on, I was falling in love with the middle-class liberal intelligentsia, if not the people themselves—I think Porter's dad was a factory worker like mine, though I could be wrong—then their style and, more importantly, their attitudes.

Being a member of the Sealed Knot may not qualify you as a Hampstead art tart, but it does show an interest in concerns outside your immediate sphere and a desire to seek out more from the world than what's just presented to you at Allied Carpets, Woolworths and on TV.

I know that there are plenty of working-class people who are interested in far more than their immediate environment; it's a ludicrous myth that they're all sullenly unconcerned with education or enquiry—you only have to look to the popularity of night schools to see that. However, old furniture, lots of old books and antiques was an alien world to me, and, rightly or wrongly, I associated it with posh people and a certain attitude to life—arty, thoughtful and, to me, very attractive.

It's worth saying a word or two about the Sealed Knot at this point. I've since discovered that membership of this organization isn't, for the Midlands, that unusual. Two other wargamers who came through our group were heavily involved in it—Johnny and his biking brother Matt from Allesley Park and Karl Devonshire from the badlands of Radford. There does seem to be something in the water that draws us to spend large amounts of time pretending to be someone else.

There are nine Sealed Knot regiments operating in London, a city of 7.5 million people. Look at any major hobby and there are more people doing it in the capital than anywhere else. I'd bet there are more surfers in London than there are in Cornwall, more skiers than there are in Aviemore. This is not the case with the Sealed Knot. There are twelve regiments in Birmingham, out of a population one-seventh the size of London. Still, Birmingham is a large urban area. But what can account for the ten Sealed Knot regiments of Northamptonshire (population 600,000), the thirteen of Warwickshire (population 500,000), the ten in Leicestershire (population 600,000)? If you compare this to professional soccer teams, London has thirteen; Warwickshire has none. There's something odd in the minds of Midlanders, something that enabled a friend of mine to explain that his wife wasn't coming to a dinner party because she was off 'wenching.'

'What-ing?' I asked.

'Wenching. Tuesday and Thursday nights she plays a wench up at Warwick Castle.'

Still, at age twelve I hadn't been exposed yet to any of this, and so the Porter house was a truly remarkable place to me, a sorcerer's cave. Andy wasn't shy about adopting the role of sorcerer, either, presiding over the table with a true sense of drama and saying things like: 'The nucleus of the swarm!' and seeming to get more *S*s into the sentence than it actually contained. He'd lean forward and say: 'The Hamddra blade of the loathsome Krelle, one atom thick, it is the *sharpest structure in the universe.*' He seemed to roll into the *R*s like a cat up a post, savouring the loathsomeness of the Krelle and having some of their vile glamour rub off on himself.

'It can't be sharper than a Sword of Sharpness,' I'd say. 'That's enchanted, and the Hamddra blade isn't, so you're talking rubbish. I have at the varlet.'

Andy would suck in his lips and narrow his eyes as if wishing he had a Sword of Sharpness, a Hamddra blade or perhaps even a blunter instrument to strike me with.

I could have avoided being so annoying had I paid closer attention to the literature I was reading. There are, for instance, lessons to be learned in *The Lord of the Rings,* for anyone who cares to take them. I was slowly absorbing some of them— women aren't very important or interesting and generally play a subservient role. A traditional feminist criticism of men is that they divide women into madonnas and whores. This isn't the case with *The Lord of the Rings*. There are no whores in that.

The only women represented there are the unattainable elf maidens or the fat and friendly hobbit mothers—interestingly, sex is entirely absent from the book. I know some Tolkien dweeb is very likely going to find some example here to contradict me, but I have read the book fourteen times. This may only qualify me as a fair-weather fan, but I think I'd have found some by now. There are lessons about what good looks like—white and Nordic as in the elves—and what bad looks like—black as in the orcs and Southrons. The Southrons even obligingly ride elephants and wear turbans to drive the point home. Also, just in case you were in danger of missing the point, they come from the south. There's a lot of stuff about class and knowing your place too, but, as in any book *that* popular, there are also bound to be some subtler connections with life as it is lived.

Had I looked harder I would have seen very clearly that *The Lord of the Rings* gives a very good lesson in how to be cool. At the beginning of the book, two characters appear. One is Tom Bombadil, who was so irritating he was axed from the film. The other is the dark and mysterious Strider, who, it eventually emerges, has decided not take up the vast wealth of his inheritance as King of Gondor and instead to spend his time as a sort of glorified park keeper trudging the soaking hills between the Shire and Rivendell. As you might.

Tom Bombadil is open and happy and full of merry song. He talks in a funny way and wears an extravagant hat with a feather in it. After a couple of pages in his company most readers would gladly point him out to a Black Rider or even stick him with a Morgul sword themselves.

Strider, however, sits in the corner, leaning back and saying little, his hood up despite the warm. Like this he wouldn't be out of place happily menacing a shopping mall alongside some modern young people. Strider is an enigma and much more charismatic for it.

The difference between him and Tom Bombadil is that Tom demands attention with his songs and his jokes; Strider waits for it to come to him and, as far as the hobbits of the Prancing Pony in Bree are concerned, does his best to dissuade it.

If Strider had immediately told the hobbits he was an exiled king and all-round dab hand with the sword the readers would have been much less interested in him. Really, this is all about seeking approval—the best way of getting it is to look like you don't want it. I couldn't see at the time that this might apply to life.

Something else I took from the book, and something it took me years to get over, was this: when it comes to language, lay it on with a spoon. *The Lord of the Rings* is full of the sort of language and description that could curl your toes through your boots and into the pavement so hard you could crack a slab. It's a world where no one is ever tired, only weary, where the sun does not come up but instead walks in the fields of the west. I loved this stuff.

Accordingly, I greeted the wargamers: 'Good afternoon, merry friends.'

'What did it say?' said Hatherley, who looked less than merry.

'Sit down and try to be quiet. We want to finish the game,' said Porter.

'Aye, thou art on thy course and must cleave to it.'

I did try to be quiet, rather unsuccessfully as it turned out.

Pete, my fellow second-year, had a cleric—the priestly half-way house between magic-users and fighters of the early game—who was in trouble with a giant bat.

'The bat swoops,' said Porter, rolling a dice, 'it hits, 3 points damage.'

Pete's character was just starting out. In D&D, the more experience you have, the tougher you are. I knew his character couldn't have had more than 6 hit points and, this late in the dungeon, must have taken more than 3 damage already.

'I hit back at the bat,' said Pete, sort of recording the damage on his pad and sort of not either.

Porter didn't pull him up on it, as he surely would have me. Pete was a good rugby player who, even at twelve, had an edge of physicality to him that made the gangling Porter, if not frightened of him, then at least slightly more respectful. On top of this, because Pete lacked my virtually unbearable enthusiasm for the game—he was merely absorbed in it—I think Porter wanted to reward him for his lack of shouting and screaming.

One of the annoying things about a trip to Pete's house in these early years was that sometimes he'd want to play Scalextric or some other non-D&D game. He had a purpose-built track including pits and garages and trees and even a skid pan chicane, most boys' dream. I'd watch the cars zooming around the track with sullen uninterest. Why do this, I thought, when there are snarks to kill?

Andy wasn't cheating by allowing Pete some flexibility. If you play D&D exactly by the letter of its law then characters tend not to last very long at all. Most people bend the rules in the interests of a longer and better game.

Pete rolled the dice, and the fourth-years rolled their eyes as I said something about the bat tasting his holy wrath. Still, I didn't mind. Among the muskets and the swords, honoured by the company of older boys and immersed in a world so much more colourful than my own, I felt for the first time in my life that I truly belonged somewhere.

All that time growing up I'd never felt comfortable with my background. I loved my parents, but I always felt a bit like the alien in *The Man who Fell to Earth*—just staying with them until I could gather the strength to fulfil my true destiny.

As I drank in the atmosphere of the wargaming room I felt that I'd at last found some fellow spirits. It was a fantasy more dangerous than anything to do with dragons.

Being Andy Porter

It was inevitable, I suppose, that my first love would look like something out of a fantasy novel. It was less inevitable that it should look like Andy Porter. Later, when the revised set of D&D was issued in 1978, it was noted that Andy looked not unlike the picture of the troll on the cover.

If the artist Quentin Blake—he of the Roald Dahl books—had seen him he'd have snapped him up for a drawing on the spot. The thing about Andy was that, as a teenager, it seemed to me he was just too long and not nearly wide enough. It was as if the Lord had got carried away moulding the height and hadn't quite enough material left for the breadth. Andy could quite easily have just stepped out of Castle Gormenghast, lanking forward with a set of keys or warning you of some terrible fate that awaited you if you went within. In the interests of balance I must say that few teenage boys are visions of loveliness. As adolescence bore down on me, I was no oil painting myself. The combination of short legs and an enormous head might have seen me included in a fair few fantasy novels. As my friend Daryl Weir once noted, with some justification, I resembled a large, mobile penis. 'The whole thing's a dick,' I believe were his exact words.

When I say 'love' I mean I had a crush on Porter. I didn't want a physical relationship with Andy. I wanted a deeper consummation than that—I wanted to be him.

It's common for adolescent kids to seek out role models other than their parents. However, my parents weren't role models for me in the first place. There was no sense of rebellion in becoming like Andy, just a feeling that I'd finally discovered who I really was. The fact that I'd discovered I was really someone else was, literally, a schoolboy error.

So who was this Andy Porter that I had discovered myself to be? What follows will sound harsh, but I'm writing it from my twelve-year-old view. Andy's attitudes appeared to me unpleasant, but then I'd missed a central fact about our relationship—he very clearly didn't like me. He had a nice side, it was just that—at that stage of his life—he never chose to show it to me. Also, Andy was immature himself and probably just as alienated from school as I was. Looking back, it's easy to see that a lot of his attitudes were the result of feelings of insecurity. Mind you, you can say that about ninety per cent of human behaviour. In fact, so much of human behaviour seems based on insecurity that it almost ceases to work as an excuse or reason for what we do.

Any criticism here, it must be said, is also a criticism of myself. I wouldn't have been able to look up to Andy if these tendencies hadn't been there in me in the first place.

Andy, at that period, lived in a very black-and-white world, where things were either exalted or damned. You can see this by the choice of his characters in the game or the dungeons he created. When they took on their gaming identities the boys showed how they wanted to be perceived by their peers but revealed quite a lot more.

At this stage of his gaming life Andy still participated as a player. As he got older he found he much preferred to be a referee—a dungeonmaster. There are two ways of interpreting this. One is that Andy had a talent for coming up with the dungeons—this, remember, is the generic name that we gave to the scenarios our characters participated in; they didn't need to be underground, they could be in a town or a house or under the sea or anything you can imagine. So by that interpretation Andy decided to concentrate on what he was good at. I personally was grateful for this because I never enjoyed creating dungeons nearly as much as I did being a player. The second way of looking at it is that you can't lose as a dungeonmaster. Neither can you be challenged: your word is final, and any time you want to kill off a player you pretty much can. In terms of the game, the dungeonmaster is god. I have to say I think that, at aged fifteen, it appeared that Andy rather fancied himself as God, from where I was sitting.

His main character was a magic-user—wizard—known as Zarlan the Ultimate. His next character displayed less modesty and was known as Zarathustra—as in Nietzsche's *Thus Spake Zarathustra,* where the idea of the 'superman,' the übermensch, first comes about.

I don't know if Andy had read any Nietzsche, but he certainly let you believe that he had, and there was something of the over-bearing, imperious attitude of the German philosopher to the way he acted. He would love to tell you something about physics, to say 'A black hole is so dense that density has no meaning; it is in the infinitely dense condition known as the singularity. The surface is known as the event horizon. There matter, space and time collapse and the rules of physics themselves fall apart.' He'd say this in a way that implied you had been very, very foolish to overlook these facts. I began to do the same and thought that I could start to call someone who was really thick 'The Singularity,' that is, infinitely dense. However, I was scared of anyone who was that thick, and the wargamers were all reasonably bright, so that one had to remain on the back burner.

In his apparent arrogance Porter wasn't unique. Walters, Hatherley and Gerling were all like this in their way, but Porter was the most charismatic of the three, and I set out to copy him.

Each of the boys seemed convinced that he himself was a genius. This was, I think, because, while they found themselves at the top of the class academically, they were definitely at the bottom when it came to style, sports or what we used to call street cred. Therefore they sank their self-esteem into their strengths and chose to ignore their weaknesses. As, under their influence, did I.

As the game drew to a close that evening after Llandudno I learned a new way of seeing myself. The soccer scores were being read out on the TV in Andy's living room, his mum having left the door ajar when she popped her head through to tell him to finish things off.

At that time virtually the whole nation did 'the football pools,' a gambling competition to predict the outcome of all that weekend's soccer games. The stakes were small, and the prize for winning was substantial—in the millions of pounds.

The comforting voice of the scores reader slowly revealing that, no, you hadn't won and it was another week's drudgery ahead rather than sipping champagne on the Riviera, was one of the rituals of English life. As the voice came through with the evocative names of the Scottish teams, 'Partick Thistle 0, Raith Rovers 2; Hamilton Academicals 2, Queen of the South 2; Stranraer 0 . . .' I saw Hatherley roll his eyes.

'Would you silence that yob, Andrew?' he said. I thought this curious, as the man reading the scores had a voice every bit as posh as the one Hatherley was putting on.

'Gladly,' said Andy, closing the door to exclude the TV.

'Don't you like football?' I said. I personally was indifferent to it. We'd always been taken to speedway, the English version of dirt track motorcycle racing, and regarded soccer as for posh kids. That sounds like I'm making it up, but, if you go to speedway, you'll see what I mean.

'Football is for morons and thugs,' said Porter. 'Superior people play Dungeons and Dragons.'

So there you had it. Not making the first team, or any team for that matter, wasn't something to be ashamed of; it was a cause for pride. Also, I liked the phrase 'superior people.' That hadn't exactly been the feeling I'd had among my classmates, but it helped explain why I felt no connection with them—it wasn't my fault, it was theirs.

'I expect you're quite a fan,' said Hatherley, 'it's the sort of thing that would appeal to a dummkopf like you.'

'No,' I said, 'D&D's the thing. I'm not a moron.'

'No, you're not a moron; you are technically a cretin,' said Walters.

Andy just glowered at me. I think he disliked me so much that he was afraid to start insulting me in case it was the first step on the path to murder.

Briefly, it appeared, I had acquired a new nickname, and the three fourth-years chortled in complicity at their cleverness in thinking it up—I was to be known as Cretin.

I can't say this scorn made me feel good, although it didn't make me feel that bad either. I was used to a lot worse at school from some of my classmates. In fact, for years my nickname at school had been Spaz. I got it at junior school and actually encouraged people to call me it when I reached senior school. To me Spaz was the sort of name possessed by an Artful Dodger type of character, an individual who had an unusual approach to life, not a leading member of the gang but essential to it nevertheless. I didn't realize that to other boys it just meant I was a spaz.

My friend Pete had actually tried to help me ditch the name by calling me 'Baz' as a contraction of my surname. I told him I preferred Spaz. Pete was a popular kid at school; it might have caught on. It was as if he'd taken the 'kick me' sign from my back, and I'd carefully reattached it.

All the way home from Andy's house I thought of what I could say to Hatherley, rerunning the scenario in my head.

'Cretin and idiot are titles given to people of low-IQ scores. Mine on the class test was 158,' I said. In my fantasy I liberally granted myself a fair slab of points over what I had actually achieved. 'That makes me a genius. And to be a dummkopf I'd have to be a German idiot. I should think even you can see that I'm not German, Hatherley,' I said.

In the fantasy Andy Porter laughed and said, 'You have to admit, he's got you there, Hatherley.' By the time I got home it was almost as if I'd said it, and Andy had been winking along at my cleverness.

This is why I say I was in love with Andy, or at least that I'd fallen for him like a boy falls for a girl from afar. I imagined us doing things together. If he had been a girl I might have imagined us tripping through sunlit meadows hand in hand, but I largely just imagined us wargaming and him liking me, sharing a joke or telling me that my character had won some interesting and exotic treasure.

I did have some dreams about him vanquishing bullies at school, but I think I knew in my heart that he was as scared of the tougher kids in my class as I was. If I think back to the fantasies I had about him it's amazing how literal they were. He was a wizard in a tower, old with weakened powers, his kingdom crumbling around him. He needed a champion and chose me, master of the dark arts, to travel through the multiverse confronting his enemies in the seventy-seven dimensions. I'd win and return, scarred by battle and experience. In one daydream I had about this sort of thing I believe I'd lost both my eyes but had one replaced with the magical eye of a long-dead wizard. I'd brought back the gem that contained Porter's wizard's soul, and, placing it under his tongue, I revitalized him. There you are; I help Andy, he turns into someone else; the pupil shows himself worthy to the master, and everyone's happy ever after.

It was me who was doing the changing, however.

I didn't know it at the time, but I was picking up another attitude from the fourth-years—that of having an opinion on absolutely everything. I think it's a reasonably adult position not to care about something one way or another, to have a new idea suggested to you and say, 'I don't really have any strong feelings on it.' Clearly it's good to have strong feelings on some things, but not on the kind of shoes someone wears or how they shake a dice. Huge passions over small things are really the province of adolescents and, through Porter and these fourth-years and their opinions on soccer (disgusting), pop music (degenerate) and conceptual rock (superior) I was learning them early. They were to stay with me for a long time.

Looking back at it now, I can see that D&D involved a whole-sale rejection of cool and a celebration of things that were, to the average schoolboy, utterly naff. In this way it was a genuine sub-culture and more radically separate from the mainstream than punk could ever hope to be. The punks wanted to confront 'society,' but they were dependent on that society for their *raison d'être*. If you're setting out to shock then you need someone to be shocked. The sensible, adult world to D&Ders was just a total irrelevance, and we ignored it in the hope it would go away, which for some of us it did.

All that mattered to us was to have an amazing and exotic character who could dust up a set of spectres in no time. The fact that another boy our own age might have had a girlfriend, a sack full of sports awards and fashionable clothing would have made us look down on him. The only reason for not being into D&D was that you were either too stupid or you were kidding yourself. You wanted to be into it really, but you were too blinded by fash-ion to admit it. When you grew up you'd sit down at the gaming table like a sensible person.

The only reason anyone of our age ever got a girlfriend, we thought, was that they were either superhuman—all boys have one boy they mark out for special worship—or that they had tricked her by pretending to be someone else.

The worst kind of pretence was to wear fashionable clothes. Andy used the word 'trendy' as a pejorative, and I soon followed him. I think one of our objections to fashion was that it was uno-riginal, that you weren't being you, just copying something someone else had come up with.

This made for some difficult trips to the shops with my mum.

'What, exactly, are you looking for?' she said one day after we'd been through every shop in Coventry city centre and I'd rejected each pair of trousers I'd seen, from burgundy Sta-Prest to jeans and everything in between. Actually, in the 1970s 'everything in between' wasn't that much.

'Breeks,' I'd said.

It was a quarter to five, and my mum stood weakly by the racks of navy blue in C&A.

'What?'

'Breeks, proper old-fashioned breeks like you'd ride on a horse.'

'You're not marching about in jodhpurs,' my mum said.

'I don't want jodhpurs. I want breeks, proper breeks like you have in *Lord of the Rings*,' I'd said.

'Find me the breeks!' she said. 'They do slacks in three styles which are good enough for every other kid in the city, so why not you?'

She gestured towards an advertising poster which showed combed youths gazing into the middle distance as if something had happened, was happening and would continue happening in their lives, unlike mine. God, I hated them.

'There aren't any breeks in here,' I said.

'So unless you want to walk about naked then I suggest you get you a pair of slacks and let us get home while the buses are still running.'

'I want breeks,' I said.

This could be seen as a straightforward example of teenage truculence. However, I think it reflected something deeper. Like many kids of my generation I wanted something that simply wasn't available. Reality just didn't have what I required.

My biggest fear wasn't that we wouldn't find the breeks; it was that we would find them, and they'd become fashionable. I know now that you could file that one under 'unreasonable anxiety,' but back then it seemed a dire possibility. Then I'd be in the unenviable position of having to tell everyone I saw who was wearing them that they were a copycat. I imagined that I might be able to get a story in the *Coventry Evening Telegraph* featuring me wearing the breeks and warning others to keep away from them. The idea of wearing something that was popular enough to be sold in a shop appalled me. Really, I think I would have been happier shopping at one of the Sealed Knot's meetings, stocking up on waistcoats and buckled shoes. I imagined the looks of approval and jealousy I'd get when I turned up to my next D&D meeting enbreeked. Perhaps Porter would even ask me to join the Sealed Knot. Now, there was a thought. I imagined me being detailed to rescue him from where he lay fallen on the field, fighting off ten roundheads and making it back to our lines. There's no way, of course, that any of us D&Ders would have seen ourselves as Parliamentarians. We were the high, the noble and the true, not a bunch of Bible-blind sheep-shaggers from the fens.

D&D was making all my family relationships more difficult. At my nan's I bored her rigid with talk of monsters and Porter. In my mind Andy wasn't someone who could scarcely restrain himself from strangling me; he was a new, exciting and glamorous friend. The closer I felt to D&D, the closer I was to him, and the closer I was to him, the closer I was to D&D. Andy was, to me, the personification of everything I wanted to be: clever, arty, aloof and arrogant. I wasted no time in practising these traits on my nan on my regular Sunday visit.

My nan had, as she always did, made me tea and furnished me with a packet of bourbon biscuits, all of which I would dunk and eat. I'd brought with me my figurines. These are almost entirely irrelevant to the game of D&D, but never mind, they provide a focus for the imagination and a way to physically interact with your hobby. I cherished them.

'There's the dragon,' I said. I also had a copy of *The Dragon* D&D magazine with me and had been drawing a dragon while wondering if there was a chance I was a polymorphed (shape-changed) dragon in human form. I had the dragon angle fairly covered that morning.

I took out the dragon, which I had 'painted,' imagining myself to be Andy Porter while I did so but also marvelling at the disparity between his abilities and mine. Years later, when my motor skills had improved and I'd practised a bit I would get an O-level U at art—unclassified, the bottom possible mark. At that age my artistic prowess was not yet that developed.

'The wings are blue,' I said, 'for deflecting lightning bolts.' This was a straightforward lie. Nowhere in the rules of Dungeons and Dragons does it say that dragons can deflect lightning bolts with their blue wings. Nowhere does it say that dragons have blue wings. Well, actually, a blue dragon has blue wings and is immune to lightning bolts, so there is some justification there. However, this was not a blue dragon. I just had a tiny bit of Baltic blue paint left from an old model of a warship, so on it went. Green all over seemed too mundane for such a fabulous beast. I had been meaning to fill the struts in with red when I got the time. These, I decided would be main arteries, and if a warrior were to cut one by mistake he'd be covered with corrosive, clinging dragon's blood.

However, from another angle I might not be lying about the blue wings at all. This was the world of fantasy gaming. If I wanted to design a dragon with blue, lightning-deflecting wings that was up to me.

'Oh, yes, they look like they'd do a good job of that. Is that in case they're flying in a storm?'

I rolled my eyes. I imagined the level of contempt Andy would summon for a mistake like that. The woman had much to learn. Still, she was my nan. There's a limit to the level of contempt you can show a nan.

'Wrong!' I said. 'Well, they would work in a storm. But really they're designed against bolt-throwing MUs.'

'Bolt throwing emus?' said my nan.

I nearly spat my biscuit. Emus! Emus! That sounds funny now, but at the time it seemed practically sacrilegious. An emu was the puppet used by the popular entertainer Rod Hull. I thought they should confine themselves to light music-hall acts and not sully the purity of D&D with their prying beaks. What the hell would Andy Porter have said about that?

'MUs. Magic-users,' I said as if she was being wilfully obtuse.

'What are they?'

'They cast spells.'

'Like wizards?'

Ahh! I put my hand on my head. 'A wizard is a tenth-level magic-user, Nan. They don't get called that until then. You can't call a magic-user a wizard. A wizard is a magic-user, but a magic-user is not necessarily a wizard. You need to be exact.'

I was puzzled by her ignorance surrounding magic-users. I'd been certain that I ran her through the basic character classes months before. I looked down into *Monsters and Treasure*. My eye alighted on the wyvern, the mythical beast that has the body of a dragon, the legs of a bird and a vicious, barbed sting in its tail. I pondered on its might for a few seconds, as it has 6+1 hit dice. This means you shake six six-sided dice and add one to your score to see how tough the beast is. You might shake 21 and add one—22 hit points. That meant that if you bashed it with a sword (which at this time did 1–6 damage, later it went to 1–8 when advanced D&D came out and convinced us that we were all, well, advanced) it would take you on average seven bashes to kill it. The least you can do it in is four.

'6 plus 1 hit dice,' I said to my nan. 'Do you realize how powerful that is?'

She didn't look like she did, so I thought I'd fill her in.

'I mean,' I said, 'a crone like yourself would probably only have D4.'

The 'crone' bounced off my nan like a non-magical weapon off a werebear. 'What's a D4?' she said. You see, that's what love can do—make you ask questions of a fantasy wargames-obsessed thirteen-year-old when anyone in their right mind would reach for a gag.

'A four-sided dice!' I said. In my mind Andy was sitting at the table next to me and we were exchanging incredulous glances.

'Dice have six sides,' said my nan.

I couldn't even be bothered to reply to that one. I just held up the triangular four-sided dice with an 'Exhibit A, m'lud' written all over my face.

'It's like a little pyramid, isn't it?' she said.

I blew out heavily. 'A pyramid has five sides, including its base,'

I said, 'this has four.' There was mild contempt in my voice, even though I'd made exactly the same mistake in front of Porter and Hatherley when I'd first started gaming and been subjected to some heavy scorn. Sharing that scorn made me part of their gang, even if it meant I had to scorn my dear nan.

'In fact,' I said, 'you may even only have one D3. A wyvern is probably twelve times more powerful than you.' That somehow didn't seem enough. 'Maybe a thousand times,' I said. A beast like that has got to be more powerful than twelve nans. My nan didn't even have claws or any venom. She did, however, have some biscuits.

'Open them others if you want 'em,' she said, nodding towards some shortbreads, 'or would you prefer some Krakawheat and cheese?'

I preferred Krakawheat and cheese like the troll prefers roasted halfling. There's something in early adolescence that's akin to being pregnant. I've heard pregnant women describe that antsy, can't do anything with yourself feeling, and it seems similar to how I felt then. And, as in pregnancy, adolescence brings with it strange crazes. Pickles, cheese and Krakawheat were mine.

So there I was, the dog at my feet, eating the food I loved the most in the warm, snug kitchen of my beloved nan. The clock was ticking; the gas fire was on, and there was a smell of baking in the room. This should be the sort of thing that your best memories are made of, and, to an extent, for me it is. However, there was something else going on underneath.

I took out another model—two dwarves side by side. Porter had painted these. He was a skilled artist and later went on to be a professional illustrator. I'd pretty much wrecked his work by adding some red paint down their arms.

'You know why that blood's there, don't you?' I said.

'From the fighting?' said my nan, not unreasonably.

I was smug. 'Sort of,' I said raising my brows, 'but not for the reasons you might suppose. A dwarf is small but incredibly strong. When he hits someone with his sword or his axe he doesn't just stop at the blow. He continues through the stomach to punch out their entrails.'

Again, don't look for that in the rules; you won't find it. It's just that beheading someone with an axe was a little tame for my tastes that morning. I think I wanted to frighten her, to feel power over her as I imagined others—Andy in particular—could feel their power over me. There, though, is my image of D&D—of me trying and failing to terrify an old lady while she feeds me biscuits.

'They often strangle people with their own bowels,' I said as my nan kneaded some dough.

'There's scones later,' said my nan. Her character sheet would record that long exposure to this sort of thing had rendered her immune.

However, I didn't pay much attention to my relationships with people who genuinely loved me. I was too obsessed with people who genuinely didn't.

Pale Exile

At lunchtime at school on the first day of the new half-term I stood in the area between Porter's house and mine. Woodlands was modelled on someone's idea of a public school. (In the UK, 'public school' means the reverse of what it means in the US and refers to a very exclusive private school.) We had ten houses where the boys had separate assemblies and lunches. There were five separate buildings, each partitioned to contain two houses, and they were spread out over the school's 50-acre site. The next-door house, which was just a double door away on the other side of a wall, may as well have been on a different continent.

After lunch there was a period of recreation, which meant standing about in most weathers—games of any sort, including running, were not allowed. At other schools future star soccer players would learn their skills in the playground. Woodlands boys were restricted to a kind of aimless mooching, although I would bet this means my former schoolmates could out-mooch almost anyone on the planet.

Most lunchtimes I tried to talk to Porter, but he often kept back in his own house's area, into which I wasn't allowed to cross. This wasn't just a rule imposed by the masters; the boys of his house would have responded badly to an outsider—particularly a weedy one. However, Andy was a D&D addict, and, as there were no fellow gamers in his house, he was occasionally forced to come and talk to me or risk going a break without mentioning an ogre.

I couldn't see Porter at first, so I took out an advert I'd cut from *Military Modelling* magazine. It was for a shop that sold the miniature figures, and I'd coded the figures with a B for those I'd bought, an O for those I'd ordered and an I for those I intended to order. I still have this advert, and there's a fourth category that I find horribly revealing. This is the category of things I can't remember if I've ordered or not, and it's recorded with a question mark. Naturally this last category makes my exercise in codification a bit pointless. I'm sad to say this sort of behaviour has never really left me. I did once put all my CDs into alphabetical order but realized this was a waste of time because I never put the disk back in the right case. I console myself with the fact that I got to the idea of randomizing the song you're going to listen to years before iPod. In fact, if you leave the CDs out for long enough you can even get them to skip tracks.

It might seem that I was a very rich boy, able to send off for various figures whenever I felt like it, but this isn't the case. My parents gave me 50p a week pocket money, which was five orcs or one and three-quarters of an ent. Also, I often walked or cycled to school and back to save my bus fare—12p there and 12p back if I remember correctly—2.4 goblins a day. I spent my money on absolutely nothing else. During my entire youth from eleven to fifteen I never bought a chocolate bar, a packet of crisps or a fizzy drink. Any cash I had went on wargaming. The only exception to this was when space dust came out—the sweet powder that detonated like tiny bombs in your mouth. I bought one packet of that. We gave some of it to an Alsatian that was tied up outside the newsagents and had planned to tell the owner that I'd cast a devil out of my friend Dave and that was what was causing his dog to leap about like a maniac snapping at the air. Unfortunately we lost courage before he came out and decided that the joke wasn't worth risking the wrath of a vengeful German Shepherd.

Other than that D&D took my whole cash supply. Even when

Fun Snaps emerged—the little paper wraps that explode when you throw them on the floor—I didn't buy any. Though they were as near as I could imagine to an alchemist's flash pellet, to me it was like wilfully throwing gaming books onto the floor.

Strangely Dave and Pete, the two other wargamers from my year, were keeping their distance from me as I padded the gloam, seeking to avoid whoever had taken it upon himself to make my life a misery at that moment and not be noticed reading the ad, which would mean someone would demand to see what it was.

I wasn't the victim of classic bullying—I almost never had a problem with an older boy—just a sort of general contempt from most of my classmates and specific contempt from a few of them.

It was then that I saw Porter, who appeared to be signalling to me. I felt my heart skip a little, but I made myself nonchalant as I strolled over to meet him.

'What news, kinsman?' I said as I approached.

Porter had something in his hand. It was my copy of *The Strategic Review* with the illusionist character class in it.

'I've brought you this back,' he said.

I looked around, fearful that I should be seen taking it. This posed me all sorts of problems. We went directly from outside into afternoon assembly in the house—orders as it was known, when school messages were communicated along the lines of: 'On Saturday evening at 7.20 p.m. two boys threw mud at a car at the junction of Jobs Lane and Tile Hill Lane. They are known to be Woodlands pupils. It will be better for those boys to come forward to accept their punishment now than if I have to send for them—the Headmaster.' It wasn't unusual for the head to punish pupils for things that happened out of school hours, or even in the middle of the summer holidays. Part of me today half expects a call to explain exactly why I was sharp with my wife the other day.

I knew I would have no opportunity to return to my bag and put the magazine in it. If I was seen with it in assembly, it would be confiscated, as it would be assumed I was reading it, and if any of my classmates saw it, they would demand to look at it, see it was all writing and very few pictures and either rip it or ridicule me. Quickly I put it beneath my blazer.

'Why are you giving it me here?' I said. 'Why not wait till Saturday?'

Porter looked shifty.

'We've decided,' he said, 'that Saturday's game is going to be fourth-years only.'

I didn't quite understand.

'What, are you finishing off last week's dungeon?' It had been interrupted by Andy's tea, but I was sure Pete still had a character left alive.

'Yeah, we are finishing that, but it's fourth-years only,' he said.

'So will it be back to normal the week after?' I said.

Porter looked exasperated. It was as if he was finishing with some witless girlfriend who just would not get the message and go.

'No,' he said, 'it's fourth-years only from now on.'

In Michael Moorcock's *Stormbringer*—a book I was then devouring—the forces of chaos go to war on the earth, and, as they pass, they change its substance. The ground becomes a thing between states, not solid, liquid or gas just a bubbling formless mess. The tarmac beneath my feet felt similar. I went pale as a haunted albino warrior king.

For the first time in years I was speechless. I just stood looking at Porter. I don't think he was ready for this response. Even though a lot of the characters he played in the game were mercilessly cruel sorts who delighted in their enemies' misery I don't think he was quite up to that sort of behaviour himself. Ideally he would have liked to have been a heartless, half-mad psychopath to insulate himself from destabilising gentler feeling, but he just wasn't. He went to put his hand on my shoulder but withdrew it. He clearly wanted to walk away, but something kept him there.

'You won't be able to play!' I finally managed to get out. 'You haven't got the rules!'

'I've got my own set now,' said Porter, 'and Hatherley's got

Greyhawk.' Even though I think he felt sort of sorry for me, he could never resist a touché.

This was the final blow. *Greyhawk* was a D&D supplement that I knew carried information on the thief character class, a class I'd been dying to play. It also had some new monsters in it, one of which was depicted on the cover—the floating orb of eyes known as the Beholder. In a rightful world, I thought, I would be allowed to borrow *Greyhawk*; I would be able to have my own thief character and . . . I didn't know what. With *Greyhawk* and a regular wargaming group my life would have been complete. Without it, it was nothing.

A Conspiracy
Unmasked

My fellow second-years seemed relatively unperturbed by the news of our exile. Both Pete and Dave said they would play with me again but not that Saturday, as they had things to do.

I found this slightly surprising as I never had anything to do nor, as far as I knew, had I ever met someone who had. Also, the idea of having something to do that was more important than D&D I simply didn't understand. They may as well have been speaking Russian to me. I had no way of interpreting what they said.

That Saturday I had nothing to do as only an adolescent can have nothing to do. When you're older you can actually welcome this state, a chance to sit down and study the wallpaper and allow the mind to wander. My mind wasn't wandering, it was bursting with D&D. The moan of my mum's Hoover made me think of ghosts, the rattle of a tea cup the rattle of dice; a passer-by in the street could be Porter coming to tell me that they'd decided I was welcome after all.

I genuinely thought that this might be a possibility, that there was no way they could continue the game without me. The light in my own front room, that seventies light that turned the world bright brown, seemed to mock me, no compensation for the cosy glow of the Porter front room, which suggested a hobbit's burrow or a priest's study.

I read the manuals, the fanzines, my own character books; I

even shook dice in imaginary encounters. Alf the Elf fought ten gnolls and won. I gave him the experience points. He fought a werewolf. I selected the werewolf he would fight—one that I had diced up with unusually low hit points (and I was fairly selective about the dice rolls that I determined would count and the ones that didn't because I 'hadn't thrown them properly') and he beat the werewolf. The advantage of throwing on a sofa is that it only takes a movement of the leg to change a dice roll you don't like. Alf went up a level, and I selected his new spells.

There I had him, a powerful fighter/magic-user ready for action, but nowhere to use him. I decided to order some more figures from *Military Modelling*. Then, with the logic of the lovestruck, it occurred to me that Andy or some of the others might want to save money on postage by including their orders with mine. The natural thing to do was to cycle up to Andy's house and ask him.

It was two o'clock, and the only outlet for the zinging energy inside me was to at least *see* someone playing D&D. Also, I think that, like a hopeless lover, I imagined that turning up on the doorstep of the object of my affections would make them suddenly change their mind.

'Good idea to go out on your bike instead of sticking your head in those books all day,' said my mum.

'It's not a bike. It's called Shadowfax,' I said.

My mum just looked at me strangely and said something about her thinking it was a Raleigh.

It occurred to me to take my gaming stuff with me, but I left it behind in a sort of lucky gesture—umbrella luck: that is, take it and you won't need it, leave it and you will.

Down Broad Lane I zoomed, this time not needing to stop to push when I reached the hill, my legs fuelled by desire. Within fifteen minutes of having had the idea I was approaching Porter's house, through the short cuts in the alleys that led to his front door.

As I approached the gate I looked to the windows of the house, and I couldn't believe what I was seeing. There at the table were the fourth-years, as I'd expected, but alongside them were Dave and Pete. I had difficulty taking the scene in.

Someone, I can't remember who, saw me, and I remember the wargamers looking out at me. No one came to the door. I was numb. The fact of the second-years' presence was too much for me to take in.

I pursued the only course of action that I thought was open to me. I went and rang the bell. No one answered so I rang it again. A shape became visible in the glass, and the door opened. It was the kindly Mrs Porter.

'Hello,' she said, 'Andrew, there's someone here for you.'

After another thirty seconds Porter appeared. I didn't know what I expected him to say or what I expected myself to say. I had no idea of the future at all at that moment and was as much in the present, that is with no conception of the next second until I was actually living it, as I have ever been.

'Yes?' said Porter coming to the door as if forced there at gunpoint.

'Good e'en,' I said.

'Good what?' said Porter.

'E'en, it's old for evening,' I said, my voice cracking.

'It's the afternoon,' said Porter.

'Though the sky is dark as dragon's blood,' I said. 'I'm sending off to Minifigs, and I was wondering if any of you wanted to stick anything on the order.'

'No,' said Porter.

There was further silence.

'Do any of the others?'

'No,' said Porter.

'How do you know?'

'We discussed it this morning,' he said.

This wasn't convincing, but it hardly mattered. It felt so utterly frustrating that everything I wanted was just a step away, but I couldn't touch it. More silence.

'There are second-years in there, aren't there?' I said. I so wanted to join them.

'Yes,' said Porter. Then his resolve cracked. Despite his hard exterior Andy was not good at being a wilful bully.

'We're banning them from next week,' he said. 'We just had to let them finish off the game.'

'Oh,' I said, before adding, 'Dave's character was dead last week.' That meant there would be no need for him to finish the game; he was already finished.

Porter looked at a loss.

'Hatherley resurrected him,' he said.

'Hatherley's character's a magic-user, resurrection's a cleric's spell,' I said.

Andy's eyes searched the heavens for something to say.

'There was a magic item,' he said. 'He used that.'

This didn't convince me.

'What sort of magic item?'

'A wand,' said Andy.

I shook my head. A wand is a magic-user's device. There's no way it would contain a cleric's spell.

He and I stood slowly roasting in the deceit.

'Can I come in?' I said.

'We're just finishing,' said Porter.

'You've three hours to go,' I said. 'That's time to start another game.'

Andy was clearly desperate for me to release him, from that moment and from my company for ever.

'You can't come in,' he said.

I can't remember much more. I was back at home, and I was crying. I can remember that, really sobbing. I believed that they meant to ban Pete and Dave the next week, but at the same time I had a sort of physical realization of the realities of the situation—that it was me alone who had been singled out for exclusion. I felt shudders going through my body, hot and wretched. I was too nerdy for Dungeons and Dragons. I'd been rejected by dweebs.

A Light
in the West

I didn't want the fourth-years to bar Pete and Dave too. I just wanted them to have me back. The problem with this sort of rejection is that all the respect and devotion I'd shown to Porter now came back to haunt me. In my mind he was the coolest, most intelligent, inventive, even well-dressed, person I'd ever met, and the evidence was incontrovertible—he hated me. What did that say about the kind of person I was?

At school on the Monday I could hardly look at Dave and Pete. However, at break time they approached me. The reaction of most schoolboys to upset in someone else is derision. We had conceived the idea that becoming a man meant atrophying the sensitive side of your character and that to display emotional discomfort was a sign of great weakness. I'd half expected them to take the piss. I was, however, in for a shock.

Pete, I've already noted, was of a different stamp to most of the wargamers. He was a good sportsman for a start and seemed to treat D&D as an interesting game rather than a life-defining ritual. Dave, at that age, was very shy and quiet. Looking back, I think part of the appeal of the game for him was its formalized social interaction. If someone speaks to you in the street you have a host of choices in your response, a host of mistakes to make. Life is simpler when attacked by a gelatinous cube, you just hit it—with an edged weapon of course. They're immune to blunt instruments, but you can find that out by looking in a book. You might die, but you've died doing the right thing. And also, of course, in D&D people tell you when it's appropriate to speak. 'It's your turn,' they say, which they rarely do in real life, particularly at a boys' comprehensive.

I could have done with a set of rules on school life, on how to get on with people, on existing, really. I just didn't know how to relate to Porter's fourth-years, and I didn't know how to relate to my own classmates. The problem, I think, was an overconfidence in my own likeability. Although I was in many ways insecure, as all kids are, a large part of me thought I was great and had something fantastic to offer the world if only the world would listen.

I didn't want the society that was on offer at my school—that of the identity-submerging working-class youth: who's hardest, who's best at sport; who's got the right haircut; who's the most disobedient? I didn't see that if you played by the rules there was actually quite a lot of scope to be yourself. You just had to be yourself in a way that people would understand.

Whatever social situation I found myself in, I wanted to be included but separate. My identity would be utterly distinct in every way and yet accepted. I'd be arty, literate, intelligent and vocal, dressed in an eccentric manner and yet liked, even valued, by the skinhead boys in the thirty-two-hole Docs.

I've had this all my life. I've never wanted to fit in. I've always got to say something that goes against the grain or that's slightly jarring. This has given me the reputation for not caring what anyone thinks of me. Of course, the reverse is true, and, then as now, I'm almost desperate for acceptance. I want to smash it all down, but I want it to be me who's standing on top of the debris after it's collapsed.

Pete and Dave were the nearest thing I had to friends. Pete was self-confident enough and Dave quiet enough to accept me. They responded with kindness.

Pete explained that they hadn't known I wouldn't be there and thought Porter had just reversed the second-year ban. Whether this is true or not I don't know, but, if it was a lie, it was a kind one. He said that Porter had no need to ban him and Dave; they didn't want to play with a bunch of stinking fourth-years anyway, and that Pete would be having a game at his house—second-years only—on the next Saturday. This cheered me up a bit, although I was worried that the game wouldn't be quite as good with only two of us as players and without such an inventive a dungeon-master as Porter.

I agreed to come up with a dungeon and set about thinking what I might put in it. At this age my dungeons were fairly basic—just a series of tunnels stocked with monsters and treasure from the D&D books with no effort at real invention.

It's probably worth having a short word on what the treasure is. Like everything else in the game it's represented by statistics. A vampire might be guarding 1,000 gold pieces (gps to us D&Ders), a suit of +3 armour, a couple of magic scrolls, a snake staff and a cursed sword. If you can carry the gold pieces, worked out according to a few satisfying calculations using D&D's often ignored rules designed to reflect the encumbering effects of weight, you can buy weapons, provisions and armour when you return to a town. The magic armour can be worn by your fighter and will make him more difficult to hit—almost impossible for some weaker creatures—the scrolls might contain spells that your magic-user can use, and the snake staff can be used by a priest. It'll turn into a snake and attack his enemies. The cursed sword, once picked up, cannot be put down without a curse-breaking spell from a cleric. It can be used as a sword but modi-fies your attack dice, removing one, two or three points from whatever you shake. The sword seems to have a life of its own, wilfully moving away as you swing it towards your target.

I had one further bright light on the horizon. My mother had been slightly shocked, I think, by how badly I'd taken my rejec-tion. Accordingly she did two things, one that I found difficult to accept, the other that I welcomed with open arms.

The first was that she stitched me together a Kermit the Frog from some old yellow corduroy. Rather than consoling me, the frog just reminded me of why I was miserable in the first place. Also, I considered that I'd left childhood, cuddly toys and anything soft behind, so to be given this frog felt like I was being treated like a child. And yet in my extreme reaction to Porter's rejection, in my inability to reflect on my behaviour and change it and in my addiction to a game, I was a child.

Luckily, my mother isn't, as she'd admit, much of a seamstress, and the frog bore little resemblance to Kermit. It had a kind of conical aspect to its head that gave it a sinister look. In the subsequent weeks I would find this quite pleasing and name it Krrrllkccr (the exact spelling) the lizard warrior.

Much more appealing to me was that she stopped into a Citizens Advice Bureau and located a wargames club at a school in the city centre. It met on Friday nights and for a ridiculously short time—half past six until half past nine in the evening—but somehow I felt back in the game. There would be other wargamers there and a chance to start a new campaign.

Naturally I didn't tell Porter about this, or see him very much at school for that matter. I also, instinctively, kept it from Pete and Dave. I thought it might leak back to Porter and that he might turn up at the wargames club and ban me from that too. I know now that, of course, he wouldn't have had the power to do that, but at the time it felt like he would.

Denied the fantasy of being Andy's friend, I felt the unpleasant reality of my situation. I'd been hopelessly outgunned by Porter and Hatherley. They seemed to be in possession of razor-sharp wits, the edges of which were invariably directed towards me. Most of this wit, as I recall, revolved around minute definitions of things and a literal interpretation of whatever you said.

At the time I was still interested in decent music. The X-Ray Spex were my favourite band, but I saw no clash with liking the wacky hippy hopping of Kate Bush either. I'd brought *The Kick Inside,* which I'd borrowed from the library, to a game and played it. Hatherley, who said he liked only classical music, listened to

'The Man with the Child in His Eyes'—admittedly not Kate's finest hour—and said, 'Has he got a child in his eyes? Well, then, he must have deformed eyes, or the child has in some way been shrunk.' This sort of thing caused hilarity among the wargamers and strongly implied that because Kate Bush had said something that was, in his opinion, inexact then the entire body of her work could be dismissed as the ravings of a moron, along with me for liking her.

Even in my exile I kept faith with this way of looking at things. I had few friends at school and went about alienating those I did have by employing this sort of humour on them. It was as if I thought that, if I could perfect the right attitudes, I'd be welcomed back into the fold. I was modifying my personality in order to impress people who weren't even there. I didn't see that all I really needed to do was to shut up.

It's at this point that I have one of those strange memories that simply doesn't fit in chronologically. My mum found the address of the wargames club on the Saturday. I went the next Friday. Nothing short of civil war—and a proper civil war of the American or Somalian sort with hundreds of thousands dead, none of your minor English armed squabbles like the Wars of the Roses or that one Cromwell fought—would have kept me away.

However, I have a distinct and clear memory of going with Dill myself to the Citizens Advice Bureau in order to get the address of the wargames club. The reason for this memory is mildly scary. My mum did indeed get me the address; I remember that right, and I also went down for it myself *after* I had actually attended the club.

I didn't, of course, need the address of the wargames club. My mum had got it the week before, and I had already visited the place. Finding myself in town with Dill—habit, and my desire to buy *Battle* magazine, saw us continue our early morning visits to the shops—I thought I'd just stop in for the pleasure of having them write the address of the club down for me personally. If I couldn't be at the wargames club, which would have needed to have been open twenty-four hours a day, seven days a week to satisfy my need for it, I could at least be connected to it in some minor way.

'The address is . . .' said the woman at the desk, looking through a Rolodex.

'Sidney Stringer School, Hillfields, Coventry CV1 5NL,' I said.

'Yes,' said the woman, looking rather puzzled.

'Knew that,' I said, as if I'd in some way achieved something. 'We don't just tabletop there, it's mainly Dungeons and Dragons we play. Are you aware of D&D?' I said.

'Are you aware you're wasting my time?' she said.

'I wouldn't call it a waste, learning valuable information you could pass on to any future enquirer,' I said.

'Next,' said the woman.

On the Friday night I was dropped off at the wargames club by my dad. I was disappointed to learn that there was no D&D on offer—they were fighting tabletop games with model soldiers—the Napoleonic Wars, the Boer War, Ancient Rome, that sort of thing.

Mercifully, in one corner two boys were taking out the familiar figures of trolls and dragons. It seemed that, in the short term at least, I'd learned something from my experience with Porter and Co. I approached the table respectfully and asked them what they were playing. It was the Wizards and Warfare rules I'd been familiar with from my first days at the school wargames club.

One of the things that has made me unpopular down the years is that, if I know something about a subject, I'm very keen to show that knowledge off. This goes down poorly with a class of thirty working-class school boys, I can tell you. It doesn't go down particularly well in adulthood either. 'Hello, Mr Mandela, your memories of prison life are all very well, but did I ever tell you about the night *I* spent in the cells for falling off a phone box drunk? Even in my darkest moments I never gave up hope,' that sort of thing. However, this time I just said I'd played before and asked if I could join in. I was pleased to be welcomed.

I was surprised, when I asked which school the boys went to, that they said they didn't go to school. Although they both looked younger than our fifth-formers they had jobs. One was an arc welder, although he looked more like an elf than the elf figures on the board. I'd always imagined welders as great brutes of men, not fine-boned creatures like the boy in front of me.

There was also the sense that he'd failed. In my mind, if someone wasn't an actor or a writer or a wizard or a pop star, then their life was without meaning. I couldn't imagine anyone wanting to be an arc welder. To me, work was like choosing a character class. Why would anyone choose anything that I considered dull? Still, I had temporarily had the wind knocked from my sails, so I was quiet and respectful and didn't say what I might have said in later years. 'Christ, you poor sod,' or something like that.

This was the first time I'd socialized on equal terms with anyone who wasn't from my immediate background, and, thank God, I showed some wariness around them. It had penetrated, I think, without anyone saying it directly, that leaping around acting out the roles of the characters in a loud voice was unlikely to endear me to people. They were friendly to me and responded well when I told them about D&D and said they'd like a go. It did occur to me to invite them down to Pete's the next day, but I thought I should clear that with him first.

The end of term approached, and the games limped on, lacking something in invention without Porter but also being slightly more indulgent towards me, so that I managed to work Alf the Elf up to twelfth level. This progress is much faster than the game is designed to allow, but Dave, Pete and I had an unspoken agreement that our characters would get on quicker than most.

I was missing something, though—namely someone to look up to. With Porter gone there was no role model in my life, and I think I felt its lack.

Christmas brought a bonanza. I ordered *Greyhawk,* which I think was the best value for money of any of the original D&D supplements. It had a wealth of reforms to the rules, making magic-users physically weaker and fighters stronger, introducing the character classes of the holy warrior—the paladin—and the lock-picking, wall-climbing, shadow-hiding thief. This greatly appealed to me, and I spent an afternoon attempting to pick the lock on my mother's vanity box, breaking it so it wouldn't open. My dad eventually had to smash it open with a chisel. Sorry, Mum and Dad.

That Christmas I was also given *The Book of Demons* by Little Soldier games. This, I think, disturbed my parents slightly. In truth it also disturbed me. It was just a list of demons, their names and descriptions, special abilities and a few spooky illustrations without any reference to the games system—hit points, armour class, etc. were missing. Some of the demons I found truly fascinating and at the same time terrifying. I'd read a bit about Luciferge Rochdale, for instance, and immediately had to close the book again, having given myself the terrible creeps. Even typing that name nowadays gives me a mild fit of the heeby jeebies.

I also had some hex sheets—graph paper with hexagonal instead of square blocks on it, for drawing wilderness adventure maps; and a Guinness mirror. I couldn't at all work out why I had been bought this mirror, along with talcum powder and some aftershave. I think my mum and dad were recognizing that puberty was approaching and trying to make me feel good by buying me manly things. I thought it was a dreadful waste of money that could have been spent on wargames. The Guinness mirror I found particularly offensive—it was just so 'of this earth,' linked to straightforward lads who wore sports jackets and got married young. It made me shiver looking at it.

Using the book of demons, I adapted its character class, the witch/warlock, for D&D. (Weirdly, the book was designed for role-playing games but not for any one in particular. They left all that to you.) I was to spend a great deal of time on this sort of thing in coming years, much of it wasted, as some dungeon-masters refused to accept my creations.

My fascination wasn't with the sort of wizard you see depicted on heavy rock album covers—wands and pointy hats—but with the old witches of England, those who cast spells that come boiling from cauldrons, a sorcery of candles, brooms and magic circles drawn in dark, storm-racked cottages, and travel by coracle through deep, wet woods. I liked the idea of the cold and the damp that I imagined these people lived in and old, dark magic.

The warlocks gain their power from communing with the demons in *The Book of Demons,* and I spent hours working out how to fit that into Dungeons and Dragons—the main problem being that, when you're being charged down by a Minotaur, you don't really have time to whip out the chalk, draw up a pentagram on the floor and project yourself into a trance in order to summon the spirits of the night. The other problem was that, when one of the dukes of hell turns up, he tends to be a bit powerful for the three half-starved goblins you're trying to defeat. Then there was the question of the cost of spell-casting. All fantasy literature shows there's a price to be paid for communing with the dark side, and, although I wanted that wan glamour for my characters, I didn't want it to make them ineffective in the game. This view of magic was hard to fit into D&D's system, but I had a lot of fun trying. Believe it or not.

I'm sure a psychoanalyst would have a field day with my particular choice of character class. Basically the warlock gets his big mate to bash his enemies up. Should Asmodeus have sauntered round my house and asked if anyone needed sorting out I might well have sent him up the road to Andy's.

It was, however, too much of a fantasy to hope that would come true. But then it did.

A Suburban Dragon

The thing about dragons, at least in the world of D&D, is that they are powerful sorcerers themselves and are capable of taking any form they choose. Often they'll appear as an old man, a young girl, an animal or even a plant. The most powerful dragon of the D&D universe in those early days was a golden dragon. If I was a fantasy author and describing a golden dragon who'd chosen to appear as a boy and wander into a wargames club then Billy Crowbrough is how I would have made him look.

I'd been slightly late for the first meeting of the Friday-night wargames club in the new year. This was some achievement, as I'd been sitting with my bag packed from about four o'clock when I'd returned home from school. Three weeks away from the club felt like a long time at that age, and, as I waited for my dad to come home from work so he could give me a lift there, the TV of *Newsround* and *Captain Pugwash* seemed almost perverse in its lack of mention of wyverns.

My dad, as dads sometimes do, seemed to take an age to finish his tea and get ready, despite my best efforts to hurry him through his egg and chips. So we were a good 96.2 seconds tardy for the opening of the club. Entering the room, I could not believe what I was seeing.

When I'd left before Christmas there'd only been a couple of lads scrabbling about with a few sad trolls. Now, at a long line of tables, sat about ten boys, all readying character sheets in front of someone who could only be a dungeonmaster—a man who appeared to be in his twenties.

'D&D!' I said, in pretty much the way Columbus's crow's-nest fellow must have said 'Land!'

'We've room for one more if you want to pull up a seat,' said the man. He was dark and very big and looked a bit intimidating to me, but he had in his hand something I'd never seen before— a D&D module. This is a pre-prepared adventure pack. In the eighties these became quite popular—why spend hours designing your own world and populating it with monsters and treasure when for £2.95 you can have someone do all the work for you? (The answer to this is very much the same as why people go up mountains.) The dungeonmaster was running The City State of the Invincible Overlord, a whole town designed in D&D terms, with a description of the contents of each house, palace or shop.

So far I've presented D&D as just a series of fights, but it wouldn't be nearly as popular if that's all it was. In these buildings you could receive requests for help, commands to perform duties or opportunities for social advancement. In fact, you could do anything that you could do in real life as long as you could work out how to relate to the social structure of the City State—much easier for me than relating to the social structure of Coventry.

I did pull up a seat, or at least I tried. It was a bit packed at the table, and I had difficulty making my way in, particularly as the only small space had been next to a very rotund youth of about fifteen who seemed to need one and half chairs for himself and another one and a half for his expansive smoking style. This was Billy.

When I say he reminded me of a golden dragon, he really did. For a start he had an amazing crop of bright blond hair, tending to long but sticking up in a shaggy plume, and, for seconds, he always had a cigarette in his hand, smoke billowing from his mouth as an accompaniment to his many, many utterances.

This was the seventies, of course, and anyone objecting to someone chain-smoking an inch away from their face would have been seen as an uptight oddball.

'Sit down,' he said, letting out a fart, 'betwixt the wind and his nobility.' He gestured to a boy on the other side of me. I sat down. No adolescent boy is truly fazed by a fart because, if he is, then he's going to spend a good proportion of his life fazed.

I squeezed in next to him and took my books from my bag. Billy looked down out of the corner of his eye.

'You've played before?' he said.

I opened an exercise book with details of my characters in it, flicking to a page that contained details of the dead third-level magic-user Mandrakus. This was a deliberate choice. I wanted to show him that I had been in the game for some time, but I didn't want him to see any live characters because the information might be useful to him at a later date if he tried to kill one of them. This was the paranoid state I'd arrived in from playing with the fourth-years.

Billy raised an eyebrow. 'Detailed, and yet disordered,' he said. 'Try one of these for size.' From a folder labelled 'Fighters'—my God, he had a whole separate folder just for fighters—he slid out a sheet. It was marked for recording the attributes of the character you were playing. Where I would just write the categories into my book—strength, equipment, spells, etc., this had a specially designed grid with neat letters spelling out each category as if it had been professionally produced.

'Gosh, where did you get these from?' I said.

'Ask not!' he said. 'I am a gentleman of the shade.' He produced a pack from his bag. 'Letraset!' he said. 'And I photocopied 'em while I was knocking out the school magazine.'

He lit a cigarette off the butt of the one he'd just put out.

'School magazine?' I said. His school had a magazine? It was clearly a very different establishment from mine. 'What school?' I asked.

'Henry VIII,' said Billy. This was the local 'grammar' school, one of two in the city that had not been closed down by the socialist governments of the 1970s. A grammar school was an elite institution whose exclusivity was based on intelligence, not ability to pay. They were free and run by the government. Grammar schools were seen as socially divisive because they selected their pupils on the basis of academic ability at age 11.

The dungeonmaster, the *man* who was playing D&D, thereby demonstrating what a grown-up activity it was, laughed and said, 'You're Falstaffian, Billy!'

'Incorrect,' smiled Billy, 'I am not Falstaffian; I am indeed Falstaff: I played him in the school play last term. They put on *Henry IV* specifically so I could take on the role.'

'Only because you were too fat for Hamlet,' said the boy to my right. I'd later find out his name was Paul—just a passer-through in the world of D&D, within a few months he would be on to girls, cigarettes, drink and other preparations for medical school.

'True,' said Billy, 'and Othello was out of the question because of the amount of black paint they'd need to cover me. It's a limited-budget production. *Romeo and Juliet* was a non-starter because they couldn't afford to reinforce the balcony.'

The boys found this a hoot, though I didn't really know what they were talking about. I'd never heard of Othello or Falstaff; they just didn't seem to come up too much in Whoberley. I don't think this marks me out as unusually uncultured. A friend of mine from a similar background to me, and who is now a successful author, had never heard of Picasso until he went to university.

The boys had the bit between their teeth over Shakespeare and strove to outdo each other.

'You couldn't do *Antony and Cleopatra* because of safety issues on the Nile barge,' said Paul.

'Or *Titus Andronicus;* they wanted it tightus but not that tightus,' said Billy, patting his belly.

This sounds like an unremarkable exchange, but I'd never heard another youth, or anyone for that matter—my family being maestros of blowing their own trumpets—making a joke against himself like that.

Billy's voice was pretty much like mine—that of a car worker, but office not staff, salary not wages. Even though our parents

were wages not salary—paid weekly, not monthly—they had
brought us up to be 'well spoken.' Paul's voice was different—in
short, it was posh. This wasn't the overstated, ridiculous posh of
Walters and Hatherley. I didn't know it at the time, but what I
was listening to was the genuine article, the unashamed middle
class in all its glory.

I looked at the sheet, 'Thanks,' I said, sliding it back.

'It's yours,' said Billy, 'you'll need it for a new character for the
City State.'

That was something I'd never encountered with the Woodlands
wargamers either: generosity.

I diced up a character and was amazed by the detail the dungeonmaster insisted on. Not only did we have our normal characteristics—strength, intelligence, etc.—but we had social level
too, and he was insistent on us all working out exactly how
much our characters were carrying in order to impose rest and
movement restrictions on us. This ate up half the game time,
but it ensured that what little time we did have for play was very
realistic.

This idea of realistic, of course, is relative in any game con-
taining dragons. What we meant was that, within that world,
everything had to be consistent. Just because we had werewolves
in the game it didn't mean that, once a man had turned into a
giant snarling wolf, his clothes were going to be in one piece
when he changed back. In our world the Hulk would have split
his shorts.

I rolled a fairly ordinary character but managed a 16 for my
dexterity score.

'I'll be a thief,' I said. I'd rather run the course on thieves in
previous weeks, but that was all the dice rolls were suited to.

'Why not be an assassin?' said Crowbrough. He produced
from his bag a photocopied version of the rules on the assassin
character class, taken from the *Blackmoor* supplement. I'd heard
of assassins and read about them in fanzines, but I'd never seen
the rules for them before. I was in backstabbing heaven with my

new character, Masokor, initiate of the Shadowblade School of
Assassins. (I made the Shadowblade thing up on the spur of the
moment and was vastly pleased with it. I determined that, in my
next dungeon, there would be just such a blade made out of
shadows.)

It was difficult to relate to the dungeonmaster, who was, as
I've noted, an adult. I had no experience of treating adults as
equals, but I felt honoured by his presence. Previously, I was so
sophisticated I hung around with fourth-years; now I was hob-
nobbing with a man who appeared to be in his twenties, one who
made his living in Theatre in Education and so had the glamour
of an actor about him. This was Mike Cule, a larger-than-life figure who later went on to play a memorable Vogon guard in the
TV version of *The Hitchhikers' Guide to the Galaxy*. Had I known
this I would have fallen at his feet and worshipped him. Mike was
a big, big, lad who Billy christened 'Daddy Cule.' He was a D&D
enthusiast who, though travelling the country, went out of his
way to play whenever he could.

I found the game amazing. Before this I'd only played D&D
that was set in underground caves and mazes—the dungeons of
the title. This was based in a city that had evocative names like
Wailing Street and Hedonist Row. Better still, you could interact
in a way other than simply attacking things. I went into a shop
and bought a wig. Other boys were fascinated by one called
Fetish, which sold things like enchanted tickling feathers and
allowed us to explore our taste for ribald humour.

Throughout the game Billy was incredible, full of interesting
things for his character to say and ideas for what our party of
adventurers might do. At eight we had a quarter of an hour break
and went out for chips. Billy had extra large with fish, a saveloy, a
meat pie and two scallops. Scallops are the Coventry speciality—
large pieces of potato fried in batter, created in a moment of
genius when someone realized that what people wanted with
their chips were bigger chips with batter on. It seemed to me
that he was capable of using his mouth for three purposes at

once—eating, smoking and opining on any subject he thought relevant—which was a lot of subjects.

Then he said something that made me almost duck as if someone had taken a swipe at my head. He declared himself politically.

'You've had rather a lot of food,' I said.

'It's the weight of history upon me,' he said.

'It's the weight of fat on your stomach, Crow,' said Paul.

'Unlike yours, Paul,' said Crowbrough, 'my class has historically been a hungry one. Today we eat for, as any socialist knows, tomorrow we may starve.' That was Billy all over; it wasn't just that he ate for pleasure—there was a socio-historical aspect to his gluttony.

'You're a socialist?' I said.

'Marxist-Leninist tendency,' said Billy, 'although I will take a little Trotsky if I have to. Only in the afternoon, though. I can never face the thought of an ice pick in the morning.'

I had no idea what he was talking about. All I knew was that anyone of his age I'd ever heard express an opinion about politics had been incredibly right wing. 'Socialist' was used by the fourth-year D&Ders as an alternative term for yob, or defective. My granddad was proud to say he was a socialist, my dad would—at that stage—probably have described himself that way, but they were from another planet. Anyone I'd known and respected was a fascist or a Nazi—of the sort that fancies itself in jackboots sweeping about in a staff car rather than the sort that does a lot of thinking on the realities of genocide. Actually, now I come to think of it, that is pretty much what a good number of the actual Nazis were like.

Also, I'd been given to understand that socialists were morons. One thing was for sure: Billy wasn't a moron.

This focus on class and politics in young boys may seem remarkable today, but it was a common part of conversation in England at the time. The far right National Front was on the rise, particularly in local government; organized labour was still at the height of its power with regular strikes and mass meetings; the

Conservative Party was going right and the Labour Party left. The politically fired young man was a phenomenon common enough to be lampooned in the TV series *Citizen Smith*. We felt engaged in the political process because it seemed to really matter. It was about a lot more than who you thought would manage the country best; it was about who you were and what you wanted to be. Politics was felt on a personal level, and it was as natural for us to talk about that as it would be for kids to have an opinion on *Dancing With The Stars* today.

By the end of the evening I was smitten with Billy and, to an extent, wanted to be like him. I wouldn't have said this emerged as a conscious thought, more just a change in the way that I was sitting, a borrowed figure of speech. That was more difficult than being like Porter, however. For the latter, it seemed to me, you just had to affect to rejoice in cruelty, be rather condescending and have looked up lots of facts about physics. To be like Billy required a huge cultural shift—as far as I could see you needed a complete knowledge of Shakespeare, the liberal arts, science and politics and the ability to say something witty every time you opened your mouth. Others may have gone away and attempted to learn something about Shakespeare, the liberal arts, science and politics. I decided I didn't need to bother with all that and could just wade in with pronouncements on these subjects anyway and spend the rest of my energy trying to be funny. Unfortunately, it's a habit that has never left me.

At school the next week Billy and the grammar-school boys felt like a golden secret. It wasn't one I was capable of keeping for long. I'd told Dave and Pete at our game on the Saturday. I'd desperately wanted to invite Billy, but, since it was at Pete's house, I didn't feel I could just slide in with ten extra players. However, I'd invited them to my house for the next Saturday already.

'Yes,' I'd said, 'we have all-day wargames. They go until . . .' I searched for a suitably late time, 'nine o'clock, sometimes.'

Billy's eyes lit up. 'Count me in,' he said. As soon as the word got around that my parents were willing to host a, well, a host, there had been a clamour to sign up. I decided I wouldn't bother asking my mum if it was OK; I'd just mention I was having ten or fifteen friends round for ten hours or more on the day.

I noticed Porter uncharacteristically hovering at the unmarked boundary between our two house buildings on the Monday lunchtime. He caught my eye and waved to me. I approached in the manner of Cinderella towards the ugly sisters with the glass slipper fitting snugly on my foot.

'Hello,' said Porter.

'Hello,' I said, 'games going OK?'

'We haven't had one recently,' he said.

'Why not?'

'Walters and Gerling have been busy,' he said, 'and Lee's got a Saturday job.'

'Really?' I said, 'I've been doing nothing but. Alf the Elf's fourteenth level: +3 armour, +3 amulet and flaming sword.'

I was lying about the flaming sword. As so often in my life, it wasn't enough for me just to win, I had to win big.

'We're getting some others along soon,' he said.

'Good for you,' I said.

In my memory I see Andy looking left and right, like a spiv about to ask you if you want to buy a watch.

'Pete tells me you've found some club in town on a Friday night.'

'Yeah,' I said.

'Where?' he said, in a rather high voice. I don't think he enjoyed the experience of being in my power very much. There was also, I think, a sort of resentment that I'd discovered something about D&D he didn't know.

I didn't have to tell him, I knew. I could have just wandered off. At that age I was incapable of thinking about the future in any way or behaving strategically. I didn't foresee that, if I refused to tell him, he'd find out fairly quickly anyway.

In those days he'd have to go to a library and then be told the Citizens Advice Bureau kept that sort of information, which would mean a trip down town. It would be a week at a minimum before he ended up at the club. Dave and Pete didn't know where it was because I'd just said it was in town and my dad would give them a lift there if they wanted. When they did find out its address, though, it was very likely that one of them would tell Porter. That would take only a week too.

However, Andy, like me, was an addict. He didn't want to find out in a week's time; he wanted to find out there and then. In fact it was worse than that: he wanted to know already and be the one who could conceal it from me. The idea of a game going on in Coventry to which he wasn't invited was an acute pain to him. For a second I had outmanoeuvred him, or at least my mum had.

When I recall this incident, the strange thing is that I had no sense of savouring my power over Andy, limited as it was. In later years I might have actually been more childish than I was then, as a child. Even now I wonder why I didn't string things out, pretend to have forgotten the address or say I'd let him know where it was when I'd assessed it to see if it was suitable for him. It might, I suppose, have been reasonable to say that since he hadn't wanted to play with me before, I saw no reason that he should have changed his mind now. There wasn't even a feeling of hesitancy. I just told him with the sort of eagerness to please and pride that young children have when they show their parents a painting they've done.

Andy smiled. 'Right,' he said, 'I'll be there this Friday, and I'll see if it's all it's cracked up to be.' His abrupt change in manner made me feel slightly cold. It put me in touch with something that I'd been feeling inside but hadn't noticed until that moment, one of those strange poisonous tremors that arise in you with rejected love. I wanted Andy to suffer as I had suffered. I wanted him to meet Billy and to be crushed.

The Gathering
of the Clouds

The rest of the week went in a blur. In English I wrote a story about Dungeons and Dragons on the theme 'my perfect day,' which started with me finding an elf sword under my bed and waking up to discover that my family had been murdered and I was going to have to fight my way out of a thicket of night gaunts. I got four out of ten for that, as I did for whatever I wrote.

Our English teacher was a tired sixty-four and one of that generation of men who had been allowed into teaching after World War II because there was an acute shortage of male teachers. Old age seemed different in the seventies. Today a sixty-four-year-old can be a gym-toned third-ager, full of vitality and vim. The English teacher was not like that. He had the air of a man who awoke every morning disappointed to discover he was still alive and was going to have to go through the tedious business of getting up and putting on a suit heavy with decades of chalk dust. The only thing he was full of was mild ale. One morning he came in for some reason with earth in his hair, leading to speculation that he had been dug up. He was knackered and looked on children as merely an obstacle between him, his pension and his pipe.

He would set us a task at the beginning of the lesson and then mark books for ten minutes. He managed to do about sixty books in this time. Later I realized that he was just marking the handwriting and never spent a second looking at any of the content at all. This caused the super-neat Andrew Richards some consternation as he discovered a huge talent for English that year, only to lose it the next when the teacher started paying attention to what he had written. When the ten minutes were up the teacher would go to sleep until the end of the lesson, occasionally waking to cane someone. Bizarrely I don't ever remember there being much trouble in his lessons, but, there again, he did allow the more fractious pupils to draw or play Top Trumps if they wanted to.

In geography I built a contour island that I planned to use as a 'Diorama' to illustrate Frodo's ascent of Mount Doom. Dioramas were very popular in *Military Modelling* magazine. They used model figures and terrain to illustrate key moments in battles—the battle for Quatre Bras at Waterloo, the death of Nelson, that sort of thing. In my mind I was going to construct a working model of Mount Doom, with lights to provide the flashes from the inside of the volcano and Gwaihir the Eagle flapping about on a piece of see-through plastic ready to rescue the hobbits. (Question: he flew them out, why couldn't he fly them in?) Unfortunately my modelling skills left me with only a shapeless pile of papier mâché that, if it resembled anything, resembled a large piece of discarded chewing gum.

In science I pretended I was a trainee alchemist and in music that I was learning runes. In art I drew a (bad) picture of a warrior, and in metalwork and woodwork I imagined that I was forging mighty weapons instead of chewed lumps of wood and steel.

Darker things were happening. One of the boys in my own class had vowed, to my face, to 'make my life a misery,' and I was completely at a loss to know how to respond. For all the theoretical fighting I did with dice and pencil it never occurred to me that I might spare myself a lot of trouble in the long term by just hitting him. Even if I'd have lost the fight I would have won some respect. The idea never even crossed my mind, and I laboured on under the oppressive weight of his presence, breathing on the back of my neck in lines, flicking things at me in class or vows to 'batter me,' vows that never led to action, but which left me hot and miserable.

The fantasy world seemed ever more welcoming. Finally it was Friday night. I donned my Derry boots and put on a felt cowboy hat I'd had since I was about nine. On the way down to the bus for the wargames club I scrunched and pulled it to make it look more shapeless and the sort of thing a *The Lord of the Rings* character might wear.

I'd arrived in good time for the beginning of the club, and so only had three-quarters of an hour or so to wait on a dark stairwell before it began. As it was, I was only just the first there. Two other boys came along after about five minutes, and we sat on the stairs outside the club's classroom discussing hit dice and likely forms of traps on treasure chests until the other wargamers appeared.

Sitting in the magical half light, I looked in through the window of the classroom to see the chairs, still stacked on the desk from the end of the day's classes, waiting to be removed so the boards could be set up. It seemed to me to be a sacred space humming with latent power. I felt like an actor looking out onto the bare stage, knowing that in an hour the theatre would be alive with an audience or like a soccer player taking a look at the empty stadium of a club he'd just signed for.

A lot of me now wants to laugh at this feeling, but I think that everyone has these places where the clock seems to stop for a second, the last look at the empty house you're moving out of, or a return to an old school. It's a bit cheesy, but it's how I felt, like I was connected to this place on an emotional level and it and I shared secrets that only each other understood. This was my fourth visit.

D&D fever was definitely sweeping the club at that point. The official start time was 6:30 and by ten past six there were already five of us waiting, all twiddling twenty-sided dice in our fingers or carrying boxes of figures. There was a suggestion that we should get a game going on the stairs, but one of the boys, Neil Collingdale, was afraid we'd do damage to our eyes straining to read the rules.

As it was we waited. At 6:20 one of the older tabletop war-gamers came along and let us into the room. At 6:25 Daddy Cule turned up and began laying out the materials for City State of the Invincible Overlord. At 6:26 I feared, for the first time, that Billy wasn't coming. At 6:26:04 I feared Porter wasn't coming either. At 6:27 I feared they'd met in the street, got on with each other and were coming to pick on me. I looked at the door, willing one or both of them to appear.

The epic confrontation I'd looked forward to, Godzilla vs King Kong, wasn't going to happen.

Then, in a rustle of chip paper and a puff of smoke, Billy came into the room.

'Hail, thou that art highly favoured,' he said.

'Isn't that what the angel said when bringing news of the immaculate conception to Mary?' said someone who clearly did more than we ever did in religious education—that is copy pictures from an illustrated Bible.

'Well, you never know your luck,' said Billy.

'If Billy were an angel,' said Paul, 'how big a wing span would he need to get airborne?'

'How many of me could dance on the head of a pin?' said Billy.

'You can't dance on the head of a dancefloor, Crow,' said someone else.

All this was way beyond me and, I carried the hope, way beyond Porter too.

The boys assembled around the table, which wasn't big enough, so more tables from other parts of the room were recruited. We had, I think, by the end of it, about fifteen of us cramming around the dungeonmaster, clamouring away for his attention like old-fashioned city traders looking to make a sale, a collision of pads, dice, pens and rulebooks.

Then, coming in to the room like the Nazi officers at the end of *The Great Escape* to relieve the failing commandant of his post, were Porter, Hatherley and Walters, or, as they were now calling themselves, the 'Black Triumvirate.' Porter and the others had mentioned this alliance several times and in hushed tones. It consisted of his character, Zarlan, Hatherley's Pyrary, named after a Moorcock character, and Dennis's character, whose name escapes me. I found the name very glamorous and slightly intimidating. To me it had a life outside of their invention; it was a feared secret society to which I didn't belong but longed to join. I didn't see at the time that, in the unlikely event that I did join they'd have to become the black square or something less sinister than a triumvirate.

Ironically enough for Hatherley and Walters, who had yet to grow out of being enthusiastic racists, the Black Triumvirate was the name given to the heroic leaders of a Haitian slave uprising against the French in the early nineteenth century. Chief among them was Toussaint L'Ouverture, surely one of the most inspiring figures of black history. It was as if the boys had chosen to call their secret society and vehicle for their fascist fantasies 'The African National Congress' or 'The Black Panthers' without having any idea that the name might have wider connotations.

In defence of Andy Porter he was, as far as I remember, never any more racist than the rest of us at that time. The average British 1970s white schoolboy was quite racist by today's standards but nothing to how Walters and Hatherley were as adolescents. It was unembarrassing to express bigotted views back then—I can clearly remember Dill's granddad complaining that Pakistanis had been given jobs as inspectors on the buses and saying they should only be allowed to be conductors. To stand out as a racist, like Walters and Hatherley, you had to go the extra mile.

I don't think that the Triumvirate got the reception they expected in that, rather than being welcomed as sage-like figures who would sit in judgement over the proceedings and then set everyone on the path to D&D righteousness, they had extreme difficulty in even making themselves noticed. It was a cacophony in there. In my mind I see boys scrambling over each other to get better access to the DM, crawling under desks, dropping from panels in the ceiling, rappelling through the windows, though that can't be right.

Andy and the others finally got the DM's attention.

'What level is it?' Andy asked. This is a question any D&Der would ask when coming to a new game. Put a first-level character into a dungeon designed for fifth- to eighth-levellers and he'll be toast before you can say, 'Fire Elemental.'

'First to fourth,' said Daddy Cule.

'Ah, I'll use my fourth-level anti-cleric,' said Andy. An anti-cleric is the name for an evil priest in D&D. At this stage of our gaming lives neither he nor, under his influence, I were capable of playing characters that weren't evil or deranged in some way.

'No,' said Daddy Cule, 'you have to start from scratch in this adventure. It's OK, I've got some characters I diced up earlier to save time.'

I could tell that neither Andy nor the others liked this at all, particularly since their characters always seemed to have a rather high proportion of attributes in the upper end of the range, Fighters with strength 18 and dexterity 17, for instance, magic-users with maximum intelligence. I plead guilty on that one too. Well, it is meant to be a fantasy game, and it's not much fun if you spend all week at school as an oppressed weed and then dice up a character with a set of abilities that leaves you playing a similar weed in the game.

Andy looked down at his sheet.

'Oh, you've even given him a name,' he said. 'Hildo, is it?'

'She,' said the DM, 'and it's Hilda.'

Andy frowned slightly. The creator of Zarlan the Ultimate didn't much like playing a hairy lady hobbit thief.

'Can't I be a male?' said Andy, with the look of a boy opening a birthday present to find a pair of washing-up gloves inside.

'No,' said the DM. I don't think this was cruelty on Daddy Cule's part, just that he was pressed for time.

This was already going pretty well. I had suspected that the Black Triumvirate would try to stage some attack on one of my characters in the game and was pleased to see the tools to do it easily had been taken from them. I wasn't at that much of an advantage, though. My assassin character was still only on the first level of experience.

One of the problems of playing with adults, I'd noticed, was that they tended to enjoy the role-playing aspect of the game far more than that of ascending the levels and acquiring an ever-more powerful character stocked to the ears with magic weapons and gold. Hence, much of the evening's adventure would be about meeting people, finding clues to where monsters and treasure might be, even establishing a business in the town.

This is what passes for realism in D&D. After all, even those we consider veteran warriors in real life have probably spent relatively small amounts of time actually engaged with an enemy. Before you can kill the dragon you need to get your sword sharpened, and it is this sort of activity with which certain sorts of DMs love to task their players. I've played adventures where we spent three days looking for a stud with which to repair some leather armour. It's not as boring as it sounds, though it is boring.

As the adventure began the boys placed their miniature figures on a large sheet of graph paper. Despite what I said about D&D being a game played in the imagination, when you have twenty players it really does help to have some way of establishing where they all are in relation to each other. The alternative, well, I'll go into that later.

Twenty is too many to play D&D, at least twenty mad adolescents anyway, and the game was chaotic, taking us the best part of two hours to fight some brigands and buy some flasks of oil. I had to wait until the break to introduce Billy to the Black Triumvirate.

There are ways of introducing people if you want them to get on. 'This is Billy. He has just bought Empire of the Petal Throne; I'm sure he'd love to talk about it,' might be one of them. I was a bit more direct. Even though I didn't realize it at the time, I wanted to see some fur fly.

Billy was chatting to his friend, the posh Paul, when I caught Hatherley's eye. Even writing this I can almost hear Hatherley behind me. 'Where did you catch my eye? It seems to me I still have two in my head, so you must be a liar,' and Walters in the background saying, 'Gas the liar!'

'Lee, this is Billy,' I said, 'You two share an interest in politics.'

'When did we share it?' said Hatherley, 'I don't recall sharing anything. I've never met him before. What percentage of this politics that we share does he own, and how much do I own?'

'It's a figure of speech,' said Billy. 'The ability to understand metaphor and elisions of meaning in language is one of the key stages of human development. Most people learn it around aged four.'

Now, why hadn't I thought of something like that?

Hatherley gave a little wobble and glanced at Porter, like you could imagine the first mate of the *Titanic* glanced at the captain as it hit the iceberg.

'Billy's a socialist, aren't you, Billy,' I said.

'Why?' said Hatherley in a tone of strong disapproval, though I think he'd been a bit rattled by Billy's blunderbussing of him.

'I get it from my father.'

'Is he a socialist too?'

'No, he's a fascist,' said Billy.

'He is too,' said Paul, 'you should see the collection of weapons he's got.'

The mention of weapons very much made me want to go round to Billy's house.

'My father's problem is that he's suffering from false consciousness,' said Billy. 'He has misidentified the cause of his miseries as the civil service, rather than the capitalist class.'

'I thought fascists didn't like Jews and blacks,' I said.

'Jews and blacks!' said Dennis, like an old colonel saying, 'A fox? On my garden?'

'Well he doesn't much,' said Billy, 'but it's the civil servants that really get his goat.'

I wondered what sort of civil servants he didn't like. Doctors?

Policemen? Dustbin men? I was later to find out it was the sort who push pens in government bureaucracies. Specifically, tax men.

'Paul's probably a socialist too, aren't you, Paul?' I said.

'Certainly not, I'm a Conservative,' said Paul.

'Is he suffering from false consciousness?' I said.

'By no means,' said Billy, 'his parents are doctors, and so it's natural for him to defend what he's got and therefore to be Conservative. We of the working class must likewise stand up for our own interests.'

'How nice for you,' said Hatherley, who was overcoming his wariness and had resumed his normal sneer.

Dennis muttered something about the proletariat but not too loud. They weren't sure of Billy yet.

'Thank you,' said Billy, in a smoky breath, 'always nice to have the approval of the bourgeoisie.'

'Bourgeoisie!' said Walters, 'We are not middle class. We are upper class!' He said this in a kind of toady bark, like someone doing a particularly belligerent impression of Churchill.

'I doubt that,' said Billy.

Walters and Hatherley looked perplexed. At my school it was an insult to say someone was posh. If they said they were posh themselves no one was going to argue with them.

'How dare you!' said Walters.

'Well, I'll tell you how I dare,' said Billy, 'if you were upper class you wouldn't go to school with Spaz here. You'd be at some private institution or have your own private tutors. What does your father do?'

'I don't see that's relevant,' said Hatherley in a sort of down-the-nose chuckle.

What I didn't tell Hatherley, in an unaccustomed fit of tact, was that I knew full well what his background was because my auntie lived next door to him in a small semi-detached. The walls of those things were none too thick, and I'd often heard rows between Lee and his father, the meat of which was Lee's dad's

assertion that his son should 'take his head out of those bleedin'
books and go and play some bleedin' rugby' and Lee's equally
heartfelt contention that his father 'wouldn't understand.'

I could grasp this sensitivity if he'd had his head in Gray's *Elegy*
or a slim volume of Shelley, but *Monsters and Treasure?*

'It's all that's relevant,' said Billy. 'If, as I suspect, he works in
a factory then you're working class. Wanting to be upper class
doesn't make you upper class, it just makes you pretentious. The
truly upper class would laugh at you and deride you, if they bothered to notice you at all. Anyway, Billy Crowbrough, pleased to
meet you.'

Billy proffered a bear-like paw which the effete Hatherley
shook gingerly.

Unfortunately Billy hadn't spoken to Porter yet, but Andy was
slightly cannier than the other two and preferred to keep his powder dry. Unlike most people Andy was in the Sealed Knot and
actually had powder to keep dry, and so I guess the experience
must have stood him in good stead.

The chat continued, and, despite this rather frosty opening,
Billy appeared to get on with the boys quite well. This pleased me
more than them arguing. I didn't want Billy to annoy the fourth-
years so badly that they wouldn't want to talk to him ever again.
I did want them to get on. In fact, I think what I wanted was a
new group, including the Black Triumvirate but with Billy as its
leading light and me as his trusted lieutenant.

The game continued, and, as the numbers involved had been
so unwieldy, the D&Ders had only had their appetites whetted.
They were desperate for more.

'We could come round to my house tomorrow,' said Andy, 'but
I'll have to limit it to eight.' I went cold. Was I still excluded?

There was a clamour of people trying to sign up for Porter's
game and lots of arguments and difficulties as Andy could take
only two of four friends and none of a group of nine others.

'Oh, don't worry about all that,' I said, 'I said last week,
everyone can come round my house tomorrow.'

'All twenty?' said Porter.

'Oh yeah,' I said.

'Your parents don't mind?' he said.

'I haven't asked them yet,' I said, 'but I'm sure it'll be OK.'

As I handed out my address I enjoyed a new feeling—centre of attention and leader of my peer group. It was only the borrowed glory of those that own the ball at soccer, the kid with the big Scalextric or the pool table, but for that moment it felt fantastic.

An
Unexpected Party

'Is it OK if I have a few friends over to wargame today?' I asked my mum as I ate my breakfast.

'How many?' said my mum.

'About twenty,' I said.

'Fine,' said my mum, 'when are they coming?'

'At about eleven,' I said.

My initial suggestion to start the game at nine was deemed too early by some of the older boys.

'Do you want me to do them any food?' said my mum.

'Some scones would be nice,' I said.

'Scones for twenty, three each, sixty scones,' said my mum. 'Sandwiches too?'

'Yes please,' I said.

My family were quite capable of having long and angry arguments about nothing at all, though things like this never seemed to faze us.

I'd already set aside, in my mind, the whole of the downstairs room, which luckily my dad had just knocked through, along with my brothers' bedroom for the games. I hadn't actually asked my brothers whether they minded, but I hoped they might be out. If the worst came to the worst, I thought, we could fit a few gamers into the bathroom, and anyone who wanted to go to the loo would have to use the one outside.

At 10:30 I feared no one was coming. At 11:30 my fears were allayed. Rather than too few boys turning up too many had. Several had brought brothers and friends. All in all I think we had about thirty boys round that day, gaming in the lounge, my brothers' bedroom and my parents' bedroom. Scone production went into overdrive.

The whole house was given over to Dungeons and Dragons; in fact the whole house was a dungeon. As a game it would have gone like this:

'On approaching the front door you can hear the cries of excited voices from within. What do you do?'

'I ring the bell.'

'The door is answered by a boy of about twelve. He is wearing a home-knitted sweater and looks keen to return to whatever he was doing before. Before you can explain who you are he says, "Come in, there's a game just starting in the upstairs bedroom. Close the door after you." Then he disappears back inside the house. What do you do?'

'I enter the house and follow him.'

'He goes into a long living room. Ten boys are sitting at a dining table. It's been extended but still can hardly contain them all. They are speaking in an animated way, rolling dice and poring over books and charts. They do not notice you. What do you do?'

'I go out of the room and up the stairs.'

'You reach a landing. There are four rooms projecting from it. One is clearly a bathroom. Closer inspection will reveal that it does indeed have the chicken tiles—a marble-effect tile that appears to have a chicken in the pattern, and the avocado suite of the day. What do you do?'

'I enter the second door on the right.'

'Inside are about eight boys sprawled around a large double bed. There is a dressing table and a mirror and fitted cupboards.'

'Is there anything unusual about the room?'

'It is too small for so many boys. It looks more suitable as sleeping quarters for a married couple. Lots of the bedroom's ornaments are spread across the bed.'

'I ask the boys what they are doing with the ornaments.'

'One gestures to a vase and says, "That's the temple of Mordragar, the make-up compact's the entrance to the sewers, the glass animals are aliens and the various heirlooms represent spaceships."'

As I recall, the boys in my mum's bedroom were playing Traveller, a variant of D&D set in space and cashing in on *Star Wars* mania. This was the first time I met Adrian Yarmouth or Chigger as he was known. Throughout this book I've tried to put myself in the shoes of the older boys I was describing. I'm very aware that any unpleasant behaviour they exhibited towards me may largely have been because I was unusually irritating, even for a twelve-year-old. I'll do the same for Chigger. However, I do feel moved to point out that Chigger was a nickname given to him at school during a biology lesson. Apparently a chigger is a sort of burrowing beetle larva that gets under the skin.

'Very few creatures can cause as much torment for their size as the tiny chigger,' said the teacher. And so Adrian got his name.

Chigger was two years older than Billy and in the sixth form at a grammar school outside of Coventry. He was quite small for his age, pale, heavily freckled and had bright red hair which he wore slightly long, giving his head the appearance of a fuse box someone had taken a hammer to. At the time we were using physical appearance charts from the independent D&D supplement *The Arduin Grimoire*. By shaking dice we could determine what our character looked like: hair colour, birthmarks, eye colour. If I had diced a character that came up looking like Chigger, I would have thrown it away and started again. It was fairly clear what the appeal of living in a fantasy world was to him. I think we got off on a bad footing because, during a break from our downstairs

D&D session, I came up to see what was going on in the games upstairs, the ideal respite from playing a role-playing game being to watch one played.

The players had just entered a bar. Twisted music spilled from a band of aliens, drinks were dispensed on anti-gravity pads and strange piratical adventurers lay around on padded seats, according to the DM. Of all the scenes in *Star Wars* that capture people's imagination it seems to be the one in the bar that sticks in the mind most, and, along with laser duels between spaceships, it was this one that most frequently appeared in games of Traveller.

I think this shows that a lot of what we were searching for in Dungeons and Dragons was a taste of the exotic, to believe that the world was full of surprising and fascinating possibilities and people, Han Solo or Aragorn sipping strange drinks in the shadows rather than Chigger munching on a chocolate bar and trying to use words that you didn't know.

Chigger, even for a wargamer, had an arrogant attitude. For a start, only a select few were allowed to play Traveller that day— Chigger said he thought it best that the grammar-school boys should play it first so that everyone in the game would be 'on the same intellectual level.' He also, and this is in my view the mark of a bounder, seemed willing to patronize my mum. On our wall we had a picture of Gainsborough's 'The Blue Boy,' complete with moulded plastic gold-effect frame. In our family this was referred to as 'Little Boy Blue,' and, to tell the truth, I had no idea of its real title or who painted it until about five minutes ago when I looked it up. This may sound like a hideous piece of decoration, and in fact it *was* a hideous piece of decoration, but, remember, this was the seventies. Given the alternatives on offer it was a triumph of good taste.

Chigger clearly didn't think so.

'Oh, that is nice, Mrs Barrowcliffe,' he said on entering the front room, 'is it real?' He said this with a sort of snigger in his voice. Chigger was labouring under two misapprehensions here.

One was that my mother was as easy to dominate as the younger boys he chose for his friends, and the second was that she wouldn't pick up on his sly sarcasm.

'I like it,' she said, 'and if you don't, you know where the door is.'

I think Chigger was a little taken aback by my mother's directness, and he spent the rest of the day in a sort of smirking attitude designed to restore the face he'd lost with the other boys.

I was embarrassed by this, though—incredibly, not by Chigger but by my mum. I didn't want her offending my new friends, and, while I could see that Chigger was being in some way snide about the painting, I was more interested to find out what was wrong with it than in being angry that he was disrespectful towards my mum. If I'd had to take a stab at why he didn't like it I would have said—in my words of the time—that it was a picture of a poof or that it was an obvious choice as lots of people had that painting. He was an older D&Der and so, to my set of values, more important to please than my own mother. I was going to write that I resolved to have a more disdainful attitude to popular art in future, but it wasn't exactly a conscious thing. I just know that I started looking at things in a different light after that.

The problem for me was that I couldn't exactly tell what was meant to be awful and what was good. To be on the safe side I started looking down on everything. Chigger, it seemed to me, was just the most extreme example of an attitude shared by most of the older wargamers, one of lofty disdain. I was on the receiving end of a lot of this disdain. I could have seen through it and wondered exactly what they had to be so arrogant about; I could have felt the rejection and the unpleasantness and vowed that I would never make anyone feel like that myself. Instead, I copied them.

Despite my mum's early tangle with Chigger he ran his grammar-school-only game of Traveller in my parents' bedroom. This exclusivity went down poorly with Porter and Hatherley, but there was nothing they could do about it. Even though they were using my mother's alarm clock to represent a spaceport, Chigger didn't think I should be allowed in the room.

'We need to concentrate and can't have spectators, especially little twerpy ones,' he said. 'This room is for Traveller players only, please leave.'

I don't know why but I did. It was, after all, my house. It was nothing to do with him being older. It was as if the authority of owning such a cool game gave him power over me.

Downstairs, however, a conflict that was about to define my life was taking shape. Andy and Billy were going head to head for the first time.

The order of the adventuring party was represented by miniature figurines—this is known as the marching order. The problem was that, in the excitement of a battle, people often forgot to move the little soldiers. This meant that we were in a position where the action of the game was neither represented nor not represented by the figures. The rules are hugely unhelpful here. The *Greyhawk* supplement notes that figures are 'sometimes useful.' And sometimes not.

A trap had been triggered by the third member of the party, causing the character to fall into a pit of poisoned spikes. We had a thing for poisoned spikes then. As we became more sophisticated our taste in traps would proceed through snakes to crushing rooms to the insides of giant carnivorous plants to time loops that would make the character endlessly repeat some action.

The dungeon was at the time being run by a pleasant grammar-school boy called Neil Collingdale, who had doubtless arrived under the impression he had come to my house to play an interesting and diverting game rather than to have the very terms of his existence questioned and everything he believed held up to ridicule and contempt. Collingdale's mistake was to be slightly inexact. He can't be blamed here. I think that a team of the country's finest legal minds specifically employed for the purpose of being exact might have found themselves 'slightly inexact' under the scrutiny of Crowbrough and Porter.

'Right,' said Collingdale, picking up a figurine. 'This wizard falls into the pit. Whose character is that? He'll have to make a saving throw.'

A saving throw is a staple of the game. The trap goes off and the DM has ruled that, unless you shake more than a 14 on a twenty-sided dice, you fall in. He'll then shake to see what damage the spikes do to you, and then you'll have to make a saving throw against the poison or you'll be paralysed, dead or—as happened at one game I played at a D&D convention—turned Welsh. This sort of thing appealed to the über-prattish, Monty Python-inspired sense of humour of many gamers at the time.

In fact, one edition of *White Dwarf* magazine, discussing the various sorts of dungeon it's possible to run, included the category 'The Silly Dungeon' populated 'entirely with humour in mind.' Recommendations for this humour included giant SS killer penguins, thieves in black fetish leather armour and homosexual pink kobolds. I never found this sort of stuff funny, not from any PC reason but just because, well, it isn't funny.

'Ha ha, Porter, you're in the pit!' I said, because it was Andy's magic-user who had ended up there. Porter gave me a look like aged spaniels do when you suggest removing their dinner half finished.

'That's not me,' said Andy.

'Who's the wizard figure, then?' said Collingdale.

'The wizard figure is me, but I'm not third in the party. That was Billy,' said Porter.

'No it wasn't,' said Billy.

'I said I was going into the middle when I came out of that room,' said Andy.

'You didn't move the figure to represent that, did you?' said Billy.

'We're not used to playing with figures,' said Andy, which wasn't strictly true. It wasn't untrue either. We normally started playing with figures and then forgot about them, so he had a point.

'It's not a matter of being used to it, it's a matter of doing it. Some cats aren't used to crossing the road, but they better do it right or it's a saving throw vs car tyre for them. You should have moved it.'

'I can't reach it, can I?' said Porter. He had a smidgen of the contempt he normally directed at me, but it was of a different quality with Billy at that point, more like a teacher saying he would have thought an intelligent lad would have known better. There was also the implication that, had he been organizing the game, the figures would have been in an easily accessible position, despite the fact we were seated around a large extended dining table with a camping table at both ends to make it bigger.

'You're as near as I am,' said Billy.

'You didn't move yours.'

'Because I was happy with its position, QED,' said Billy. That was a first. I'd never heard Porter QEDed before. 'You didn't move your figure, Dave. Were you happy with your position?' Billy was going by the barrister's maxim of never asking a question that you don't know the answer to. Dave hadn't fallen into the pit; so of course he was happy with his figure's position. Anyone who hadn't fallen into the pit was happy with their position.

Dave was my super-quiet second-year friend. If Dave had been happy with the position of his man he wasn't happy with his own position between Porter and Crowbrough. He made a sort of grunting noise that could be interpreted by either side of the argument as a token of support.

In the latter years of our play I attempted to bring a greater role-playing element into the game and asked each character to provide a description of what they looked like and their general demeanour whenever I ran a dungeon. Some were very inventive, although you could guess Billy was never going to say, 'A well-toned bloke who's a hit with the girls,' because Billy didn't want to admit to himself that well-toned blokes are, on the whole, a bigger hit with the girls than chip-devouring fatties, and Andy was never going to say, 'A self-effacing, rather timid and nervous priest who just wants to help people.' Dave, for every single character he ever played said, 'He looks like a man in a cloak.'

Sombre monk? 'A man in a cloak.'

Cheeky thief? 'A man in a cloak.'

Elf warrior? 'A man in a cloak.' Surely the elf warrior must look more like an elf in a cloak, Dave. 'This one looks more like a man.'

'What kind of man? Bald, hairy, tall, short, black, white?'

'Just a man.'

Dave, I feared, was never going to be much help to the police if he witnessed a robbery.

At the time this seemed quite unremarkable, just another dose of adolescent tunnel vision. We played with one chap who used to have tomato ketchup on everything he ate—I recall him putting it on a Kit Kat once. That didn't seem remarkable either.

'Collingdale, you heard me say that I wasn't standing there, didn't you?' said Porter.

Neil Collingdale, oblivious as only a well-brought-up boy who has been raised to believe everyone should be as nice as possible to each other all the time can be, said, 'Yes.'

I don't think he understood the pandemonium he would unleash. Porter sat back with a smile. What this meant was that, where the argument as to who had been in line for a spiking was originally confined to Porter and Crowbrough, it now spread to the whole table. Any of us were in the frame, apart from Porter, who had seemingly been given a free pass.

Billy had, I think, an exaggerated sense of fairness, one of those attitudes that look well on paper but can get you steamrollered in real life or at least make your day-to-day dealings quite difficult. This, to him was an abhorrence.

'It's not me who was there,' said Billy. 'Either the figures mean something or they don't.'

'I think we've just established that they don't,' said Porter with a chortle. I chortled along with him and felt good to be sharing someone else's discomfort with Andy, rather than being the discomforted one myself. Andy, as older boys will, shot me a look that said I should get off his chortle and find something to chortle about of my own if I wanted to chortle at all.

Some situations, I think, require victims if any progress is to be made. This was one of them. A trapdoor had opened; someone had to fall through it. Unfortunately Collingdale didn't see it that way. I think he liked Billy and didn't want to offend him. He was beginning to wish he'd never mentioned this pit of spikes in the first place, and, ironically enough, he looked a little as if the floor had just fallen away underneath him.

'I didn't say that it was you,' said Collingdale, trying to look as though he was in control.

The room erupted with shouts of 'Well it wasn't me!' and 'I'm the one with the bum-shaped hat, you can clearly see I'm at the back.' 'You're not the one with the bum hat, you're the slave girl.' 'My character's male!' 'Yes but we'd run out of figures, and you said you didn't mind having your magic-user represented by a slave girl until someone died.' 'I said you shouldn't mind having your magic-user represented by a slave girl, that's very different.'

No one there was actually living the possibilities of the game. The game is a story, and stories have beginnings, middles and endings. We didn't want an ending for our characters, just to go on and on undying and ever more powerful. This is an unsatisfying way to play, like going through a video game with all the cheats operating.

Porter and Crowbrough were arguing like that was all they'd been made to do. In fact, given their shapes and colouring, it seemed that maybe they had been designed to fight each other by some god with a taste for the burlesque. Even the way they sat was different: Billy wide and expansive, like Father Christmas waiting for the next child, Andy more contained—limbs tucked in to suggest the sort of crouch that precedes a pounce.

'What is the point in having the figures at all, then?' said Billy, 'wipe them away,' he made a dramatic gesture, 'take them all away now.' There was always something theatrical about Billy. He looked like a Kabuki actor displaying 'brooding anger.'

'The point is that the dungeonmaster needs to be more attentive and clearer.' Andy, in common with all—well, men, really—could never admit to a mistake. 'A flaw in the system doesn't mean that the system needs to be completely discarded, only amended.'

'This is weak dungeonmastering indeed,' said Billy, pointing to Collingdale, who looked appalled, like a well-bred English gent being accused of spying for taking a few snaps near a Greek airfield.

'It is weak, but that's not my fault,' said Porter. 'We needed someone with more experience. You're not up to the job, Collingdale.'

'Probably his upbringing,' said Hatherley, 'liberal parents leaving him weak-willed. We should mark him with a suitable symbol.'

'Pink triangle,' barked Dennis.

'Go and fetch Chigger,' said Billy.

'Hang on,' said Collingdale. This was a bit outrageous. It's like being in court (a lot of our D&D arguments reminded me of two rather unsuccessful barristers slugging it out) and suggesting that you throw out the judge if you don't like the way the case is going. Most D&D books recommend that, if a player cannot accept a dungeon-master's decision, the player should be expelled from the game. That kind of presupposes that the dungeonmaster isn't a boy who has simply come for a pleasant day's fun, and the people to be thrown from the game aren't individuals of iron will to whom it is a matter more important than life or death.

Chigger was sent for. Most of us accepted that sort of thing. At that age you think of yourself as an adult, but you behave as a child, and we were going to the oldest boy there as a kind of appeal to a surrogate parental authority. Chigger loved an argument, saw that it had sort of been settled in Andy's favour, so he took Billy's side and said that Andy should have moved the figures. This put us back at square one.

'Well, if you can't play the game properly, Andy, then perhaps you should choose something less mentally demanding,' said Chigger, who loved to say things like that.

Porter looked like he was about to explode. He didn't appear to like being on the receiving end of this stuff very much.

'I'm used to games where the DM's on the ball,' he said. Collingdale very soon after took up badminton, I believe, where the disputes are more straightforward. It's in or it's out, a shuttlecock, isn't it? No one announces half-way through that they thought everyone was agreed they'd given up using the net.

'I am appealing to simple logic,' said Billy.

'The logic in this case is far from simple,' said Porter. 'The DM needs to make a decision right now and the correct one.'

'You can't change the rules half-way through,' said Billy. 'It's like saying, "I don't like gravity, I should be allowed to float around." Anything else you don't like? The relationship between time and space, perhaps? Maybe we should have that altered for you.'

I don't know what became of Neil Collingdale, but I suspect a career in the diplomatic service would have been rewarding.

'You're saying Andy definitely falls into the pit, Billy?'

'I am,' said Billy, on clouds of wrath.

'I don't accept . . .' said Andy.

'Right, the spikes were illusions, and there's a magic wand at the bottom. Andy's in the pit undamaged by the fall,' said Collingdale. This is the thing about being a dungeonmaster: you can, if you want, just make things up.

'I test the wand,' said Andy.

'He just said he wasn't in the pit,' said Billy.

'And you just said I was,' said Andy.

'You don't understand, do you, Porter?' said Crowbrough, 'I'm giving in to your argument.'

'Oh no, Crowbrough,' said Porter, 'it's you who's won.'

And off they went again, arguing the opposite of what they'd been saying ten minutes before.

I think we got to about the fourth room of around fifty we

could have explored of that dungeon before everyone had to go home. I didn't know it at the time, but this sort of argument was going to go on for a long time—nearly four years. In fact, it became, to paraphrase Michael Moorcock, an eternal argument that seemed to exist independently of whoever was actually arguing. At times it seemed we weren't people at all, just expressions of a position, parts of a machine that could be worn out and removed but would just be replaced by new parts to keep the engine of disagreement running.

I would have chosen to be on Billy's side in these confrontations, but, I was to learn in the coming years, you don't always choose your side in a row; sometimes it chooses you.

Out, Daemon, Out!

I'd had a sort of intellectual and spiritual lust to be Andy Porter. With Billy it went deeper.

Most of the wargamers had to return for their tea by seven at the latest. Billy's parents granted him a greater degree of independence, and he was allowed to stay as long as he liked. When the clamour of the day's gaming had died down we'd sit in the cigarette smoke and play the D&D-like Empire of the Petal Throne together—him as the dungeonmaster and me as the player. We were alone in our own world, give or take a few shen, ahoggya, ssu and pe choi.

We'd be at the dining table—hardly ever used for dining—in the back half of the lounge. This was no sitting room; it was a full-on lounge complete with a glass coffee table and an ashtray on a stalk that looked a bit like one of those really tall Soviet buildings with a bulb on top and that had jaws that opened when you pressed a button. While my parents watched *Sale of the Century* we'd explore the underworld just a few feet away.

The evening would go something like this.

TV: 'From Norwich—it's the quiz of the week!'

Billy: 'From down the corridor you hear the sound of chimes and the dusty smell of cinnamon wafts towards you on a breath of foul air.'

Me: 'I take out my eye.'

This drew an odd look from my mum, who didn't know that an eye is Empire of the Petal Throne's answer to a ray gun.

Mum: 'Get us a coffee, Roy.'

Dad: 'The show's just started, why can't you ask before it begins?'

Mum: 'Oh, wait till the break, then.'

Billy: 'The strange metal door that you tried to open a moment ago now appears to be sliding back, centuries of moss and grime cracking as it moves. A dim blue light is emanating from behind it.'

TV host Nicholas Parsons: 'You are a bricklayer?'

Me: 'As soon as the door opens I'm going to fire.'

Mum: 'Keep it down.'

Nicholas Parsons: 'For one pound, which clarinetist is well known for "Stranger on the Shore?"'

Billy: 'The door cracks back, and before you is a hideous three-footed monster with three arms. It appears to be clutching a metal device in its hands. Acker Bilk.'

Dad: 'I knew that!'

Mum: 'Why didn't you say it, then?'

Me: 'Fire! I fire the eye!'

Billy: 'Roll initiative.'

Mum: 'I'm trying to hear the question here.'

Nicholas Parsons: 'For three pounds. Which football league team is the only one ever to play in chocolate brown?'

Mum and Dad: 'Coventry City!'

Were they? It was news to me. They were, I found out years later. It prompted the not-unasked-for observation from opposing fans that if you were going to play like shit you might as well look like it too.

Billy (shaking dice): 'The ssu, for it is they, shrivels under the eye's heat blast, its fleshy outer integument peeling away in layers. It's dead.'

Nicholas Parsons: 'Let's see what you can buy in the mini-sale!'

Mum: 'That's nice; it'd look well in here.'

Dad: 'Try getting them for two pounds. Our optician's got one, but he's an optician.'

Contestant: 'I'm going to keep my money for the big prize.'

Dad: 'Very wise.'

Me: 'This could be the queen I've been sent to kill. I inspect its genitalia.'

Mum: 'Jesus Christ, our Mark!'

Nicholas Parsons: 'You're going to let us keep the nest of tables?'

Billy: 'It bears the vacant groin of a worker-fighter. (In Monty Python voice) Coventry City have never won the FA Cup! Around its neck it has a vial of clear liquid.'

Mum: 'Which reminds me, where's my coffee?'

Although the game is ideally played with more people, I often thought this was its purest form—the presence of my parents aside. There was none of the backbiting and arguments that you got with a large number of players, no ego clashes and recriminations, just the game as it could be.

Empire of the Petal Throne is the creation of M. A. R. Barker, a linguistics professor from California. It brings an unprecedented level of detail to role-playing gaming and it is set in a world very unlike the medieval European one of Dungeons and Dragons. The mythology of D&D is a hotchpotch—figures from Greek and Roman mythology appear alongside those of Chinese and Celtic fables and creatures of the author's own invention. Empire of the Petal Throne is systematic and entirely invented. It is set on a planet that was once an interstellar trading post where aliens and humans lived side by side. Then it was sucked into a pocket universe; the stars went out, and most of the technology collapsed. The players join the game thousands of years later, in a society that is a sort of hybrid of ancient South America, ancient Egypt, India and the Far East, where magic is possible (thin walls between the dimensions, as you might guess), and the remains of the high technology of the spacefaring days have a divine aura. The prof had been working on this world since he was ten and, with the advent of Dungeons and Dragons, turned it into a game.

An idea of the detail it goes into might be seen in the shape of the game's domestic animal—the chlen. Few games I've come across before or since bother to actually tell you what herd animals exist in the world, and almost none would consider a beast's place in the economy that supported it.

Barker gives us the chlen, a six-legged hippopotamus-like beast which is used as a pack animal. Its hide is used as a metal substitute—metal is scarce in the world of Empire of the Petal Throne—and when it's treated it can be used to make swords and armour. Pieces of the hide are taken from the living animal and they grow back, like a human regrows a fingernail. This is where most of the weapons in the game emerge. So Barker has gone from one fact—that metal is scarce—to imagining a substitute for it and coming up with the basis of trade on his planet. He can tell you what is drunk in the world of EPT, what people wear, the names of the cloths they use, how things are transported (the sakbe roads—tiered so that upper-class users need not travel with the peasantry), the various political parties and the clans.

The prof can also—and I don't think any game before or since has tried this—teach you to write in the script of the main race on the world—the Tsolyanu—and how to pronounce things—the game is full of names such as Timandalikh hituplanMitlandalisayal and Tletlakha. No one would want to embarrass themselves by saying Timandalikh hituplanMitlandalisayal with the stresses in the wrong place. And surely it is impossible to get through life without knowing that when an EPT name is spelled with a p it should be a voiceless bilabial stop with little aspiration or that the q is similar to that of the Arabic 'Qaf.'

This is geek heaven. You don't have to stop playing the game when your friends go home. In fact, you can turn it into a study.

With the help of fanzines and close attention to the text of the game you can actually learn to speak Tsolyanu while wondering why the school still makes you learn French—it's not like you're going to use it.

I think this is the soul of why role-playing games like D&D and EPT were so popular with young boys. They provided a trellis work for the imagination to climb upon and thrive. Unsupported, your day dreams can wither; backed up by rules, pictures, model figures and the input of others, there's no end to the amount of brain space they can consume.

The thing about fantasies, from thinking about what you'd do if you won the lottery to dreams of flying on a dragon's back, is that they're fugitive things; they come and they go, and they're hard to fix in the mind. In my experience they don't like a narrative imposed upon them, and, even if you're trying to dream about winning the biggest prize in sport or, my favourite, hurtling in freefall towards the earth, then all you get are glimpses of images which often replay themselves. To get myself to sleep I often dream of jumping out of an aircraft, but all I can sustain is that first vision of the earth as I exit the plane. I've never gone through to opening the canopy or even held a picture of the jump in my head for more than a few seconds.

The power of the story, either writing or reading or listening to one, is that the imagination is tied to something that makes it go forward. I might not be able to imagine much of jumping out of a plane, but, if I had to write an account of a jump, I'd easily be able to see myself going all the way down to the earth.

D&D is, I believe, something virtually unique and unprecedented in human history. It's a story you can listen to at the same time as telling it. You can be surprised by the plot's twists and turns, but you can surprise too. It's more interactive than any other sort of narrative I can think of. If its subject matter were more serious then it would be considered a new art form, and it's probably surprising that nothing beyond murder mystery dinners has ever been evolved from it. This is why D&D is so addictive when it's played right. It's like the best story you've ever read combined with the charge a good storyteller feels as he plays his audience.

I think there's a basic human need to listen to stories, but also to tell them. In D&D you get that tingle you imagine when you think of the ancient storytellers, dusk falling, the camp fire burning and the first line being read. It's not like hearing 'In a hole in the ground lived a hobbit,' it's like saying it for the first time and to a rapt audience that is dying for your next sentence.

I have finished games feeling physically drained and actually wanted to continue to have my characters buy food at a shop or smoke a pipe in a tavern just to calm down before breaking with the game world entirely. And sometimes even that wasn't enough. The crucial difference between conventional forms of storytelling and D&D is that D&D doesn't have to finish. Ever. It's an open-ended story, and, if you're emotionally engaged with it, the temptation is just to keep going.

Billy and I worked very well together—although Porter and Chigger were at their best equally capable of initiating and participating in truly riveting encounters—and he and I became immersed. So immersed, that we were loath for him to go home, particularly when I'd just discovered the tomb of Mnekshetra, the Lesbian Mistress of Queen Nayari of the Silken Thighs.

Billy had a total reluctance to ever finish the game and, when it did finish, a total reluctance to stop smoking and drinking tea and go home. My dad to this day mentions the 'tactics' he employed to get Billy to leave. Simply saying 'Billy, go home. Now!' wasn't enough.

We'd always work out some way to get him to stay.

'Just after this encounter,' I'd say.

'OK,' would say my dad, not realizing that an 'encounter' could be with an entire foreign clan that would lead us to some ruins that would lead to the underworld, fighting monsters, swiping treasure, negotiating on behalf of the Tsolyanu princes, gaining information on a political party, starting a family, arranging school for our imaginary children, growing old and seeking potions to reverse the ageing process.

'Go now,' my dad would say, 'this second. My wife and I want to go to bed. Give us back our lives.'

We weren't yet trusted to perform important tasks like turning off the gas fire for the night by ourselves, so my parents wouldn't go to bed before I did.

'Just let us dice this.'

'Now!'

'As in *maintenant*?' said Billy, raising an eyebrow.

'Mainten-nothing,' said my dad, 'this instant. Toot sweet, if you prefer it in French.'

I'd shake a dice. There are wargamers who would have picked me up for that statement and said 'shake a *die*,' but I still think the singular of that noun has atrophied. I digress.

'In the outline of the bas relief you can faintly make out a square of lighter dust. You have discovered a secret passage,' said Billy.

'Heaven help us,' said my dad.

'Prayer for divine intervention, requiring nought nought on D100.' I'd shake again. '36. Sorry, Dad, you can't just never go to church and then expect Jesus to appear in your front room whenever you click your fingers.' I'd say.

I'd look at the clock. If Billy could make it to ten o'clock he wouldn't be able to catch a connecting bus to take him home.

'Can I have a cigarette, Mrs Barrowcliffe?' Billy would say, knowing that my mother could not bear to see someone smoking without a cup of tea or coffee in their hands and that, as a keen smoker herself, she was very sensitive to the plight of anyone left without. A cigarette would be brought, and Billy would begin to work some tactics of his own. He'd use a different set of stories to engage my parents, to make them as reluctant to see him go as I was. My dad, being a sucker for funny stories, would always listen to him.

'My family are, as you know,' said Billy, 'supporters of the National Front.'

It was a myth we subscribed to at the time that his dad actually held some position in this neo-Nazi party, but I've since found out that wasn't true.

'My uncle's also a clay pigeon shooter.'

Billy's dad was West Midlands champion at the sport for a while. Also 'uncle' didn't mean his actual uncle, just a friend of his dad's.

'Anyway, living next door to him is this vegetarian teacher. As you can guess, they don't get on, and there's been a lot of bad blood between them.'

I think nowadays vegetarianism still comes with an implicit set of other values, but back then it was impossible to imagine a vegetarian who wasn't a sandal-wearing, Campaign for Nuclear Disarmament-supporting leftie. Well, other than Hitler.

Billy would continue. 'My uncle's very proud of his garden, and he's always suffering with cats coming on to it, crapping everywhere and digging things up. There's one cat in particular— a huge tabby, who he particularly dislikes after he chased it away, slipped and did his knee in.'

The 'crapping' went over my head like a rifle shot. My parents were of that generation of working-class people who regarded swearing of any sort as very bad form indeed. I was surprised to see they didn't mind 'crapping,' though, and thought I might try it in the future, maybe even venture a 'shitting' or a 'pissing' and see what the reaction was.

'So this day,' said Billy, 'he comes down to find his garden all a mess, and he finally snaps. He goes up into his bedroom with a twelve-bore and waits for the tabby to appear. After four hours of waiting,' (Billy's family were nothing if not determined) 'the Tabby appears on the fence, nips over and walks up the path like he owns the place. My uncle sees red and opens up on it with both barrels. He's normally a dead shot, but he's so angry that he misses, and he shouts after the cat, "I've warned you before, you bastard, if I see you round here again I'll fill you full of lead."'

My mum and dad laughed. Perhaps 'bastard' was OK.

'Unfortunately,' said Billy, 'at the very moment he lets loose the teacher has just been returning home from up town. He's walking up the path, sees my uncle fire the gun and thinks he's talking to him. He runs inside the house and calls the police. Result, an armed siege. My uncle thinks the commies have come for him and won't come out until his wife comes to the door.'

It's an interesting fact that, at a period when the police were routinely referred to as 'fascists,' the real fascists viewed them as communists. Billy's dad described them as 'glorified social workers.'

'What happened to him?' said my mum.

'He explained it and just got a warning.'

That was the seventies for you—a warning for discharging firearms and issuing threats on a sunny Saturday in back-to-back suburban gardens.

'I'm surprised they believed him,' said my mum.

'He said if he'd have been trying to kill the teacher he wouldn't have got angry. He'd have done it in cold blood and wouldn't have missed.' The sort of thing that must have been very comforting for the teacher to hear.

Billy had a very engaging way of telling these stories—all of which had titles like 'The Milkman and the Bayonet,' 'Free Embalming Fluid for Auntie Pat' and 'Emptying an Irish Village Using a Land Rover.' My mum and dad were naturally inquisitive people who would question him closely in the way you do with a good anecdotalist, wanting to relive the shock and surprise of the story, probing for more interesting facts, more funny revelations. By the time he'd finished it was often twenty past eleven, and all the buses were down.

At this point my dad had a choice—drive Billy home, which he did quite often, or allow him to stay the night, which he did more. This would mean the wargame could continue to two or three in the morning, provided we went on without the fire. My parents were of the opinion that, if left to burn, the gas fire could start a blaze that would level half of Coventry.

'It'll be safe,' I said.

'That's what they said in Pudding Lane,' said my mum.

We'd enter a sort of hypnotic state where the hours would seem longer than normal when you were living them but then, when you looked back, would seem to have gone in a tick.

I felt honoured by Billy's company and, unlike with Andy Porter, liberated by it. It was as if I could be truly myself with him, and, instead of being barely tolerated, I was sort of celebrated.

I don't exactly know how much we shared. I think we had very little idea of each other's interior life. I certainly never mentioned to him the difficulties I had fitting in at school, and it was impossible for me to imagine Billy having any doubts about himself at all. What we did have, I think, was a true friendship—my first. Most childish friendships are based simply on where you live and what sorts of toys you like playing with. It can be a surprise, as your personalities take shape, to find you have little in common with the people you've grown up with. Billy and I were united by our love of fantasy role-playing games, but it was more than that. I found him immensely funny and engaging, but not in an exclusive way. It was important for Billy to think he was associating with remarkable and interesting people. I was associating with him, therefore I must be a remarkable and interesting person. So even though vast areas of ourselves were closed to each other, we still forged a strong bond based on the giving and receiving of respect.

I think that Billy actually became a father figure to me. He was big enough to be one, and he seemed to know the answer to anything I might be interested in. This isn't to say that my own dad stepped out of the role. He didn't. It's just that we really had no point of shared interest any more, no common language and, short of him taking up D&D himself, then we weren't going to have.

Billy's was my first real friendship based not on where I was—school or the back entries of Whoberley—but where I wanted to be. In short, I think that was the middle class. Billy and I were both from working-class backgrounds, but we had a definite longing for something more. For the first time in my life the place I was walking towards became more important than the one I was coming from.

I was still slightly puzzled by Billy's socialism. As far as I could see it stood up for the poor, the disadvantaged and the needy— in other words, a bunch of losers. Why did he want to associate himself with them? The fact that he and I were actually directly from the group that socialism sets out to champion never occurred to me. In my mind I was a high elf, not the son of a factory worker.

Later, of course, I did have my Marxist phase and regretted not rallying to the red flag earlier. If I had I would have been able to say to serious girls in university bars: 'Yeah, I read *Das Kapital* when I was fourteen.' I said it anyway, but it would have been nicer if it had been true.

Most importantly of all, Billy seemed to set the standards high for what he wanted in a friend, and I had to live up to them. In this world it wasn't embarrassing to want to be clever and to talk about clever things; in fact it was necessary. Next to Billy's sparkling wit my classmates seemed dull and vindictive. My day-to-day life seemed ever more unattractive, and my link to D&D grew ever stronger.

Vigils

I don't think it's an exaggeration to say that, at this time, my devotion to the game became almost religious.

Puberty finally descended on me, and the illustrations in Empire of the Petal Throne provided ample fantasies—the Empire, you see, is a hot place, forcing people to go around scantily clad. These illustrations were far better than the ones in the D&D books, though still not that good. Virtually all my Empire of the Petal Throne characters became followers of the goddess Dlamélish—the green-eyed mistress of sins and, as you might expect, obsidian princess of the damned.

Dlamélish aids those who are perverted and engage in sorcerous orgies, orgies I wouldn't have minded participating in myself if they could have guaranteed no other blokes there.

This was the period of the all-night wargame, many of which were held at Billy's house. It was just as much a window on another world as Andy Porter's place had been. His dad's taste in ornaments was a little eccentric and included, among other things, a .303 rifle with a Turkish leaf bayonet attached, a British Army helmet and a live hand grenade.

The hand grenade had pride of place on the mantelpiece, above the fire, and was, Billy assured me, entirely safe owing to the fact his dad had put a metal band around it to make sure that it wouldn't go off. I recall one of the older wargamers, Steve Boscombe, saying he didn't feel comfortable with it in the room and us all wondering why he was making such a fuss.

Years and years later, when I met up with Billy again, he told me what happened after his dad's death. Billy is a pacifist who has very little use for an arsenal of weapons, so he decided to dispose of them. I don't use the word arsenal lightly here to indicate a trifling collection of, say, ten or so guns, knives and associated ammunition. Billy's dad had enough to equip a small army. Well, to be more precise, a large platoon. That may have been what he was planning. His dad had, it was said, in addition to his sporting shotguns, World War I and II pistols, a Bren gun (a 'light' machine gun capable of downing a low-flying aircraft), several rifles and a sten gun (a submachine gun of brutal elegance). It was rumoured but never proven he also had a rocket launcher. He definitely possessed a quantity of World War II shotgun ammunition that had been issued to farmers. Instead of the normal pellets inside the cartridge it contained a large steel ball. The idea was that it would enable farmers to shoot down German parachutists. Whether it ever worked is another question, but I wouldn't fancy one hitting me.

A lot of this stuff was very illegal in the UK, so Billy rang the police and asked them what they wanted him to do with the weapons. He was put through to a firearms officer who told him that he was really busy and didn't have time to come down and collect anything personally.

'Just pop it in a bag and hand it in at a police station,' he said.

'There's rather a lot of it, and I have to come on the bus,' said Billy.

'It'll be fine,' said the policeman, 'just make sure no one sees it.'

'OK. What do you want me to do with the hand grenades?' said Billy. 'Should I take them on the bus too?'

There was a pause on the phone. 'I'll be over immediately,' said the policeman.

The police, apparently, have forms on which they record weapons they've taken. Normally most people's collections fill up two or three boxes on the form. Billy's dad's ran to four sheets.

Of course, being surrounded by all these guns thrilled me no end, and Billy's dad, like all men with collections, needed little encouragement to discuss it.

In some ways Billy's dad fitted the stereotype of the earnest fascist. He was very heavily built, fat, and suffered from pleurisy, so he gasped and hacked whenever he moved around. However, he seemed quite a kind man and never mentioned politics to me or criticized Billy for his spectacular and ardent socialism. I have a picture of him in my mind sitting with his rifle across his knee, saying, 'Come the glorious day I'm going to go out and shoot me a civil servant with this.'

For the all-night games, we'd sit in Billy's house from six in the evening until midday, madly gaming, enjoying fighting the tiredness and the monsters together. In the early hours of the morning the game took on the feeling of a rite.

It sounds stupid, but I think something happens to the brain around dawn. When I've stayed up sober—working late on newspapers for instance, or driving long distances, I've seemed capable of a higher level of concentration. It's as if you're tapped into the flow of feeling that exists between people, and, as the intellectual faculties tire, then the emotional ones take over.

It was in these late-night sessions that we were most likely to cooperate as players and feel something beyond selfish concern for our own skins—a loyalty to the adventuring party. It was on one of these adventures that my berserker Nogbad the Seven Million Nine Hundred and Ninety Nine Thousand Nine Hundred and Ninety Ninth died, as a berserker is meant to, wounded but charging the enemy anyway to save his blood brothers. It was the first time I'd really role-played—that is, thought about what my character would do rather than just tried to preserve him at all costs, and it felt like I'd learned something about life.

When Elric had died at the end of *Stormbringer* I'd felt actually upset and wished that Moorcock had preserved his hero's life. Similarly I'd been pleased when the hobbits had been rescued on Mount Doom. After Nogbad died, though, I began to see things differently. One of the flaws in *The Lord of the Ring* is that only one person the reader really cares about cops it. If I'd have been Tolkien I'd have left Sam or Frodo dead on the mountain. Mind you, with 100 million sales and my spell checker recognizing the author's name, what do I know?

Still, after fourteen hours' gaming, when everyone had worked as they were meant to work—the thieves unpicking the traps, the clerics healing and the magic-users laying waste to the teeming goblins—it felt good to have fulfilled my role and met a glorious death. It was almost a shame when they dragged my body back to the town to have me resurrected. A few weeks later, when Nogbad died again, it wasn't nearly so interesting. I'd experienced that sometimes it's right for things to end, though I wouldn't say I had yet learned it.

I remember Billy's house as peculiarly comfortless and unadorned, pineapple grenades aside, and it looked as though it hadn't been redecorated for years. If I recall it now, it always seems to have been in its own half-light, more Victorian than 1970s, with a bareness to things, everything there for a function rather than to please the eye.

There were some things that pleased the eye, however, in that Billy's dad had an enormous collection of 1950s pornography which he had handed on to Billy. There was nothing here more daring than a topless shot, but, seeing it by the side of Billy's bed, I felt like a hobbit thief opening a trove of gold. My only breaks in these marathon games were to take one of the magazines to Billy's outside toilet. This is the madness of youth. I can't imagine interrupting a social gathering nowadays to say, 'I'm just stepping outside for a wank.' Back then, and in that company, it seemed utterly unremarkable.

I think this is a serious point, although, God knows, it doesn't sound like one. I have in my life done so much that I have absolutely no connection with whatsoever now that I wonder if it's even accurate to say that those things were done by me. I'm tempted to refer to my teenage self in the third person.

There are other questions here—at what point exactly did it cease to be acceptable for me to slip out for one off the wrist with no more embarrassment than a worker nipping out for a cigarette? At what time on what day did that change?

If I make it to eighty, how will I look back on myself now? I pray to God that the way I feel today isn't just an interlude. Imagine if I'm sitting beneath my tartan blanket in the old folks' home and turn to the nurse to say, 'Could you just wheel me into the lavs? I fancy I'll have me some solo delight.'

The thing is that, like it or not, I am connected to that little boy. But think of this—every cell in the human body renews itself completely once every fifteen years, according to Billy anyway. That would mean that I'm not even the same person physically as I was then, let alone mentally. I come to the uncomfortable conclusion that the only thing that ties me to my fifteen-year-old self is a soul.

In these early all-night wargames it was usually only Billy and me who lasted the course. Occasionally some of the older boys would stay, but they would normally get the first bus home. It was only me and Billy who would still be gaming at midday.

Eventually, tiredness would overcome us, and I'd have to go home. Falling asleep in the afternoon, the knowledge that I had an Eye of Incomparable Understanding tucked into my priest Vridrir's backpack, I really did not see how life could get any better.

Pilgrimages

The summer of 1978 saw punk slouch up the M1 from London to Coventry. Admittedly it had been around in pockets since the year before, but things travel slowly to the provinces from London. I can still remember an argument in a music lesson over who was better—the punk band The Stranglers or the pop group Showaddywaddy. In '77 it was still a debate. By '78 it wasn't.

It was important to define yourself through a favourite band, and I settled on the X-Ray Spex since others had already bagged The Stranglers and The Sex Pistols.

This didn't diminish my interest in D&D; I just incorporated it into it. I developed a character called Poly Styrene, my female cleric—named after Poly Styrene of the X-Ray Spex. At this time, under the influence, I think, of Hatherley and Walters, I'd decided that I was a Nazi myself and, despite the fact that I only knew one black person, who had always been very friendly to me, would no doubt have expressed some pretty hair-raising views on race. As I've noted already, given the fact that Hatherley and Walters were relentlessly unpleasant to me and that Billy, my mentor, was an avowed communist, you'd have thought I might have started to find membership of Anti-Fascist Action appealing. Instead I started to imagine my sweltering Derry boots were jackboots and to note that I was Aryan in appearance. Not for the last time in my life, I identified with my enemies more than I did my friends. In my defence, I think that by imagining myself as a Nazi I was imagining myself as liked. The other boys didn't want me in their group, but I put myself in it anyway.

I still listen to the X-Ray Spex, and there's definitely something in the quality of Poly Styrene's voice that sends all my nuclei fizzing to this day. In having a character named after her I was combining my two passions. One thing that had completely escaped my attention, however, was that not only was Poly Styrene an ardent anti-racist campaigner, but she was mixed race as well.

I can only think that I had a highly developed ability to see only what I wanted to see. I recently reread *A Wizard of Earthsea* and realized that I'd made a similar oversight in that. Despite reading the book about six times before, I'd been completely oblivious to the fact that the central character in that was dark-skinned as well. The text clearly says so. My preferred mythology was Celtic, cold mountain tops, ancient magic drawn from stone circles, callow youths made old beyond their years by the knowledge that they had to bear, and pale ladies of the mist-filled glades. So that's what I imagined, ignoring Ursula K. Le Guin's explicit, inventive and clear descriptions of a world based on a sort of early Mediterranean/African culture.

I often think of this when I see people talking about how you 'get through' to teenagers. I think the answer is: you can't. They are so immersed in their own world that whatever you say just gets interpreted in a way that you can't even guess at. They're seeing things that you don't see and missing things that you feel are obvious. It's not far off feeling enchanted.

I did feel like I was under a spell, though not as much as I would have liked. I'd reached that point of obsession with a hobby when playing it all the time and talking about it all the time simply is not enough. I needed a more physical connection with the D&D world, and this desire led me to my first independent travel.

We began to visit wargaming shops. It was long before Games Workshop had a slick operation selling all its own products in every town. Then there were only two shops I thought I could visit—Dungeons and Starships in Birmingham and Games Workshop in London. There were, in fact, more shops than I imagined. It was probably just that someone's dad could be persuaded to take us to London and that Birmingham was the furthest we could envisage going on our own.

These excursions had the air of pilgrimages, the shopkeepers the cardinals of our religion, interpreting the words of Pope Gygax the First.

Dungeons and Starships, I think, got quite sick of us. They had erred to an extent in including in their advert the words 'much more in stock, call for details.'

I called.

'Hello, I was wondering what you had in stock.'

'Well what are you looking for?'

'Nothing in particular, I just wondered if you could run me through what you have.'

'What, all of it?'

'Yes please.' I had a sandwich and can of pop by the phone, and I'd brought out a chair as I'd anticipated it might take a long time.

The man refused and said I should come down and see, but I would have been very happy to sit there while he said, 'Tunnels and Trolls, Ogre, Bunnies and Burrows, Chivalry and Sorcery, The City State of the Invincible Overlord, Tomb of Horrors, Dungeon Geomorphs, Runequest, Palace of the Vampire Queen, twenty-sided dice sets, Dwarven Glory . . .' I would have loved to question him on the exact content of each game, to imagine myself playing them and to tell him of my gaming experiences.

We did take the trip to Birmingham and Dungeons and Starships. Eighteen miles away, it felt like another world: strange accents, a bigger city.

'This is probably how an adventurer would feel coming into the City State of the Invincible Overlord,' I said to Dave, getting off the train and imagining a cloak around myself. I don't think I was far wrong.

Dave and I looked around nervously as we made our way through the Bull Ring shopping centre, which to me seemed packed with ghetto-blaster-toting Rastafarians ready to slit you from ear to ear in a second. The presence of these other boys living different, rawer lives frightened us a lot. I wished more than ever that I had a sleep spell or a fireball at my disposal, although I think I would have been too scared to say the words to defend myself.

We made our way up to Snow Hill the only way we knew how—walking. It would never have occurred to us to take a bus in a strange city because it was simply outside our experience. I knew only two bus routes—the 13, which connected my house, town and Andy Porter's, and the 18, which went to my nan's. Unless the bus had 'Dungeons and Starships' written on it we would never have got on it, afraid of where we might end up. The idea of asking was out of the question. People would then know you didn't know where you were going, which would be, in the words of the time, 'a show up.' Embarrassing, in English. Also, of course, buses cost money, money that could be spent on D&D equipment.

When we finally did arrive at the shop it was closed. Half day Wednesdays. Naturally we hung around for two hours outside it, pressing our noses into the window to see any game we could see and hoping that the owner would come back and open it up.

'Perhaps he's forgotten something and'll return,' I said.

'It's a chance,' said Dave. It wasn't. I couldn't understand this bloke. He had the opportunity to be in a games shop twenty-four hours a day, seven days a week, and yet here he was taking a half day off. I supposed he might have a game, but why not have the game in the shop? Perhaps he didn't want his mates rifling through his stock, mucking about with it and throwing it around, like occasionally happened at our games.

We did, however, go to the second-hand bookshop next door, where I bought Michael Moorcock's Swords Trilogy, featuring the hero Corum. This was exactly what I'd been looking for—a

Celtic warrior with a magical silver hand, war chariots, weapons made from the heads of the enemy, druids, mist and cold woods, the works.

There's also, if I recall correctly, a deal of sardonic laughter in Moorcock's work. I looked up sardonic in the dictionary—'grimly mocking or cynical'—and then became more sardonic myself. I ate my breakfast sardonically, spoke to my mum sardonically and rode my bike sardonically to school, where I was sardonic. The strain on those around me must have been considerable.

The books sustained me for the week and a day until we could visit Dungeons and Starships again. This time we went on a Thursday, when we knew it was open. I'd phoned to inform the man that I was coming, and I was slightly disappointed not to hear him turn to a bugler to tell him to keep his instrument good and ready for my arrival.

I had a bone to pick with this man anyway. I didn't see why he had called his shop Dungeons and Starships. I loved Dungeons and Dragons and was quite smitten with the science fiction version of the game—Traveller. (I particularly admired the restraint of that title, along with its sleek black box bearing a tasteful single stripe, and was very glad they hadn't called it something like Space Wars or MegaTraveller. Later, of course, they did call it MegaTraveller, and that annoyed me.)

In my mind, though, fantasy and science fiction were separate categories that should on no account be jumbled. It was like gravy and ice cream, lovely separately and even one after the other but together, never. I couldn't bear the combination of laser guns and wands, spaceships and galleons, and it really hurt me to think of someone mixing them.

I decided to confront the man about it when I got there and spent a while thinking about what I would call a games shop if I owned one. The Dream Forge I thought might be a good one, and I made up my mind to let him have it if he'd give me a copy of the game Ogre, which had just come out. This wasn't a role-playing game; in fact it wasn't really much of a game at all, as far as I recall. It was set in a world where giant tanks—the ogres of the title—fought against armed hovercraft and self-propelled guns. The ogre started at one end of the board and had to make it to the other before being destroyed by the guns and the hovercraft according to a set of rules. As far as I recall there wasn't much in the way of tactics to this—I might be doing the game a disservice here, I am relying on my memory of nearly thirty years—but I found it morbidly fascinating, an early version of a 'shoot 'em up' video game without the video. I'd played it at Andy Porter's house and wanted a copy of my own.

Billy came with us that day, and we discussed a suitable name for the shop on the way. I was interested that Billy, who always seemed such a creature of refined tastes, veered to the earthy and the pungent in his fantasy life. 'Blast 'em All!' he said, or maybe 'The Kill Zone.' I didn't like this, it seemed too obvious to me. I liked the name of a comic shop in London I'd read about: Dark They Were and Golden Eyed. Marc Bolan's album *My People Were Fair and Wore Sky in Their Hair but Now They're Content to Wear Stars on Their Brows* was the sort of name I was looking for. 'How about the Halls of Elven Kynde,' I said, 'or The Silken Web?'

'Sounds like a haberdashery shop,' said Billy.

'What do you reckon?' I asked Dave.

'Shop'd do,' he said.

'Well, no one would know what it sold then, would they?' I said. 'You can't just call it "shop."'

'It'd keep the crowds off,' said Dave. Still to this day I don't know if he was joking.

'How about The Most Excellent Gaming Emporium?' said Billy, trying to copy the ornate verbal style of the Empire of the Petal Throne.

I nodded.

'Or Tek himiranyi's Path of Opening the Way,' I said.

'The stress in Tek himiranyi should be on the *ran*, not the *him*,' said Billy. 'Tek himi *ran* yi. Tek *him* iranyi sounds ridiculous.'

We argued about that for the rest of the journey.

One of our titles had to work, I decided. I'd have presented them as a sort of portfolio to the bloke in the shop, but I didn't have a pen.

Dungeons and Starships was, I have to say, something of a disappointment when we finally made it through the door. I had imagined a sort of sorcerer's cavern, rules piled in tottering stacks, strange things in dusty jars, masks and animal heads staring down from the walls, at the centre of it all a wizened figure with too much of the wrong sort of knowledge in his eyes.

Instead I found a well-ordered, tidy shop with a fairly normal, studenty sort of bloke behind the counter. When I say normal, studenty bloke I mean one of those you don't really see any more, the sort you can imagine having his own tankard behind the bar in a pub and liking folk music in his socks and sandals. It was pleasingly ill-lit and had a security grille blocking out the windows. I couldn't help wondering how many hit points the screen would have and how resistant it would be to an enterprising gamer bent on booty. I really did think about coming and breaking in but in the secure knowledge that I wouldn't actually do it. My bravery has always increased in inverse proportion to my proximity to adventure.

I say it was something of a disappointment because it was very far from being a complete let-down. It was stacked with games whose names I'd only read in magazines—Runequest, En Garde, Lankhmar, War of the Star Slavers, Godsfire, Nomad Gods, Tegel Manor—the latter the haunted house done by the same people who did the City State. This is what I coveted—particularly as it had a relatively well-drawn picture of a spooky house on the front. One of the charms of these old games is that, rather than looking like a game, they actually resembled the sort of map you might find scrawled on a piece of bloody papyrus at the bottom of a treasure chest. Their amateurism makes them seem more authentic.

Unfortunately, having spent all my money on two sets of train fares and three Michael Moorcock books the week before, I only had £3 left. Tegel Manor was £3.50. To me 50p might as well have been a million pounds. Later, Pete bought Tegel Manor, and I was placed in the unbearable situation of being able to see it but unable to read it because it would spoil the dungeon.

The man running the shop said hello, and I thought it best to show him that we were no mere browsers. I went up to the counter and introduced myself.

'I'm Spaz Barrowcliffe,' I said, 'I called you earlier on. D&D magic-user level 25, EPT priest level 4,' (Billy was a bit of a martinet when it came to seeing the rules were followed) 'Traveller marine with a pretty good platform of skills, if I say so myself.'

The man looked blankly at me. At the time I thought it was because, as a powerful shop-owner, he had much more experienced characters than that and wasn't impressed. Now, though, I can interpret his look. It sort of said, 'What am I supposed to do with that information?'

'I know what you're thinking,' I said. 'Elves can't go beyond ninth level as magic-users, so why have I got one of twenty-fifth level? In one word, "Wish spells."'

'That's two words,' he said, unbeknowingly opening a Pandora's Box.

'Wish-es is what I meant,' I said. I wasn't offended by what he said. Compared to the pedantry of most of my friends, he was exhibiting a laid-back and easy-going attitude.

'"That's" one word,' said Billy, as if emerging from the Pandora's Box.

'Wish spells is two words,' said the man.

'But you said, "That's two words,"' said Billy, 'when "that" is in fact one word.'

'He said "that's,"' I said, 'which is technically two words condensed.'

'"Which" isn't technically two words condensed, it's a parenthetical determiner, normally used with a noun.'

'Which goes,' I said, casually using it with a verb, 'to show . . .'

'Would you like to buy anything?' said the man.

I did want to buy something, but I also desperately wanted to talk to him about D&D, to get his stamp of approval that I was a knowledgeable and dungeon-hardened player. I'm not sure kids think like this any more, but to me he was a figure of authority who could give me the endorsement that my peer group withheld. I think this is a very common thing for men. In the world of motorcycling, for instance, the man in the flat cap who comes along and tells the youngsters about the amazing side-valve contraption he had in the 1950s is a cliché. Similarly, many soccer fans are never quite satisfied until they've established that *that* goal from 1973 is the one they admire above all others, so showing their depth of knowledge and their unimpeachable credentials as a fan.

Billy smiled and put his hand across the counter.

'Billy Crowbrough, Hunca Munca, thirtieth-level fighter, possessor of the Invulnerable Coat of Arn. I also DM EPT, and some other RPGS, occasionally Traveller, though in that field I only dip a paw,' he said, illustrating his words with a dip of his paw.

The man nodded. 'How about you?' he said to Dave. 'Do you want to tell me anything about your characters?' I don't know if he was being sarcastic, but I suspect he was.

'Just a man in a cloak,' said Dave.

The man behind the counter nodded.

'Maybe a ranger, then,' he said.

'A man in a cloak,' said Dave.

The man blew out, like a half-submerged hippo wondering how it was going to keep its children entertained during the school break. 'Is there anything you particularly want?' he said.

'I've got £3 in my pocket, and I intend to spend it,' I said, expecting him to start acting like a hard-up silk merchant in the presence of a lord bent on soft-furnishing his castle.

'Not that much you can have for that,' he said, 'but we have these.'

He held up a set of arcane-looking cards rendered in a parchment yellow.

'What are they?' I said.

'Tac cards,' he said.

I felt my temperature going up. For a second I couldn't remember what Tac cards were. I was going to have to ask him, and then he'd think I didn't know the first thing about D&D and had only just come to the game and so had no real right to be in an expert's shop. Then it came to me. Each card had the name, encumbrance value and damage characteristics of a weapon or piece of equipment on it. The players laid them out in front of them to show what they were carrying.

'*White Dwarf*, number 3, Open Box review. I believe they thought they might be useful but could make the game slightly clumsy,' I said.

'Oh no,' said the man, 'we've played with them and they really are superb. They remove all those arguments about what weapon someone has out or what they're holding in their hand when a surprise attack occurs. They also let all the other players see whatever visible equipment each other has.'

I wasn't sure I liked that. If Andy Porter noticed I had, for instance, some magical armour, he might decide he'd like that armour for himself. And 'all those arguments about what weapon someone has out.' Well, we'd had those arguments, but, considering the prevailing atmosphere of the games at that point, getting rid of one set of rows would just allow extra time for others.

'I don't know,' I said.

'In a year's time you won't be able to game without these,' said the man, 'games that don't have them will just look unsophisticated.'

I certainly didn't want to look unsophisticated in front of this man. I adjusted my battered felt hat and tapped my Derry boot against the counter. I had no choice but to buy the cards. He'd said the u word and sold me. I bought them on the spot, splashing out 35p on an *Underworld Oracle* fanzine and feeling annoyed that there was nothing I could spend my last 15p on.

Dave bought Boot Hill, a role-playing game set in the Wild

West, and Billy bought an Empire of the Petal Throne supplement—the Nightmare Maze of Jigresh. We'd been in the shop
ten minutes, and there was no real excuse to stay any longer.

'I'd love a cup of tea,' I hinted.

'There's a café just around the corner,' said the man. We
paused, looking at each other. I wondered if it was some sort of
test, if there was a word I was supposed to say in order to get
invited to some secret game that was going on by candlelight in
the back of the shop. We stood looking at each other for a while.

'Need any players for your games?' I said. I didn't know how
I was going to get over to Birmingham—eighteen miles away
may as well be the moon when you don't have transport—but I
thought such a rich shop-owner would be bound to have a car.

'I don't get the chance to play as much as I used to,' he said.

'Yeah, right,' I thought.

'I went all the way through the Halls of Testing for fighting
men in *UO*, issue 2, and came out fourth level,' I said.

Again, he looked at me blankly. What did he want me to say?
He moved, sat down and began to read a magazine. I was
slightly surprised to see it was the *Radio Times,* nothing to do
with D&D. Why would he read the *Radio Times,* I wondered. It
sort of implied he was going to watch television, and I couldn't
imagine any D&Der doing anything that dull.

'Is that it, then?' I said.

'Unless you want to buy something else,' he said.

'No. Have you thought of calling this place The Elven Web?'
I said. 'Sorry, the Silken Web, or the Halls of Elven Kynde?'

'No,' he said.

'How about Killzone?' said Billy.

'It's Dungeons and Starships,' he said. 'We've made the sign.'

I couldn't help feeling that, with a different name, the place
might have been more full on a wet Thursday in a cold spring.

All the way back we were full of our adventure.

'I could tell he thought we were going to buy Tunnels and

Trolls or some bollocks like that,' said Billy. 'I think it safe to say that he judged us creatures of discernment when he saw our interest in EPT.'

'Yeah, and did you see his face when I got my three pounds out,' I said. 'He obviously takes us seriously. We'll probably get invited to a game next time we go.'

'I think he liked us,' said Dave.

'Why do you think he didn't want to tell us about his characters?' I said.

'Probably saving it for a surprise when we play with him,' said Billy.

'What characters do you think he'd have?' I said.

'Fiftieth-level human cleric, no races. I think he likes to play things straight,' said Billy, 'probably with the Mace of Cuthbert and some other one-off magical items. I wouldn't have thought he'd be overly laden down with potions. Invisibility, maybe, but he'd have CLW and CSW as spells so he'd more than likely trade them in for something more magic usery.' CLW and CSW were cure light wounds and cure serious wounds.

'He's not the barbarian sort is he?' I said.

'No way,' said Billy, laughing and shaking his head as if the very suggestion was ludicrous. This phrase 'no way' had come in with the detective Frank Cannon and still sounded either new and fashionable or contrived, depending on your point of view.

'I wonder how you get into running a D&D shop,' I said.

'You'd need a stack of qualifications and a bucket of money. Forget it Spaz, it's a dream,' said Billy.

'They might want an assistant,' I said.

'They'd want someone who had been gaming for years. They wouldn't want to risk employing a dilettante,' said Billy.

'I'm not a dilettante,' I said, though not knowing what a dilettante was. At school you get to recognize bad words when they crop up and disassociate yourself from them. This is a hard-learned lesson for some. I'd once been asked if I'd eat a winnet and said 'yes.' Those of you who don't know what a winnet is are lucky in your ignorance. I believe the more usual term is gruffnut or dingleberry. Clag is occasionally used too. I was more of a laughing stock than normal for a week.

I returned home happy, dealing out my Tac cards on the table again and again—torch, sword, rope, crossbow. I imagined myself holding them like a gambler holds his cards—the concealed items in my rucksack close to my chest, the sword I was carrying out on the table.

Then I lost a couple, I don't know where. I still have no idea where. Our house had an ability to swallow these things. When I was eight I was given a die-cast model of a German Stuka dive bomber. It had a detachable bomb which you could drop to detonate a cap while neoooooooowing the plane about. I used it once on Christmas Day. The bomb went down the back of my mum's bed and, despite hours of searching, could never be found again.

The Tac cards, in fact, were one of those products that seemed to have been devised solely with the aim of separating boys from their pocket money. We tried to use them once and gave up. I think they could have worked, with perseverance, but the other wargamers were never going to persevere, particularly with something I'd bought. Strangely, the cards seemed to follow me around for years. One would pop up in a university file or fall out of a notebook when I was first working as a reporter, little symbols of the triumph of ardour over good sense.

Wargames saw me buy a few things like the Tac cards over the years. We'd visit Dungeons and Starships every week over the holidays—35p for a return to Birmingham leaving me with 15p, plus whatever I'd saved by not eating, to spend on things. Often I just bought a dice. Often, even when I had birthday or odd job money to spend, there was nothing worth buying. I bought things anyway—the game Citadel, for instance, with its intricate floor plans (never understood it, never played it); White Bear Red Moon—enjoyed it but no one else was interested, so I played it on my own.

These solo games were bizarre. As far as I recall White Bear

Red Moon was a board game that pitted the Lunar Empire against, I think, the Beast Riders. Since I was much more struck on the imagery of the moon than I was of sweaty beasts I'd stage five-hour-long battles where I wouldn't allow the beasts to win a single encounter. Destiny, for the duration of the game, was in my hands.

The other game I bought and never played was The Emerald Tablet. This was very appealing to me because it used occult symbols on cards as part of its way of settling battles. Obviously it was a combination of a miniature game and a card game, but I loved the inscriptions and the magic circles that were drawn on the cards. However—and I've just paid through the very snout on the internet for one—it is immensely, incredibly complicated.

Today, if a kid wants to play a wargame he can buy a PC game for his computer—one of the Total War series maybe or Age of Empires—master which keys he needs to press and away he goes, giants steaming into harpies with abandon. The outcome of the combat is decided by unseen calculations within the computer. Mapping out the action on a tabletop, we had to do the calculations ourselves. D&D possessed table after table, but games like Emerald Tablet were on another level. They were basically a long description of how to do sums.

Here is something I once read for fun, as a break from my maths homework:

A Cleric of level 1–5 cannot turn (scare away) a vampire and this undead nasty is affected only by weapons with a +1 bonus or greater; it has the hit probability of an 8-dice beast (10/12 against AC2).

$$(D3) = (50 \times 40)/9 \times 1 = (810) \text{ iv, } (A4) =$$
$$900/3 \times 11/20 \times 27/2 = (2160)4$$

The Ma bonus . . .'

It goes on in very much the same vein for a very long time indeed.

This was the Monstermark system, a *White Dwarf*-designed set of rules for evaluating the toughness of monsters found in dungeons. The above is not an actual quote, and I made up the figures in the equation because I got bored copying out the real ones.

I never managed to read past paragraph 3 of this feat of mathematical gymnastics—spread over three issues of the original *White Dwarf* with the aim of 'emerging from a morass of subjective judgements' about how dangerous monsters were. There's a terrific paragraph that begins 'the calculation for a hell hound is actually quite easy' and then goes on to contain what seems like 500 calculations in one very long sentence.

If you ever wanted to feel clever about yourself, this was guaranteed to do it. I'd leave the relevant copy of *White Dwarf* out on the sofa turned to the Monstermark system.

'Yeah, Mum,' I'd say, 'it's a much more scientific method of calculating the D factor and A factor of a monster so as to lead to a more equitable way of handing out experience points. Look, there's the easiest equation you can do. It's for a hell hound. What, don't you understand it?'

The fact that I had no idea what it meant never stopped me trying to make out that I did and that, really, it was all straightforward once you got into it.

One of the strengths of any hobby is the number of ways it offers you to relate to it. Just as model train collecting must have something to support it other than just looking at model trains, D&D has a whole raft of things you can do while not playing the game. Of course there's dungeon design, reading fantasy novels and painting figures and, one of my favourites, designing character classes. (I still think my Melnibonéan—inspired by Moorcock's Elric of Melniboné—in *Illusionist's Vision* 1 is something of a classic, but maybe that's just me.)

Here was something for the mathematically minded. You could combine sums and monsters. For some boys this was heaven. And they didn't stop there. Redesigning the game's system became almost a mania with some people.

The holy grail of fantasy wargamers is, well, the holy grail actually. That aside, many aspire to making things as realistic as they possibly can. One of the main causes for arguments in our D&D was that, at any one time, we could be playing a mishmash of two or three combat systems—most notably the D&D original, plus some stuff from the *Greyhawk* supplement and things taken from publications such as *The Arduin Grimoire* with its critical hit (you've had his eye out) and fumble (you've had your own eye out) system. These were introduced to make a combat between an Imp and a magic-user who had turned himself into a giant armadillo more realistic.

Some D&Ders could be more than a little animated when it came to combat. Here's a letter from *Underworld Oracle* that reflects the broad attitude of many of us. After a complaint about the ecosystem of a dungeon—how monsters can live close together without attacking each other, it goes on:

'Also, *I nearly went incoherent* when I saw that the playtest party had wiped out 8 ghouls with only one man wounded. Against AC2 a ghoul will miss with all three attacks only about 30 per cent of the time. Sometimes it will hit more than once. Considering that low levels may be paralysed even if not killed, I can't figure out how your boys did so well.'

The italics are mine, by the way. The letter then continues, without a pause, to change subject completely.

'Why do you say DM?' The wilderness is half of D&D. GM (Gamesmaster) for ref is much better.'

I find it amazing that people could be so passionate about the minutiae of the game, but there again, in catering for the maths heads and the pedants, there was something for everyone. Well, maybe not everyone.

There was definitely something for me, though. I was more interested in imagining myself casting spells and the delicate and beautiful descriptions of exactly how my enemies could be eviscerated. Rather than maths, I was drawn to magic.

As my adolescence bore down upon me I looked at myself—schoolboy, weed, über-runt of the collection of runts known as the D&D group, perspirer over charts and tables—and came to the obvious conclusion about who I was. I was a magician. Obvious, really, I'd always known it. Now it was just a matter of reaching out for my destiny.

Moonchild

My first attempt at casting an actual spell was centred on a fast during the dark of the moon—the time of Lilith, lady of vampires, according to a pile of old tush I'd taken out of the library. The book assured me that I could expect all sorts of interesting effects from this—the ability to see spirits in trees for instance—though it warned me that it was possible to encounter 'blocking forces' in the shape of demons that would tempt me from my path of enlightenment.

The fast was, according to the book, a druid ritual, but I've since discovered that it's also observed in ancient Jewish and in some yogic traditions as well. It's never really fitted into spotty English schoolboy traditions, and I was to find out why.

We'd acquired a dog—Sam the Springer Spaniel—who required walking every day. So every day I set off down the A45 road and over the fields to my nan's house on the Canley Estate. These were older council houses, two-up two-down, small but smart, semi-detached and each with its own large front and back garden, built to the quaint notion that a house should be pleasant to live in as opposed to reflecting an architect's bold and radical vision.

It was easy enough to miss breakfast—my house was always a turmoil in the morning, and no one was going to notice if you'd had your cornflakes or not. At lunch I claimed to have forgotten my sandwiches. This was nothing unusual; I very often did forget my sandwiches.

All the way down the highway (as the A45 was called as it passed our area) I checked for signs of impending expanded awareness. I was sure that I could detect a purpley glow over the landscape, and I paused in the middle of a soccer field to try to hear if the gates were opening to the land of Faerie. Nothing.

Hello, a crow landed. This was probably Hugin or Munin, one of the Norse god Odin's spies. I was absolutely starving. The starvation I'd expected was a sort of glamorous longing of the soul. This just felt like I wanted some biscuits and quick.

'Hail Hugin or Munin,' I said.

It flapped off in the direction of the swings, leaving me wondering what crow pie tasted like.

I kicked on to my nan's. I'd been prepared for the blocking forces to present themselves as a faint odour of soot, the nagging feeling of something you valued burning, a strange feeling of discomfort like it said in the book. I had been unprepared for them to appear as a nan carrying a tray of scones. The ancient druids couldn't have had nans, I would have thought, because if they did the whole basis of their fasting religion would have been scuppered. A shaman isn't going to spend three days and nights starving himself into expanded consciousness up a tree if there's a kindly old lady rattling the tea cups and offering him fruit cake and biscuits at the bottom, is he?

A nan sees a non-eating grandson as an abhorrence in her sight and will do anything to force something past his lips. I resisted the Bourbon Chocolate Creams. I slavered over but resisted the shortbread. The ham salad came out, and the fast was off. As so often in this life the needs spiritual got a fair trampling from those carnal, and I sank my fangs into a generous hunk of meat between two slices of Gladdins finest crusty white garnished liberally with mayonnaise and salt. Then I had the Bourbons and shortbread for afters.

It was hotly debated in the 1980s whether D&D led people to an interest in the occult. It doesn't seem unreasonable to suppose that, if you spend your entire imaginative life caught up with magic, then sooner or later you're going to end up wondering what it might be like to try it out for real.

The opponents of D&D—overwhelmingly American—failed to see that an interest in the occult doesn't arrive out of the blue for most people. I'd been fascinated by tales of witches and wizards from early childhood. From the age of nine I'd been taking out books from the library with titles such as *The History of Witchcraft in England* and *Dion Fortune's Psychic Self Defence* or *Astral Projection*. *The History of Witchcraft* would leave me fascinated and a bit scared by some of the illustrations, and the other, more practical, books would give me the distinct feeling someone was watching me.

I don't think an interest in the occult is a bad thing. That doesn't make it a good thing either, but it's just another phase for a lot of teenagers, like going about with your hood up or tucking your Marlboro in the sleeve of your shirt, and you'll grow out of it fairly quickly. The overwhelming majority who are drawn to the occult either scare or bore themselves silly fairly quickly. It might be dangerous, for some, but it's much less dangerous than horse riding or wind surfing, and no one seems to bother too much about those.

Also, it doesn't take a book of spells or D&D to fire the imagination of the obsessed teenager. The imagination is already up and burning, and it will take anything at all as fuel.

I first tried astral projection—sending the soul from the body in the way that is sometimes seemingly experienced by people on operating tables—after reading an article about it in the *News of the World*.

I tried communing with the holly tree in our garden one night after thinking I could see a face in it when I looked out of our back bedroom window. I sat cross-legged in front of it wishing I had some mistletoe to consume to help me see the spirits more clearly. After half an hour it began to rain softly. Undeterred, I went into the house and emerged to continue communing in my anorak. After about an hour my mum brought me a cup of tea.

She didn't bother to ask what I was doing sitting in the freezing damp; I think she had given up all hope of an intelligible answer at that point.

A certain sort of religious nut does try to steer children away from occult influence, overlooking the fact that most will steer clear of it of their own accord unless their parents make it glamorous by warning them against it. To some adolescents, everything is an occult influence. To me the spice rack in the kitchen might have held the key to the spirit world if I could find the right mix of ingredients, a strange-looking kitchen knife was perhaps a misplaced ritual dagger, messages of foreboding or promise could be read in the sky or in the patterns I saw when I closed my eyes. For a time I was sure I could step through a dimension door by simply screwing up my eyes and pressing down on their lids. This, to me anyway, gives a weird checked effect from which emerges a blob and from there some swirls, which could well be runes, and on to a sort of black and white grid that I took to be the dimension door through which I would travel.

Even the *Exchange and Mart* magazine played a part in my magical imagination. This was a classified magazine where people sold goods. It seemed full of possibilities. A child has only possibilities, so the little glimpses of other destinies it offered—sexual, spiritual and social—seemed very tangible to me. Among the ads for trailer tents, cars, pets and musical instruments, various sex products and manuals were advertised. I hope I won't discover one day that the ads for the 'Non Doctor' marital aid system (four interchangeable heads) were all in my mind.

Weapons were for sale too, and I considered sending off for a telescopic truncheon 'as used by the Gestapo' or an SS dagger. Luckily I needed the money for D&D. I guess Kevin Gerling might have got his Nazi marching songs from this outlet. They were certainly for sale.

Also in the *Exchange and Mart* was an ad for a shop called The Sorcerer's Apprentice in Leeds. I longed to live in Leeds, which I imagined to be a citadel of gleaming towers similar to Tolkien's Minas Tirith. I wanted to visit this amazing shop, which offered crystal balls, altar bells, and oils for skrying—the initiate's word for looking into a pool and seeing visions. My memory is that there were various animal claws for sale too, but I might be wrong about that.

Pretty much like a kid with a Toys R Us catalogue in November contemplating Christmas, I'd look down the lists and imagine the beauty of an Athame sacred dagger or how amazing a sword of power or protective talisman might look. I read the ad again and again—in my mind it almost seemed to speak to me from inside the pages as the magazine lay in the rack.

Every month when we got the *Exchange and Mart*—my dad didn't often buy much, but he did like to browse—I'd look to see if something new was for sale, a book on occultism or a home temple kit, a thousand-dream dictionary or a guide to the Kabbala (the scary stuff, not the Madonna-influenced lifestyle religion). The frustrating thing was that the ad said you had to be over eighteen to order anything. However, a way out loomed when my mum asked me what I wanted for my birthday. I drew up a list.

1. Crystal ball 4″ diameter
2. *Grimoire of the Shadows* (book)
3. Hypnosis pendant
4. Sword of power
5. Aftershave

I'd added the last because I was beginning to think that it was about time I sprouted some hairs on my chin and thought that splashing a bit of smell on might encourage them to come out. I decided not to put the kit of erotic spells down because that would have involved talking to my mother about sex and indicating that I was, in some way, interested in it.

'There's the birthday list, Mum,' I said, handing it over.

'Right,' she said, 'have you written the codes down?'

Normally we bought our gifts out of my mum's 'club' or catalogue because prices were cheaper there, and I think you got some sort of discount the more you shopped at it. Each toy had a code, and this was what she wanted. I think she suspected that a hefty order for D&D material would be put in but hoped that I'd come in with a bid for a Simon toy or a remote-controlled car like a normal boy.

'These don't have codes,' I said, 'they're from the *Exchange and Mart.*'

'You are *not,*' she said, 'having anything second-hand.'

Second-hand items to people of my mum's generation were a sure advertisement of poverty, cars aside.

'They're not second-hand,' I said, forwarding the *Exchange and Mart,* 'they're in here.'

I tapped the ad for The Sorcerer's Apprentice and watched as it had a magical effect on my mother, that of causing her eyes to come out on stalks.

'Absolutely and totally not,' she said. Other children would have heard this as a 'no.' I, however, viewed it as a reasonably encouraging bargaining position. Three or four hours of repeating the word 'why?' 'oh, but why?' and the trenchant 'it's so unfair' over and over again would normally have her seeing things my way. However, she was unusually firm on this one.

'What's wrong with you?' she said. 'Other kids ask for a bike. Why are you drawn to the macabre?'

My mum was very capable of unknowingly flattering me. For several weeks after she said this I couldn't pass a mirror without looking into it, raising a raffish brow and saying 'drawn to the macabre' as if it was some caption for my image in the glass.

'I don't want a stupid bike,' I said, 'I want a *Grimoire of the Shadows* and hypnosis pendant. What am I going to do with a bike? I've got a bike. I mean horse.'

'What are you going to do with a bloody hypnosis pendant, that's my question to you. I'm not having your brothers walking around the house like zombies doing your bidding, whatever that might be, and I'll tell you that free, gratis and for nothing,' she said. 'Why not have a Pong?'

I think she felt that, if I was offered the stuff that the kid she thought she'd have would want then I'd become the kid she thought she'd have.

'I hate Pong,' I said. This was a computer game that was already out of date, but I didn't want a modern computer game either. Why would I play on a computer when I had D&D? The idea seemed sick.

Unfortunately my mother was unmovable. Really, she missed a chance to put me off the occult for life there and then. If she'd have bought me these items I might have quickly realized that magic doesn't work, particularly the erotic stuff, and dropped the interest. As it was, the ad in the *Exchange and Mart* seemed to twinkle at me like some forbidden fruit on a strange tree.

Still, there were consolations. I satisfied myself with getting a few things from *White Dwarf* magazine and renewing my interest in perfecting my warlock character class.

Weirdly, D&D didn't encourage my leanings towards trying magic of my own at all. In fact, it frustrated them. Even the most pompous and ambitious historical magicians, from the Zaroastrian Magi through John Dee, Francis Barrett and Aleister Crowley, never claimed to be able to throw fireballs or lightning bolts like D&D wizards can. So D&D was never going to feed the fantasies of practising magic in the real world. That is all about gaining secret knowledge, a higher level of perception or inflicting misfortune or a boon on someone rather than causing a poisonous cloud of vapour to pour from your fingers (Cloudkill, deadly to creatures with less than 5 hit dice, for those who are interested). The game, as we played it, just doesn't support the occult idea of magic.

In fact, it might even be argued that, by giving such a powerful prop to my imagination, D&D stopped me from going deeper into the occult in real life. I certainly had all the qualifications—

bullied power-hungry twerp with no discernible skill in conventional fields and no immediate hope of a girlfriend who wasn't mentally ill. It's amazing I'm not out sacrificing goats to this day.

However, I did discover some very practical ways to conjure magical effects, with a little help from my friend.

The
Sorcerer's Apprentice

Billy was, I discovered, quite the amateur chemist.

His father was a very skilled toolmaker—he undertook some serious freelance engineering projects at his house, and there were a number of outbuildings stocked with lathes and grinding wheels, more like a small factory unit than a conventional shed—a mega-shed, Billy called it. 'Mega' had just caught on as a word and everything was 'mega' at that point. Billy had his own shed, and his father had encouraged his interest in science by allowing him to stock it with chemicals exceeding what you'd find in your average school lab.

'Gosh,' I said, 'do you use that for making explosions?'

'I used to when I was young and immature,' said Billy, 'but now I conduct more important experiments.'

'Like what?' I said.

'Titration,' he said, 'using pipettes.' I nodded as though I knew what he was talking about.

'Gosh, perhaps you'd be an alchemist if you were a D&D character,' I said. We'd just got *Dragon* magazine number 2 with the rules for the alchemist character class in it.

This led to the usual almighty squabble that attended the launch of a new class, as everyone wanted to take alchemists into the dungeon and no one wanted to be a boring old fighter.

'I'd probably be a magic-user,' said Billy.

'That's what I'd be,' I said.

Billy shook his head. 'You haven't the intelligence,' he said.

'You only need an intelligence of 12,' I said. This was annoying to me. Porter had said the same thing when I'd told him of my choice of class.

'I think it fair to say,' said Billy, 'that the grammar-school entrance exam would be about the level of the test to get into magic-users' college. You failed that, therefore your intelligence is not above 12,' he said.

'I only failed through bad handwriting,' I said. Actually, 'bad' doesn't do justice to my handwriting. Neither does 'handwriting.' 'Desecration of paper' about covers it. Whether or not this was the true reason for my failing the grammar-school test, it's the one I clung to.

'Handwriting would be required for drawing up magical symbols,' said Billy.

I frowned. I didn't like this line of talk at all.

'Do you think you could make a flash pellet?' I said, changing the subject. Making flash pellets was a first-level skill for alchemists. The alchemist would throw one on the floor, and they would explode and blind an opponent.

'Yes,' said Billy, 'but I prefer a more subtle chemistry.'

A measure of what that chemistry might be came one day when I'd cycled over to Billy's, and his dad decided he wanted the house to himself. This meant that, for once in our lives, Billy and I were forced to find something other than D&D to do. For the first and virtually only time in my adolescence I was at a loose end.

We cycled out over the parkland in the east of the city, mooching about in the grey and the cold. I thought I was going to die of boredom in that washed-out light until Billy turned to me and said, 'How much money have you got on you?' My mum had given me a pound for dinner, so I pulled that out. It would, of course, never have even crossed my mind to actually spend this valuable cash on dinner. Food could be had for free if I waited long enough.

'Excellent,' said Billy, 'let's get some lighter fuel.'

'What for?' I said.

'You'll see. We'll need some nodders too.' I went red at the very word. 'Nodders' was the slang for 'condoms.' 'Or some balloons,' he said with a wink.

Nowadays I understand that more imaginative and inventive children than we were sniff lighter fuel to induce hallucinations. I would have done that in an instant had I known it was possible—hallucinations were definitely in the same mental compartment as magic in my brain, that is, the 'good' box.

Billy and I went to a newsagent's and bought a can of lighter fuel and a party pack of balloons. We then went below a very low concrete bridge in the park, just above our head height, though quite broad, and attempted to burn ourselves to death. We didn't actually think that was what we were doing, but any impartial observer watching us would have been forced to that conclusion. Billy blew up each balloon slightly, then filled it with lighter gas and tied it with a flourish.

'I am going to show you, oh eager initiate, how to throw a fireball,' he said.

He released the balloon and cast it up to the ceiling formed by the bottom of the bridge. Then, in a quick movement, he lit a match and applied it to the balloon.

There was an intense explosion, not loud but hot, as the underside of the bridge filled with fire. I felt my eyebrows singe in the sudden heat.

'And so it is done,' said Billy, as you might expect a wizard to say it.

'Give me a go,' I said through the fug of burning hair.

There is a mathematical law that operates whenever young boys engage in this sort of activity, and, given the education, you could probably plot it on a graph. It states that the boys' desire to pump more and more gas into the balloon will only be offset by the diminishing amount of gas available in the bottle. If you take the initial amount the boy puts into the balloon as a standard dose, there are perhaps thirty of these doses in the can. You will get nowhere near thirty explosions out of it, however, because doses 2–5 will be of ever-increasing size, doses 6–8 eking the last out of the can in a series of shakes and bashes. Finally the boys— and this is simply a law of nature—will try to set fire to the can.

There is also a psychological phenomenon at work here that I believe is peculiarly male. A woman or girl—presuming one could be induced to take part in this sort of activity in the first place— having burned her hair and eyebrows would conclude that she had been lucky and reduce the amount of gas she put into the balloon next time. The man doesn't come to the same conclusion at all. He, singed and blackened, arrives at the point of view that *he still has a margin of error to play with.* After all, he isn't dead, and he's hardly likely to burn his eyebrows off again. They've already gone, history; he's moved on. There can be but one deduction—the dose needs to be increased. This is just like when he misses disaster on a corner by inches in his car and turns to his female companion to say, 'Not bad, eh?' In his mind, the closer he comes to disaster without actually triggering that disaster, the better a driver he is. Next time he goes through the corner, never mind missing the wall by inches, he'll do it by millimetres. Should he end up in the wall, of course, it won't be his fault. He was only doing what any reasonable human being would do. The mistake was down to a bobble in the road or, in the case under discussion, the lack of a long taper with which to light the balloons.

'Fireball!' I said as I applied the match to the balloon.

There was a tremendous flash and the world disappeared momentarily. When it reappeared, the bag of sweets that Billy had in his hand caught fire. I was curiously unharmed, only slightly blinded, a sign, I was sure, of my magical power. Perhaps I was naturally resistant to fire, or maybe my forty-five minutes of fasting the week before had conveyed supernatural protection upon me.

'That,' said Billy, trying to stamp out the sweet-bag fire in such a way as to not damage his chocolate éclairs and giving the impression of a hippopotamus doing a paso doble, 'is almost exactly what a baby red dragon's breath would be like.'

'OK,' I said, 'well, let's see what a young adult would do. Five squirts for the baby. How many do you reckon for the young adult?'

'Fifteen at least,' said Billy, wiping away the remains of his eyebrows.

'We could put the lot in and see what an ancient dragon would do,' I said.

'I don't want to die,' said Billy, showing commendable caution.

'Poof,' I said.

As it was, we had little left in the can and so had to content ourselves with a smaller explosion.

We returned to Billy's house smouldering but happy. I had a fantastic idea, I told Billy. Next time we were at Porter's house I'd give him a fright by filling a balloon up, putting it in my bag and then whipping it out quickly and exploding it over the gaming table at his house—the house full of muskets and antiques, perhaps with horns that had stored gunpowder for his battle re-enactments lying about, you know the one, and the gaming table full of paper, that one. It seemed a splendid idea to me. If I did it quickly enough he wouldn't even realize it was a balloon.

Today, of course, in the unlikely event that I should wish to explore that hinterland between practical joke, demonstration of dark powers and arson, malice aforethought, I'd more than likely choose to experiment in a large field, wearing goggles and protective overalls. To my teenage self, though, Andy's bathroom looked like a prime spot. The bathroom was tiled, I reasoned, and therefore had nothing that could catch fire. Other, that is, than the curtains, the odd towel, a decorative toilet roll holder and a bathmat.

I had the balloons and lighter fuel in my bag so, when Andy was out making coffee—a rare event—I took it up to the bathroom.

Dave and Pete noticed me taking the bag up and asked me what I was doing with it.

'I've just got some dungeon plans I don't want anyone else to see,' I said.

'A mucky book more like,' said Pete.

'No,' I said.

In the bathroom I locked the door and set about my work. When I recall this it's a split-screen affair: me working on the balloon, the boys downstairs in the front room, Andy making coffee, the fire brigade playing volleyball in the station while some fast music plays.

Again, I fail to understand my teenage logic. If you're experimenting with letting off fireballs in someone's home, well, just don't. If you really, really must, that is, if you won't get the serum to save your dying loved one unless you do, then do it small. The clue to the danger in this sort of activity is seen in its description: playing with fire. If something is a metaphor for taking unacceptable risks, then it's a safe bet that it is an unacceptable risk.

The thought that crossed my mind, however, was this: 'I've got one shot at this, best make it a good one.'

I can see the balloon now; it was pink. I wanted to save the only remaining red one because I thought it would look more realistically like a fireball and that they might not even notice it was a balloon at all if I exploded it quickly enough over the table. Unfortunately I was no expert on lighter fuel, and, instead of the gas I'd used with Billy, I'd got liquid. 'What's the difference?' I thought.

I half blew up the balloon and then added a generous draught of fuel before blowing it up some more. Then I tied a knot in the end of the balloon, took out a box of matches, put the balloon in the bath for safety, lit a match, applied it to the balloon and set fire to Andy's house. Or at least, that was how it seemed. Vision died under the tongues of flame. I remember thinking that the effect would be very much like the spell 'Wall of Flame,' which confines an intense fire in a small space.

The flash and the intense heat in such a small room briefly brought me to my senses. At first I thought that I'd got away with it and could proceed smoothly to the dining-room explosion. There had been a bathmat draped over the side of the bath, and in some strange logic that utterly defeats me today I'd left it there because I didn't want Andy's mum noticing it had been moved and asking who had been at the mat. It was one of those frondy affairs. Should anyone be looking for suitable material to start a bonfire I can recommend one of these mats wholeheartedly.

The mat was on fire, and I was in a dilemma. I didn't want to turn the tap on in the bathroom in case I drew attention to myself. In my mind it was almost as if the bath taps were alarmed and that Mr or Mrs Porter would come clumping up the stairs to demand to know why I had been interfering with their plumbing.

The only logical thing to do was to throw the mat into the bath and try to stamp it out, which I did. At thirteen years old I was a good one hundred and fifty pounds and no ballerina. I stamped and stamped and eventually got the fire out. By this stage the bath was such a mess with charred mat that I realized I was going to have to turn on the taps. I did, cleaning up the mess from the bath but wetting the mat. I tried it over the side of the bath, but even I could see that it was never going to pass muster. One edge was terminally charred and it was clearly soaking wet.

Then there was a knock on the door.

'What are you doing in there?' said Porter.

'Mucky books!' shouted Pete from below.

'Andrew!' I heard his father's voice. Mr Porter clearly didn't want a mention of mucky books in his home.

For a second I thought I was done for. Then I saw my brief chance of a way out. I still had my bag. However, that would mean putting a wet bath mat on top of my D&D books, something I was completely unprepared to do. I'd have rather been sliced with the blade of the Krelle.

In a flash I saw the necessary course. I took off my sweater, emptied the bag, put the balloons and lighter fuel in the bag, the mat on top of them and the jumper on top of the mat. I then put the plastic-bound D&D books in. I decided to go downstairs with the magazines and papers under my arm.

'Come out!' said Porter at the door.

'I'm on the loo.' I opened the window and wafted a towel around.

Andy knocked again. I don't think he wanted his dad getting involved.

'What was all that banging?'

'Constipation,' I said.

There was a silence from behind the door. I think Andy was working out if that was a reasonable explanation or not. The bathroom looked fine to me, if a little hazy through the smoke. I wafted some more. Now all I had to do was get past Porter with his mat, like Obi Wan Kenobi going past the stormtroopers on his way to meet Han Solo.

'This isn't the mat you're looking for,' I played over in my mind.

I opened the door. Andy was on the other side.

'Have you been wanking?' he said, in a low voice so his dad wouldn't hear.

'No.'

'Yes you have. That's disgusting. Why does it smell of smoke?'

'It always does,' I said.

'No it doesn't.'

'It should,' I said. 'I should get it seen to if I was you.'

I think Andy was so puzzled that he said no more about it, nor even the fact I had my bag with me and lots of D&D stuff under one arm. Although later on in the day he did ask Pete: 'When you wank, does it smell of smoke?'

'If I've been eating smoky bacon crisps,' said Pete, with a straight face. Andy looked deep in thought, and that was the last we heard of the subject, although I did notice that, though I regularly saw him with crisps, I never saw him eat smoky bacon.

The mat was thrown away when I got home, and, as far as I

know, the Porters put it down as a laundry casualty, one of those items that you can never quite remember getting rid of but just disappears one day, missing in the wash.

There in Andy's living room I did feel a little smug. I regarded what had happened in the bathroom as a mild success and was considering going on with my plan to explode a balloon at the table. From my point of view I had nearly burned Andy's house down, but I hadn't, had I? That was the crucial point, everything had turned out OK apart from the death of a bath mat that was only armour class 9, one hit point anyway and so would have worn out quite quickly, I thought. I still sustained the illusion that I knew what I was doing, that everything had been under control. Fortunately the lighter fuel was under the mat, and I was afraid it would be seen if I tried to get it out.

By the next week we had other things on our minds—fun snaps, space dust and the science fiction game Gamma World. The plan to detonate a fireball in Andy's house was forgotten.

A wiser boy than me would have learned that some things are better left as ideas.

In the Cave
of the Svartmoot

Life at Coventry wargaming club was becoming more difficult. The older tabletop gamers who played with model soldiers representing the Roman or British Empire armies were becoming sick of the level of whooping and shouting that went on at the average D&D game.

I have some sympathy for them. What had been a sedate refuge from the world, a gentle hobby for gentlemen dreamers, was beginning to resemble a battle itself. At times the room sounded like a fire at a zoo. The oldest member of the club was so disgruntled that he earned himself a nickname from Billy—General Buggery, owing to his habit of going around the club muttering 'buggery, buggery, buggery' under his breath. They approached us in order to ask us to keep it down a bit. The suggestion was met with outrage.

Considering that we were all playing a game of strategy, our next move was slightly surprising. Faced with an attack from an enemy—which is certainly how we perceived them—we immediately gave in. The fact that we thought we were making their worst nightmare come true has nothing to do with it, what we did was completely capitulate. They wanted us to be quiet; we decided to be silent.

'That does it!' said Crowbrough in high dudgeon—I have rarely seen anyone before or since in high dudgeon, but Billy was definitely in that state and wore the expression of an old-fashioned nursing sister discovering dirt beneath a bed. 'We'll show them—we'll form our own club!' he said.

The rest of the D&Ders were in agreement. We'd conceived a disdain for the tabletoppers, as humans do when they live alongside people of similar but different habits. They, we thought, were playing with toys. D&D was more than a game. D&D was important.

We spent several weeks rubbing our hands together at the prospect of taking ourselves and our precious fees away from the wargaming club, and Billy even came up with a suitable venue. This all depends on your definition of suitable, of course. To Billy it was a good-size venue near to his house. To the rest of us it was a freezing scout hut in the Outer Hebrides.

Then there was the name. I came up with 'The Most Excellent Order of Pearlescent Blue' and Billy came up with 'Coventry League of Alternative Wargamers'—CLAW for short. Again, I didn't like this. It was too visceral for my liking, not fine enough. Too late, Billy had printed some flyers to hand out at the wargames club the next day.

I rang the *Coventry Evening Telegraph* to enquire about placing an ad and was put through to a reporter. A short article appeared, disappointingly lacking the bile and invective I'd directed at traditional wargamers and just recording that we were forming the club, and it was for role-playing games only.

I'd made it absolutely clear that tabletop wargames were for people who weren't intellectually equipped to handle Dungeons and Dragons. The article had me saying that it was for D&D and that we hoped to attract a good crowd. What I'd actually said was 'a superior crowd,' and it annoyed me that they'd made it sound like the sort of place a well-balanced human being in full possession of his senses might want to go.

Far from being sad to see us go, the older wargamers seemed indifferent. I thought they were putting on a brave face. Now I can see that they were simply waiting until we'd gone to crack out the champagne, or at least enjoy a bit of peace and quiet.

Our revolutionary zeal was undimmed by the experience of the first week in the scout hut, even though it had been too cold to actually conduct a game. This meant that it was so cold that your fingers didn't work properly, and leafing through the sheets of paper became difficult. Billy promised to get a gas heater the next week, but, when he realized there was no chip shop in the immediate environment, his confidence in the rebellion was diminished.

It was two buses to get to the new venue, and by the end of week two we were cracking. The heater hadn't materialized, and numbers were down to four of us. Sidney Stringer School, with the good lighting, the warmth and the fast-food outlets nearby, seemed ever-more alluring. By week four Billy called a meeting.

'We are, strictly speaking, not able to vote on this, Spaz, because we are not quorate,' he said.

'What does "not quorate" mean?' I said.

'It means there's only me and you here.'

Billy had prepared a speech which he read to me and, ironically, the heater.

'We have learned a bitter lesson,' he said, 'that sometimes opposition is easier than government. We have crossed a threshold that we should not have crossed. However, how are we to know where the limits are if, occasionally, we do not go beyond them. I propose a vote to return to Sidney Stringer.'

'I propose one too,' I said.

'You can't propose, you have to second,' he said.

'I second it,' I said.

'Ayes to the right, two, noes to the left, nil. I'll draft a letter to offer them terms.'

'We could just go,' I said.

Billy pondered.

'We could, couldn't we? Right, let's get the bus down there and call in at the chipper on the way,' he said.

I imagined that when we came back it might be like one of those scenes where deserters are recaptured by the French Foreign Legion, being made to crawl to the top of some battlements while the rest of the troops kick you and spit at you. As it was the man who collected the money—as he was an adult and a non-D&Der it never occurred to me to learn his name—said 'hello' and General Buggery said 'buggery.' And that was it.

This is the world of the teenage boy. To us we had rejected the older wargamers, bravely fought a battle, lost, offered terms and returned defeated but with our colours flying. I don't think they'd even noticed we were gone.

My return to the club saw me develop my favourite-ever character in D&D. I had a fighter/magic-user called Effilc Worrab. We were playing The City State of the Invincible Overlord, but this time Andy Porter was running it, as Daddy Cule had moved on to act in another part of the country. Andy was in a particularly irritable mood with me that evening, and it wasn't long before my character was in trouble from a wandering band of beggars. Reduced to no hit points, I did the only thing I could with my dying breath—call for divine intervention. This is where a character shouts out the name of his god and hopes the god pops up and saves him. You need to shake 100 on a percentage dice to do it. Still, one in 100 seems pretty generous odds for the appearance of a deity.

'Divine intervention!' I shouted.

'Shake, then,' said Andy, who thought he'd got rid of me. I did and the 00 that indicates 100 to us D&Ders wobbled into view. This annoyed Andy considerably, as he was duty bound to spare me now.

'Yes! Yes! Xiombarg is here!' I shouted. My character worshipped the female deity from Moorcock's *Stormbringer*, allowing me to think quite a lot about dark-haired naked goddesses.

Andy frowned. 'Right,' he said, 'well I think Xiombarg is going to be pretty annoyed to have been disturbed by a worm like you. She asks you what you want.'

At this point Andy had no need to describe the terrible beauty of the chaos goddess incarnate. We'd all read the print off *Stormbringer* and could imagine it for ourselves.

'I want to live,' I said.

'Xiombarg tells you that you're really irritating,' said Porter, 'and that if you call her again you can expect to pay the price with your soul. You're alive and on one hit point.'

'That's not right,' I said. 'Gods should restore you on full hit points, they always do.' This had been the convention whenever it had happened before.

'He has a point,' said Crowbrough.

'I want more than a point,' I said. 'I should be on 12.'

'No, I meant you have a case, an argument, *un raison juste.*'

'Are you agreeing with me?' I said.

'*Oui,*' said Billy.

'That's 'yes' in French,' I said to Andy.

'I know what it is,' said Andy. His eyes narrowed. He reminded me of a troll who has just found out an orc has been at his pickled dwarf hams.

'Right, full hit points,' he said, 'but she calls you a dolt and a cretin, and, to show what she thinks of you, she turns your head into that of a mule.'

Andy found this rather satisfying, I could see. He gave a brief laugh—a noise like someone had knocked the aerial out of the TV—and took on an expression like a pedigree cat carrying off a kipper while a neighbourhood stray watches from the other side of a window.

For once wisdom prevailed. I said something about that being my favourite character and how he couldn't do that and that it didn't say anywhere in the rules that Xiombarg could do that. In fact, it did say that, as Xiombarg can use polymorph spells—the term for shape-changing enchantments. Secretly I was delighted.

I loved the idea of a character with a mule's head and thought that it was massively glamorous. I never let Andy know this, though, because I feared that if I did he would announce that it was only a short-term spell or that after a week my head exploded. Muleface, as he was now known, became my signature character. I'd taken a badge of scorn and revelled in it—not for the first, or the last, time.

One thing that did come out of the CLAW was that we got to know Frank Warner, a much older wargamer. Frank saw the story in the paper and contacted us. He was a mad science fiction fan with a flat that seemed full to the ceiling with books. He surrounded himself with futuristic things. I saw my first microwave cooker at Frank's and my first flock wallpaper. Well, not everything was set to last.

Frank was something of an anomaly: a man of around twenty-five who was into role-playing games and willing to play with young teenagers. If you put those facts alone down you'd start to get a slightly sinister picture, perhaps, or at the least suspect that he was ill-adjusted. Weirdly, Frank was a self-effacing, good-humoured northerner who ran some brilliant campaigns for Traveller based on his wide reading. Almost everyone else I knew well that had anything to do with the game in a serious way was somehow off kilter. Frank was just a major science fiction buff who leaped at the chance to participate in that world in a different way. It says something about the kind of people that I met through the game that I have difficulty explaining Frank. He was normal. He should have been interested in something else.

The same could not be said for Steve Boscombe, another older wargamer of, I think, around twenty-one with a mad enthusiasm. I haven't attached that description to any object because it seemed to me that Steve had a mad enthusiasm for everything. Absolutely everything. He spoke in a way that seemed to indicate that the radio of his brain was receiving more than one station at a time. If I had to attach one word to Steve it would be 'relish.' Everything he did, he did with relish. Occasionally *I* actually found his zeal for acting out parts in the game embarrassing. This is the equivalent of Keith Richards advising you to lay off the Jack Daniel's. You know something is seriously awry.

Steve ran this hugely ambitious campaign—a campaign is the name for a series of adventures leading on from each other, all set in the same world—and wrote huge fantasy novels piled in stacks of paper that seemed to tower to the ceiling. Whereas Dave, invited to describe his characters, would say 'a man in a cloak,' Steve would say something like: 'At first, on entering the bar, you may consider him worthy of slight regard. This limber fellow sits with pipe aglow and a lusty tankard of foaming ale that he lifts not infrequently to his lips. His cloak is of motley, and his breeks are spattered with the mud of a hundred journeys. Tall is he, and imposing of stature, though he sits unassumingly. Perhaps you might not remark him on first glance until your gaze lingers a little longer and you see the *burning coals that are his eyes!*'

'Well, thanks, Steve.'

'What is in that bulging pack that lies at his side, you ask?'

'We have to get on to the others, Steve.'

'Apples from the harvest or something of more sinister mien?'

'Steve, really we . . .'

'Slender is his sword and its handle well worn, so many times has it sang its song of blood that it has moulded to the shape of his fingers.'

'Shouldn't it be "sung" its song of blood?' said Billy.

'No matter,' said Steve. 'The buckles on his boots may go unremarked at first glance, as may the tiny mole on his left hand but . . .'

By the time it got to me I was ready to say my character was a man in a cloak.

Frank had a calming effect on the games; they were more civil and purposeful and actually more like games than protracted squabbles when he was playing. Steve, however, had rather the reverse effect. He would actively encourage people to shout, to 'make the most of the experience,' as he put it.

This caused some alarm among some of the mums, who didn't have that clear an idea of exactly what it was we were doing. We were gaming at Pete's house one day. He had a games room off the main lounge that was ideal for us to play in. One day when we were being particularly noisy his mum came in, in the way mums do, to find out what was going on under the pretence of offering us a cup of tea.

We were playing EPT and had been fighting an undead temple hr'u (don't ask, it's just a hr'u, a monster, that's all you need to know. We can have the argument over whether it's pronounced 'hroo' or 'huh-roo' later). Steve had been getting into the action in a big way, calling out, 'Die! Die! Die foul pestilence!' at the top of his voice. The hr'u had taken quite a while dying, so Steve had spent a long time shouting 'Die!' and my priest, Vridrir, had lost his wife to it.

In my mind this woman was the most beautiful, sexy, good-looking, fanciable, fit, gorgeous, lush—you see I'm not dwelling too much on the personality here—woman I'd ever encountered. I had actually fantasized about having sex with her, despite the fact that her only physical form was as a string of numbers in an exercise book I'd stolen from school. I'd bought her as a slave girl but freed her and married her. To see her in the clasp of that vicious undead was torture. Why had I allowed her to wander off? That was so unlike her.

Worse, far worse, Pete's mum was dishing out the tea at that moment, so I had to be polite, all my questions burning in me, no colour in my cheeks.

'Do you take sugar, Mark?' she said, looking at Steve and clearly wondering why a young man so much older than the rest of us had been shouting 'Die!' at the top of his voice in her house.

'Sugar!' I felt like screaming. 'Bloody sugar! Someone's dead, woman, and all you can talk about is sugar!'

'So how are you boys getting on?'

She intended to hang around.

'Splendidly,' said Steve, in evil genius mode.

'What exactly is this game?' said Peter's mum, looking down at *The Player's Manual* as she poured. I could see the picture of the grinning devil on the front didn't exactly meet with her approval. Was she never going to go, though?

'It's EPT, like D&D, Mum,' said Pete.

'Oh yes, you're always on about that, aren't you?' she said, leaning forward with the tea pot and flicking open the Empire of the Petal Throne rules with her other hand. She turned straight to a picture of a naked woman about to be sacrificed by a priest in a death mask, as mothers will. She muttered words which sounded like 'not entirely suitable' under her breath.

I'd had enough. I couldn't keep it in a second longer. I could see the corpse of Tiel Hi-Vrinyani, my wife, rotting in front of me. I'd get someone to come and resurrect her.

'Is there anywhere to store the body?' I wailed.

'What body?' said Pete's mum, dropping the tea pot.

Time
of the Hawklords

1979 dawned, and Coventry was in the headlines. Hometown boys The Specials—a ska outfit—were the trendiest band in the country, and suddenly our city had something to be proud of. Presented with this gilt-edged opportunity to go with the zeitgeist right on our doorstep, to be able to say to future generations of music fans, 'I was there,' the wargamers wasted no time in missing the chance. Ska, like soccer and punk, was for dolts.

Unfortunately, there were other musical lures out there which to us were much more attractive than Two-Tone. All I'll say is that nowhere in the work of The Specials will you hear tell of a nymph, wizard, demon of the pit or any other figure from fantasy. All they had was really great music, a fantastic sense of style, cool and an interesting political message. To me they were just too thick to sing about goblins.

Andy Porter did many things that annoyed and depressed me in my youth, but I attach no blame to him. He was a boy himself, coping with his own adolescence, and few manage that well. There is one crime, however, for which he cannot be forgiven. He got me into heavy metal.

Given the fact that I was walking about with a head full of elves anyway, that might not have been a very difficult thing to do, but Porter was the first through that particular skull-encrusted door.

Andy's choice of band showed very good taste, within the zone of bad taste that is heavy metal. He was very keen on Hawkwind, a hippy combo who had metamorphosed into a more hard-rocking outfit. I've already noted Andy's power-hungry tendencies at that age. It is no coincidence, I believe, that one of the songs his favourite band was best known for was 'Master of the Universe,' where the singer reveals that he is the said master and that the winds of time are flowing through him, everything moving relative to him. We could all claim the last statement, I suppose.

Hawkwind were a D&Der's dream—songs about wizard-sages, interstellar horses, space rituals and warriors on the edge of time.

In fact 'Master of the Universe' could almost be taken to be about D&D, as the singer tells us we're all a figment of his imagination, in a world of his design. The song that did it for me, though, was the magnificent B-side of their one 'hit,' 'Silver Machine': 'Seven by Seven.' A lot of Hawkwind's imagery came from science fiction, but this was fantasy themed. I've still no idea what it's actually about, but it conveys the idea of magic like no other song I've ever heard. (And I'm including 'Magic' by Pilot, a band I used to think should be shot for doing such a lame song about such a great theme and who I now think should be shot for purely musical reasons. I had the same thing with Earth, Wind and Fire's 'Fantasy.' I wrote to *Sounds* newspaper asking if there was any way it could be banned. I now realize that a good deal of my ire was caused by the fact I quite liked it and couldn't stop humming it. Billy told me that Earth, Wind and Fire were kung fu experts who actually levitated during their shows. This I could respect.)

To cap it all, who wrote words and played occasionally with Hawkwind? Only Michael flippin' Moorcock. Could it have got any better? And for those boys who might be afraid they were going to have to confront any uncomfortable emotions in the songs, lead singer Bob Calvert, in a 1977 interview with *Sounds,* said, 'Hawkwind does have a clearly defined area. For instance, we've never done a love song.'

I'd get home from school and play 'Seven by Seven' over and

over again in the couple of hours before my mum would come home and make me turn it off. The medium, in this case, contributed to the message. I played the record on our then-fashionable radiogram, a sound system built into something designed to look like a sideboard. When I opened the top and saw the controls glowing out at me, it felt like I was about to operate something from a Jules Verne novel, as though the combination of wood and early electronica might conjure up, instead of Radio Luxembourg, the twelfth century.

I was having that peculiarly adolescent relationship with music whereby you're not really listening to the tune or the words but becoming someone, defining who you are through the song. Adults have this with music, and part of the power of a Sinatra, say, is to make the listener feel for a second like they are cruising with the goodfellas at The Sands. When the song ends, though, we know it's back to the washing-up. For some teenagers, however, there's no difference between the fantasy the song offers and their real lives. Somewhere in the mad collision of echoing voices of 'Seven by Seven,' I felt, the real me was lurking.

Hawkwind were a sort of back door into heavy metal. Their 1977 album *Quark Strangeness and Charm* (sub-atomic physics terms, you know) could, in places, easily have been taken for New Wave. You got into that, and then you went back to listen to *Astounding Sounds, Amazing Music*, and before you knew it you were head-banging along to 'Master of the Universe' and 'Magnu (Horse with Golden Mane).' From there it was a short step to Rush, who swallowed a dictionary and spat up a lot about pleasure domes and the Temples of Syrinx and, God help us, Rainbow, the lead singer of which had been in a band called Elf and who looked to me like a gnome.

The trouble with heavy metal, or at least the way it was presented at that time in Coventry, was that you couldn't just take it or leave it. You were either wholly devoted to it, or it didn't want you. There was no way you could like Black Sabbath and think that The Dickies had done a good cover of 'Paranoid.'

I bought 'Silver Machine' by Hawkwind in November 1978 at the same time as X-Ray Spex's 'Germ Free Adolescents,' but by April 1979 I was ready to ditch New Wave and embrace Heavy Rock. Another opportunity to be cool kicked into touch. I can remember watching Blondie on *Top of the Pops* and trying to convince myself that I didn't like 'Heart of Glass' and that I fancied Motörhead sidekicks Girlschool more than Debbie Harry, which I just didn't.

I had looked like an idiot before without trying. Now, putting my full creative powers behind it, I was starting to resemble the rarest sort of berk. I bought a denim jacket and cut the arms off, wrote 'Black Sabbath' on the back with correction fluid and started wearing motorcycle gauntlets on my pushbike, figuring that these had the dual benefit of looking biker-ish and like something a D&D character would wear. I sped round to Porter's for approval of my new outfit.

'Very good,' he said. I felt like a new recruit who has finally earned a word of praise from the drill sergeant.

I also took to wearing two pairs of jeans at the same time—a biker fashion. The top ones would be very ripped and the bottom ones more or less intact. This is OK on a motorbike but a little sweaty on a pushbike, particularly when combined with Derry boots. The effect was not unlike one of those sweat suits people use to try to lose weight.

The other wargamers caught the fever too, but they were generally content to simply wear a denim jacket, grow their hair as long as the school would allow and buy a band T-shirt. A couple of them would wear lab coats on trips to gigs and discos in homage to Hawkwind, but I felt the need to go further.

I think at the back of my mind I always had a dread of being accused of being a part-timer, not the genuine article, or of failing to have the name of some essential band written on the back of my jacket. Accordingly I wrote the name of just about every band I knew there, including one I'd made up—Plague Messiah. Plague Messiah was the name of the band that my character had formed in the sci-fi game Traveller and who played gigs featuring fights with thermic lances and plasma guns. To me they were real.

I wrote two execrable songs on my Bontempi Hit organ, knocking out a tune one reedy note at a time: 'Death to Life,' which bore the pithy observation that there was no tomorrow and that I bathed in sorrow, and 'The River of Death.' I played the songs to my friend Bill Richardson, a part-time wargamer.

'What do you think?' I said.

'Really, really, really, shit,' he said.

'Most people try to be as nice as they can about this sort of thing,' I said.

'I am doing,' he said.

This incident shook my faith in Bill's taste.

Not everyone was as approving of my new look as Porter. I bumped into a childhood friend of mine who happened to have a camera with him. He was so amused by what I was wearing that he took a photo of me.

I was aware that he was laughing at me, but I told myself I didn't care what other people thought and would dress how I liked. Of course, like many self-consciously wacky people, I was in fact paralysed by fear of the opinions of others and made the effort to appear as the maddest of the mad headbangers just in case anyone had the slightest lingering doubt as to the depth of my devotion. In fact, I think my disguise felt so fragile I couldn't allow it a single crack. If I did it might fall to bits and leave the real me shrivelling under the evaluating gaze of my peer group.

I also felt something of a fraud. Bikers were supposed to be tough fighters and, essentially, to have motorbikes. I wasn't tough and didn't have a motorbike. I made up for it by trying to out-biker the bikers in my appearance, thinking that if I built the edifice the interior would follow.

Heavy metal, of course, fitted seamlessly with D&D. Take the artwork from a late seventies or early eighties HM album and swap it with the front cover of a *Dragon* magazine and you'd never tell the difference. The lyrics, too, fit perfectly into that world—Led Zep's 'The Battle of Evermore' with its ringwraiths or 'Immigrant Song' with its heart-pumping beat and stirring imagery of ice and snow and, best of all for the D&Ders, the line 'Valhalla, yes I'm calling!' which is at least what I thought it said, and mention of the hammer of the gods. Then there was Thin Lizzy with their glens and overlords and rapiers and even Motörhead, who were peddling this stuff at the time with the brilliant 'Metropolis' and their fantastic-looking logo, a snarling skull adorned with savage-looking tusks. Very quickly I was running a half orc character called Baron Motörhead after the Lemmy character in Michael Moorcock's *Time of the Hawklords*. Andy Porter insisted on pronouncing Motörhead as Moteurhead, to reflect the umlaut in the band's name.

It was now possible for me to not only think about fantasy, read about fantasy and play a game about fantasy but to listen to music about fantasy too.

Casting a giant shadow over all of these, of course, was the band that was just made for me. Interested in witchcraft? Prefer dark, doomy imagery to wizards building towers and men on silver mountains like what Rainbow do? Wavering between attraction and repulsion when you see the art of Pieter Bruegel the Elder? Want to be sure you're following a band not with *a* nutter at the helm but with *the* nutter. You'll be wanting the Black Sabbath, sir. I was particularly captivated by the gatefold sleeve of the first Sabbath album, which shows a blurry image of a figure in a churchyard. This, I decided, was how my magic-users would look.

I don't think it's a coincidence that three of the monsters of heavy rock come out of the Midlands. Black Sabbath, Judas Priest and Led Zeppelin are all Birmingham boys. Like I said, there's something in the water.

Heavy metal fed my interest in D&D; D&D fed my interest in heavy metal. Then, when you would have thought my attachment to the game could go no deeper, it went deeper. I knew the original rules by heart. After two years of play this might have resulted in boredom, or at least in a less obsessed youth, but then

D&D was revamped, giving me a whole new catechism to learn again. I went to the task with relish.

The Monster Manual came out, detailing many new fiends with which to populate the D&D universe. It still showed D&D's addiction to bad art, but the illustrations were a vast improvement on the white box edition. Then *The Player's Manual* was published in a much more professional presentation than the original set and finally, later, *The Dungeonmaster's Guide*—a tome packed with information about the game and thick enough to do serious damage to a dog should it drop on it from a table. Want to know how brave the blacksmith at the local forge is? Want to know how to determine how helpful a bureaucrat might be? Need advice on interior design for dungeons? It was all there.

The redesigned game reinforced our view of ourselves—the title was no longer Dungeons and Dragons but *Advanced* Dungeons and Dragons, and Gary Gygax offered the comforting words: 'The game's major appeal is to those persons with unusually active imagination and superior active intellect.'

'Crikey!' I thought, once more, 'that's almost an exact description of me.'

We grappled with the new rules, designing new spells, coming up with sea and underwater adventures and slavering over new treasures like the magical Ioun Stones, gems which orbit their owner at a distance of about three feet, bestowing sorcerous enhancements and protection.

I loved the opportunity to go more deeply into my fantasy and the chance to reaffirm my commitment to the game in purchasing the new edition. I bought *The Player's Manual* from a D&D shop that had appeared in a Coventry arcade.

'They say this is much more than a conglomeration of the original three books, *Greyhawk, Blackmoor, Eldritch Wizardry, Gods, Demigods and Heroes* and several years of *The Dragon* stretching back into *Strategic Review*,' I said to the owner.

'You've played before, then?' said the man.

'Yeah, you might say that,' I said, attempting huge understatement, but adding 'like Björn Borg has been on a tennis court before,' by way of huge overstatement. I wonder if Borg did spend more time on a tennis court than I spent playing D&D. Probably not.

I've never grown out of this, really. A couple of years ago, on impulse, I went into Forbidden Planet to see what role-playing games they had.

'Do you have Empire of the Petal Throne?' I said to the man behind the counter, someone who had clearly spent a great deal of time trying to look a bit like a super-villain in an attempt to clearly signal to the outside world he had a strong interest in fantasy.

'What's that?' he said.

'The original role-playing game,' I said, 'published just after D&D in 1975, though after Chainmail. You have heard of Chainmail? First available through the *Owl and Weasel* fanzine, precursor of *White Dwarf*?'

'We've got Call of Cthulhu and D&D,' he said.

'Yeah,' I said, 'bit mainstream. I clearly need a specialist shop.'

'You deserve horsewhipping for that,' said my wife when we got outside. And I suppose she was right. Why do I feel the need to do that?

For the same reason that, when it came to heavy metal, I didn't think it enough to just wear a leather jacket, grow my hair as long as the school would allow and go to a few concerts. It wasn't enough for me to be obsessed. I had to be seen to be obsessed.

That summer, a biker on a pushbike, a wizard of the Whoberley projects, a creature of fantasy, I thought I was experiencing huge changes, that my destiny was set and I was on my way to being a Hells Angel and an occultist. Had I known it, my life was about to transform in a more significant way than that.

Character Assassination

Porter and Billy were not getting on. That sentence shows me where my sympathies lie now. Porter, second name as used when referring to criminals, and Billy, first name, informal, friendly. However, I didn't necessarily behave that way at the time.

The problem was that, whereas Andy had always been head of the group, the one designing most of the dungeons, full of ideas, Billy now provided a challenge. I'm sure this isn't what Andy thought consciously—he probably just considered Billy irritating or pedantic—but I think that at its heart his relationship with Billy was a power struggle. Billy didn't want to be the leader of the group, but he didn't want to be led either. The result was ever more intense arguments and, like as not, Andy doing his level best to kill off Billy's characters whenever he could.

This sort of thing is always bound to happen when things change. These days businesses spend millions on 'change management.' Without change management conflict is inevitable. With change management it's inevitable and expensive. We went for the cheap variety.

It would have been better if there had been a split, two groups of people fighting it out. Instead it was as if Andy and Billy were the eyes of a couple of storms butting up against each other, around which the rest of us swirled. For years it went on, never calming, only growing worse. Grudge piled upon grudge and resentment on resentment until Billy and Andy reminded me of a couple of rutting stags who'd got their horns locked together.

Some people are natural politicians. They see on which side the bread is buttered and proceed to lick it. I was more like someone who saw on which side the bread was buttered and got beneath the table to eat it from the underneath of the plate. I sided with Andy.

I think it was a combination of factors—childish ones such as the fact that Andy went to my school and so had to be defended against the posh grammar-school boys, and that he lived near me—and some half mad. Billy was the only real mate I had at wargaming, that is, the sort of person I would have found myself spending time with if it weren't for D&D. Andy didn't like me, so logically I should put myself in Andy's camp. Billy's friendship was in the bag; Andy's was still to be won. I should, of course, have sided with Billy—loftily staying above the argument was not in my make-up then or now. He was the best friend I'd ever had.

The problem, as so often in my life, was one of perception. From my point of view Billy absolutely demolished Andy in most of the arguments. There was no need to side with Billy because he always won. In fact, I could test myself by arguing against him and curry favour with Porter at the same time. It was a win-win situation, I thought.

What I didn't know at the time was that Billy actually didn't see it that way and also that he didn't like arguing even when he won. Strangely, he felt picked on and bullied by Andy and was beginning to dislike playing with him. I simply lacked the mental equipment to see this. If Billy won the arguments, I thought, then Billy must enjoy them. If I'd won one against Porter once ever then I'd have been cockahoop.

Of course, to say that Billy won the arguments depends on your definition of 'won.' Had I been smarter, I would have seen that Billy's tactic in any argument was an appeal to reason, common sense and logic; weak cards to play in some disagreements. Against this, the 'It's my game; I do what I like, and I do what I don't like, which means I do you' argument seems fragile, but often it's the one that prevails. The problem, of course, is that you're arguing from different standpoints. The logician appeals to the world as it should be. The 'It's my gamer' appeals to the world as it is.

At the time I thought the winner in an argument was the person who put forward the most logical support for his position. Of course, this isn't true. Human history, from gardening disputes to genocide, is full of examples of people with the most decent, well-argued stance ending up with their face in the mud in front of a naked display of power.

The Dungeons and Dragons rules are full of sage advice on what to do with disruptive players. They are silent on the topic of disruptive referees.

The rows had been intensifying for weeks when the split finally came. I've said already that we were playing a mish-mash of rules taken from the original books, new rules, fanzines, official supplements, unofficial supplements, rules we'd invented, rules we discarded. We hardly ever worked out encumbrance factors, for instance, so our characters skipped about in plate mail carrying chests full of gold as if they weighed nothing.

This isn't entirely our fault. The first set of D&D has holes in the rules—nowhere, for instance, does it explain what a character is. The rules assume that you are already playing the game and fully up to speed on all its concepts. Also, when it comes to things like encumbrance, you are given information such as 'moves as an armoured man,' but nowhere does it say how far an unarmoured man moves. The strange thing is that we knew this information, gleaned from the ether maybe. I've just looked through the original booklets, and I can't find it anywhere. I know an unarmoured man moves ten inches (to scale) per turn, but I don't know how I know that. Perhaps it is in there, but my addiction is truly cured, and I can't force my eyes to the print with the same adhesion I managed as a teenager.

Then there were the fanzines and supplements by the score

with special rules that we could at any one time be playing or not playing. No one, of course, ever clarified exactly what rules were in and what were out from game to game. It's a bit like having a game of soccer and then deciding if you are going to play the offside rule or not after the first goal is scored. This is a recipe for arguments, to which you can add a couple of boiled egos.

The dispute arose because the dungeon had been coming to an end and Andy had set one of the strange creatures he occasionally came up with on Billy. This creature had appeared from nowhere, and there was the strong suspicion that its presence owed more to the fact that one of Andy's characters had died in Billy's dungeon the week before than to any throw of the dice. I'm not saying Andy was cheating; I'm just saying I perceived him to be moulding the events to suit his own ends. That's not against the rules, but it's not all that nice.

I think the creature may have been something from the Cthulhu mythos of H. P. Lovecraft. Andy had become very keen on this and in particular the fictional books *The Necronomicron* and *Cultes des Ghouls,* the madness-inducing tomes of arcane knowlege. The prevailing themes of Lovecraft are insanity and dark horrors lurking under ordinary exteriors, naturally attractive to Andy.

Billy's character was very weak from other encounters, and he decided to run away, as did the rest of us. I was playing my lightly clad berserker, Nogbad the Eight-millionth, Glebe had a kung fu-ing monk, a passing gamer a wizard and Dave and Pete thieves. Only Billy was hulking along as a paladin—a holy warrior—in full plate armour. Dweebs will note that a neutral berserker can't be in the same party as a lawful good paladin. We ignored the rule. I ran for it because I'd got my berserker up to third level and wanted him to make fourth. Running isn't very berserker-like behaviour, but I was favouring practicality over authenticity.

Up until that point, of course, we hadn't really been using the movement rules either. D&D has a lot of complex stuff for this, and most of it isn't really necessary to running a successful game— especially if you're treating it more as a fantasy story with dice rolling than you are a wargame. Suddenly Andy wanted distances measured out, the encumbering effect of Billy's arms and treasure worked out, turns calculated, even the slope of the dungeon passageway he was running up accounted for. All these things are perfectly reasonable and within the laws of the game, but we'd been through ten or eleven combats before that without using them.

There was lots of arguing about the fact Andy didn't immediately throw to see how far away the monster was or whether it was blocking the exit from the dungeon or not. It just appeared behind us with a bang and immediately went for Billy after a couple of very quick dice rolls from Andy.

Everyone said they bolted for the exit. Most monsters you meet in the underground are there for a reason and, by convention, won't pursue people very far in the wilderness—D&D's catch-all term for anywhere outside the underground. Eventually, after an age of arguing and counter-arguing that could have filled ten episodes of *Perry Mason,* it was agreed that Billy's fighter had made the door with about fifty feet to spare before the Ancient One got its teeth into him.

As it was so near, Andy shook another dice, modified by things like the hunger of the beast (+1) and the fact that as a paladin Billy was an alignment enemy (+1) and said that if he shook a 5 or 6 on a six-sided dice—which only actually needed to be a 3 or over owing to the modifications above—the monster would follow him for one more turn. Andy shook the dice—a 6, which cleared up any arguments Billy might have had on the weighting of the score. Billy was an encumbered man, moving at three inches (to scale) per turn. The Ancient One wasn't quick but had been moving at six inches a turn. This meant that Billy would be mincemeat in one turn. Except . . .

D&D is a bit odd when it comes to movement. When you're in an underground or indoor setting one inch represented by the figures is to scale ten feet. When you're in a wilderness setting one inch is ten yards. This information, like a lot in the original version, is buried, but it's there, and it was carried over into the advanced rules.

According to a very strict interpretation of the law, Billy's fighter suddenly became capable of thirty yards a turn whereas the Ancient One—still underground—was only moving at sixty feet a turn until it got to the door. This presented a formidable feat of maths to work out whether the monster got hold of Billy or not. Never mind, we would have relished that. There was, as you might have guessed, a complication.

Special rules apply during combat. Each turn is divided into ten rounds. Only Andy had used the word 'turn' when he threw the dice. On top of this, the rules never make clear whether a wilderness round is longer than an underworld round or whether they're the same.

Argument and counter-argument raged. Like the worst kind of lovers' tiffs, things that had been said years ago were brought in. Then rows about who said what and who had meant what and the spirit versus the letter were invoked. I wondered what Dave got out of this, silently watching people argue for months on end. He didn't even join in.

Finally, Porter looked into his notebook.

'I'd forgotten that,' he said.

'What?' said Billy, who I now see in a sort of molten state, dying to go out for a fag but unwilling to allow Porter sway over the rest of us while he was away.

'This Ancient One has a rage ability. Once every three turns it can either double movement or double strength. It doubles movement. It's got you.'

They say that chess, at its highest levels, comes down to a battle of wills. In D&D this can be the case a week after learning the game. I could see what had happened. Billy thought Andy was lying. He didn't have that written down at all. According to the rules, of course, the DM doesn't have to have anything written down. It's just taken that he will or that anything he invents off the cuff will be to enhance the game. This development seemed for one reason only, that Andy could triumph over Billy.

For once there was a real sort of magic in the air. For all our arguments, for all the nit-picking and backbiting and poring over minute definitions of things, no one had ever called anyone else a liar. To summon up that word was like inviting a demon into the room. You never knew where it might end.

Billy quivered like a mighty jelly. In my mind I see the whole room shaking with him, as if he was about to undergo some fantastic transformation, to become a werebear or reveal himself as the dragon I had always suspected him to be.

'I don't believe you,' he said.

Dr Faustus at midnight, Elric stabbed by his own sword, Dracula gazing up from the coffin at the descending stake, King Arthur felled by Mordred's hand, all these images seemed to flood in on me and spill out through my lips with a mighty 'Oh, Blimey!'

I thought Andy would erupt, but he just seemed to get even paler.

'You should believe me, it's here,' he said.

'Then show me the book,' said Billy. I'd often imagined how the air must feel the second before a demon materializes. This was it.

Andy shook his head. 'It's got a lot in it I don't want you to see,' he said.

This was a perfectly reasonable defence, and, I must stress, I have no idea to this day if Andy did have anything written down or not. Plenty of DMs like to keep their inventions from their players.

'Then give the book to me. I'll take it home with me. I'll ask my dad what it says, and I'll promise not to look at it,' he said. This sort of suggestion would have seemed fine to Billy, and I knew that once he'd given his word there was no way he'd go back on it. He'd often quoted the Viking stance on oathbreaking—that is, go back on your word and find your lungs splayed out in a blood eagle in pretty short order.

'No,' said Andy, 'it's my book, and I need it.' He shook a dice. 'The Ancient One hits.' He shook another. '17 points damage.'

That was shoving it, I can tell you. Very few creatures in D&D, particularly at that level, hand out that sort of a whack.

Billy shook his head.

'No way,' he said, 'I never thought I'd do this but, "Amulet against Chaotic Dungeonmaster."'

A gasp went round the table. No one had ever played that rule before. This was something we'd found in a fanzine. It meant that Billy was declaring his participation in the dungeon null and void. He would accrue no treasure or experience from it, but his character wouldn't be dead either. It had been designed for just such an instance, when the DM seemed bent on killing you no matter what and you felt you were being unfairly treated.

'You can't do that,' said Andy. 'We don't play that in my dungeons.'

'The point is,' said Billy, 'you can play it in anyone's dungeon.'

Andy twitched. This was serious stuff. The air was charged. You imagined that at any moment a fork of lightning might crackle across the room.

I'd never seen a relationship disintegrate before. When children fall out the worst that happens is that they fight and then go away. Because associations aren't that strong in the first place then breaking them means little. It really did seem that we were playing for high stakes. However, I had a pressing question.

'Can I have his treasure then?' I said. I wasn't meaning to be irritating, as people who are really, really, irritating often don't.

Andy made a noise that I've only heard once since. It was on a sleeper train in China, and a man was snoring, sounding rather like someone inhaling a goat. Andy recovered his poise. He was left with only one way to hurt Billy, which, painfully, meant he had to help me.

'You get the treasure,' he said.

I'd just seen the two leading lights of my wargame circle enter an irretrievably awful phase of their relationship. Two people I respected hugely, even if at that stage I only really liked one of them, had reached a point of no return. I had a +1 Spear, a Gem of Seeing and a whole heap more of gold than I'd had before. I was ecstatic.

It was only around three in the afternoon. Normal human beings would have called it a day there after such an emotionally draining time, but we didn't. We were D&Ders, the damned. We had another few hours before we'd be expelled and Billy and I would make the short trip down the hill to my house for chips and Empire of the Petal Throne.

There was nothing for it. Another dungeon.

I think it was provocative of Billy to select his paladin to play with, but he said that was the character most suitable for the party make-up. I wouldn't have believed anyone else, but, despite his apparent worldliness, Billy had a certain literalism to him. He couldn't see that an argument in one game would ever spill over into an argument in another. Andy's character, one of his wizards, I think, had never met the paladin before—why would he want to kill him? One look at the seething Porter should have told him the limits of his logic.

I'd prepared my 'Grove of Enlightenment' dungeon, a forest-based scenario I'd gone to some lengths to design. My best way of getting ritual magic into D&D, I'd decided, was to put it in my own dungeons and to make the characters have to gather the components for a huge demon summoning they'd do at the end. Actually, I'm chickening out here. The dungeon was called 'The Grove of Twisted Enlightenment: The Ballad of Irony Blacksword.' I wrote that; I have to pay the price. Nevertheless, I'd researched it at the library, putting in new magical items taken from folklore such as Witch Bottles and a host of spells that didn't kill the characters but affected their minds and decision-making ability.

Taking in my taste for elaborate description, the quest began like this: 'It's been a hard four days in the Savernake Forest.' (I'd somehow come into possession of one of those tourist maps of ancient Wiltshire and decided to set my magical world there. I included Stonehenge, Avebury Stone Circle and even stuck in a monstrous version of Longleat Safari Park.) I went on.

'It's been cold, wet and the very trees themselves seem to sense your presence.' (I know, but this is the sort of stuff you come out with if you read enough fantasy.) 'On the morning of the fifth day there seems something wrong with the thin mist that attends your passage.' (General hilarity, it takes another twenty minutes to be able to continue.) 'You can't quite say what it is, but it's doing something to the light. It's flatter than it should be. Everything seems to slip into two dimensions. What's near and what's far becomes difficult to say.

'Time passes slowly, and, when the mist reluctantly and oh-so-hesitantly lifts, you see in front of you what appears to have been a large dip in the forest floor, almost like a giant bowl made from the roots of the trees. Now, though, it seems that all the mist from the rest of the forest has been sucked into it so that it seems almost to boil with fog. Could this be the Cauldron of the Woods, the gateway to Faerie, that the witch in the town mentioned? Or is it some elfin deception?' Guilty as charged, that's what I wrote. To get the full horror of this, imagine 'elfin deception' being said in a sort of high-pitched voice, like someone failing an audition as a baddy on *Dr Who*. I sat thumbing the thick pile of ritual cards I'd cut from The Emerald Tablet and adapted over five or six nights for use in D&D and continued. 'Nature seems more intense here, the colour that was gone in the morn has returned tenfold in its iridescence, and it seems that ancient, older senses are awake in you this forenoon. Your vision seems to crackle with colours and possibilities of colours, the wet leaves and the grass fill your mind with their ancient scent, and birdsong bursts on your ears like waves against the shore but tweeting. What do you do?'

'I attack Billy,' said Porter.

So he did, and Billy's character was killed. In fact, he was put into Porter's alchemist's Mirror of Life Trapping. This is a mirror which, if you look at it, magically transports you inside it to dwell for eternity, or until the mirror breaks or its owner calls you forth, in a sort of limbo.

The problem with this was twofold. Now the party had only

three people to complete a dungeon that was meant for a minimum of four; Andy's character was injured, and no one would cast a heal spell on him in case he had a go at them. I was glad I was dungeonmaster. Failing to heal Andy wouldn't be something he would easily forget. Also, the convention was that, if a character was killed really early in an adventure, the player would be able to join in again with another character. If you don't allow that to happen then someone can end up just being a spectator at a twelve-hour game.

Interestingly, one of the innovations Andy had come up with for his original self-designed game was that all the players went into the dungeon separately and at different points, only meeting up by chance and often mistaking each other for monsters. I still think this would make an interesting scenario for a game today. Oh dear, I'm not thinking of playing am I? I fear I am.

The trouble was that, if I let Billy bring another character in, he was only going to have a chop at Porter the first chance he got. At least, that was what Andy feared, and he argued against allowing Billy to rejoin. If Billy came in with a fresh character he could easily defeat the weakened Porter. That would leave us with Billy's character injured and Andy allowed to bring in someone else. His new character would attack Billy's character, and the whole merry-go-round would begin again.

Billy maintained, and I believed him, that he wouldn't attack Porter's character because logically, according to the role-playing side of the game, his new character would have no loyalty to his old one. He'd therefore have no reason to attack Porter. Andy didn't operate like that at all. Killing his characters, even if you were the dungeonmaster and had done it entirely legitimately, was an attack on him. Retribution would need to be exacted.

It seems to me now that Andy felt reasonably threatened by life and came to the game to feel invulnerable. You could see this in his signature character, Zarathustra. This wizard got to about level 40 very quickly and built an indestructible Wizard Blade using rules from *The Dragon* magazine. Then he used a spell to put his soul inside it and other spells to make it move. This made the character utterly invulnerable, and, if he fell out with you, all he had to do was say, 'Teleport, my sword appears through your chest,' and you were done for. He seemed happy to play the game from this position of complete domination. No one ever let him use this character in a game, but Andy seemed to revel in the idea of simply having thought him up. It's not a bad idea, it has to be said, having a magic sword for a character.

Even weaker characters than his wizard were often aggressive and would always get you before you'd even thought of getting them. Someone should have stopped this, but our problem was that there wasn't one person running every game. We all took turns as dungeonmaster. There was no central authority to rule on anything.

During the 1980s, the campaign Bothered About Dungeons and Dragons—I'm not making this up, that's what it was called—said the game was simply a feeding ground for the occult. It would be controlled by one dungeonmaster, and, when questioning your wayward teen on the subject, you should not rest until you found out who this sinister leader was. As with almost everything else they said about D&D, it was misinformed. In fact, our game had a desperate want of a leader, sinister or otherwise. That's what we needed at that moment—someone to take the lead. I did, and on the wrong side.

'I'm sorry,' I said to Billy, 'we can't have your character coming in again because I think there's a fair chance you would attack Andy.' In fact there was every chance that Andy would attack Billy again, once he got his strength back, taking the opportunity to fill his enchanted mirror with most of Billy's favourite characters.

'I wouldn't, though,' said Billy.

'Well, we can't take that risk,' I said. I was very proud of what I'd done with the dungeon and wanted a chance to show it to the others. Would they be able to collect all the pieces of the mystic pentagram to summon the earth spirit? Or would they mistakenly assemble the magic circle that would call The Dead Year, spirit of winter and decay? I was tired of all the squabbles and wanted us to actually play the game. The only way of ensuring that with Billy and Andy at each other's throats was to exclude one of them.

Billy went forlornly outside and stood smoking, and Andy congratulated me for making the right decision. As I looked at Billy through the window I was reminded of myself, a few years earlier, looking through at the others when Andy had shut me out. Better people than me would have felt sympathy for Billy. I didn't. I was too happy basking in the warmth of Andy's approval. After nearly three years of solid gaming he was treating me as a friend rather than as an annoying little pest. I had, I thought, come a long way, and now it was someone else's turn on the other side of the leaded glass. The relief at finally being allowed into the club swamped any fellow feeling I should have had for Billy.

I made sure Andy did well in the dungeon that followed and felt sure from his mood that I wouldn't be meeting a sticky end at his hands for the immediate future.

Billy mooched around until six, when it was time for us to leave, boiling with resentment but, through a sense of fair play, unwilling to disrupt our dungeon. I thought at the time that he was just interested in what I'd designed and that, as an addict, he couldn't go.

I didn't know it, but he was making an important decision, one that would have serious repercussions that went far beyond the playing of the game.

At the end of the day we cycled home. Billy ate his chips at the bottom of the hill but said he didn't fancy coming back to my house for more gaming; he'd had enough for one day. Finally, it penetrated. Something was really wrong.

'See ya,' he said.

'See ya,' I said.

I did. Twenty-five years later.

The End of Days

Surely girls would have done these things differently. They'd weep and hug and promise to write. That's not what happened with me and Billy. He just phoned and said he was going to wargame in Chigger's group on the other side of the city.

I can't remember if this group was formally grammar-school only, but that was certainly the impression I got. Anyway, my relationship with Chigger had ended after he vandalized some fanzines of mine and, after a fall-out over a dungeon, attacked me in my own front room when my parents were out. I was giving away little in size and weight but three or four years in age, and I took a solid beating. Still, I was such an addict that, if he'd invited me round there, I might have gone. The older boys he'd begun to play with didn't argue as much as Andy's group and ran some interesting dungeons.

However, I wasn't invited, so I said I'd see Billy around. I can recognize now that I was stunned by Billy's departure. At the time, though, I just couldn't think about it; I had the same difficulty turning over its implications in my mind that non-mathematicians do in envisaging the fifth dimension.

I did, I think, feel sad, but not for our relationship. There had been splits before, like when we broke from the wargames club, and I might have supposed he would have come back. The nearest I can get to it is to say it was like the feeling of having forgotten something important. You know it was important, but that's all you know about it. I couldn't at all focus on what I thought. I found it more irritating than upsetting, particularly because I had the idea that Chigger, who I found it impossible to like despite my talent for admiring people who were less than pleasant to me, had got one over on me.

There were compensations. The fact the wargamers had divided along comprehensive/grammar-school lines meant that I was at least now part of a group.

Given the conflicting emotions I felt about Billy's departure, my brain just shut down. I put down the phone, still not at all comprehending that I'd lost my best friend. I went and had my tea, read some D&D books, watched the TV and listened to a record all at the same time.

So why did Billy go? It's tempting to say that he wanted to grow up, and, in a way, he did. He wanted to get away from the bickering and in-fighting that had come to blight our game. He never, though, wanted to get away from the game. Chigger's group was full of older boys, men in some cases, who wanted to play the game properly. Billy went so he could immerse himself in the game more.

I still believe I was closer to Billy than almost anyone else in his life, but, like me, he was an addict. The purity of the game came before our friendship. The fantasy world was more important than the real one.

He and Porter had different reasons for coming to the game. Porter reminded me of one of those soccer fans who doesn't support his home team but follows one of the big clubs who win things on a regular basis. They have a psychological need to be on top and are drawn to success. Billy was more like someone who follows a lower-league side fanatically, to whom the taking part is more important than the winning. In fact, losing can be quite enjoyable too as long as it's not all the time. Billy had no more fun playing with someone of Andy's attitude than a high school American football team would have playing in the NFL every week. Eventually, it would get to hurt.

Billy had sort of slipped out of my life, gone in a blur of

assumptions that I'd see him again at the wargames club at the end of the summer holidays or that he'd argue with Chigger. When the blur cleared he wasn't there. The big stuff in life sometimes doesn't happen with crashes and bangs; it just happens, and it's only later that you feel its impact. It certainly had a large effect on me for several years afterwards and, I think, maybe an equally large one on Billy.

Billy comes back to me now as a series of images and snatches of conversation.

I remember him trying to eat a pound of lard for a bet. Billy had said he really liked lard, often had it on sandwiches and could easily eat a pound straight out of the pack. As it was he only got about half a pound down but wasn't actually sick. Pete won 10p off him for that, I think. He won the money back the next week at Andy Porter's house over a bet that he could eat a frozen chicken pie. That is, an unthawed frozen chicken pie. This was actually more than a bet. We'd come across the frozen bodies of some orcs on a wilderness adventure. As our characters had run out of food two days before, we decided to eat them. Andy said this could prove poisonous, and, to prove it wasn't, Billy ate the pie.

I remember Pete pretending to shoot Billy while Billy was opening his bag near to the glass door that separated Pete's back room from the lounge. I think I only need to provide the two major elements of the story for readers to see what happened: mimed shooting and theatrical fatty with back to plate-glass door. We had a long debate afterwards about whose fault Billy's demolition of the door had been. Was it his for keeling over backwards like a turtle pretending to be shot or Pete's for pretending to shoot him?

Then there was the time, in a test of whether we'd have the courage to be D&D characters, we took the cables out of our bike brakes on the top of Allesley Hill, where Johhny lived—he was another Sealed Knot wargamer who we briefly played with. Well, Billy unclipped his brakes. I said I simply wouldn't use mine. Billy wanted absolute conclusive proof of his bravery so the callipers were disabled. This is a one in ten hill of about half a mile's length, although in my memory it appears at about forty-five degrees and much longer.

The trouble with this sort of thing as an assessment of courage is that it's easy to be confident at the top, where you unclip your pads with a flourish. When you really need your pluck is approaching terminal velocity about three-quarters of the way down. Courage doesn't come into it if you've disconnected your brakes. You're in for the ride whether you like it or not, mate.

Again, memory is a funny thing. In my mind I see a Billy-shaped hole in the advertising hoardings at the bottom of the hill. As it was, he just sort of bounced off them, having abandoned the bike with a cry of 'Blood and Souls For My Lord Arioch!' in the brief interlude between him mounting the kerb and striking the signs.

'Did you notice how I saved the bike by throwing it away from the hoardings?' he said as I drew to a controlled, braked halt. His bike didn't appear that saved, having a large dent in the front wheel. I looked at Billy.

'Is your arm meant to be at that angle?' I said.

'Yes,' said Billy, waggling it straight.

'Oh,' I said. I'd been hoping for a dramatic break that I could turn into a story later.

He wasn't the only one to have bike trouble, though. As I've said, to me my bike was a horse of various forms depending on which particular fantasy game or novel I was immersed in at the time. In fact I think it was a steed rather than a horse. It's OK to refer to horses as steeds in the world of fantasy.

On the way from Johnny's house to mine we paused in the valley between our two hills. When I say valley, don't picture anything too bucolic here: we stopped on the concrete bridge just past the chip shop and betting shop, at the back of the supermarket car park.

I was waiting for Billy for some reason and pulled up on the bridge. Because I thought of my bike as a horse then I didn't think I needed to put my feet down to stop. I just leaned the bike against the side of the bridge railing. Unfortunately there was more of me leaning above the rail than there was below it. A simple mechanical equation came into play involving directions of force, friction coefficients of tyres on concrete—that sort of thing—and the tyres slipped, flipping me head first over the railings into the brook, a fall of about eight feet.

Billy said that I'd just inverted in a quick whoosh, the bike landing on top of me. Luckily my one talent physically is that I've so far been quite difficult to hurt. Billy pulled me out of the brook. I was only mildly concussed.

'That,' said Billy, 'is about how quick you'd go down if taken by a troll.'

'It's also how quick a thief can disappear if the need arises,' I said, kind of intimating that I'd done it deliberately. I looked at the bike. Perhaps, on another plane of existence, my bike was in fact a horse. Perhaps its horse nature had suddenly leaked onto the material plane, and the shock had made it buck, throwing me over the bridge. This, I concluded, was the most likely explanation. Even though I was so clumsy that my history teacher had named me, in a popular phrase of the time, 'a walking disaster area' and the woodwork teacher had called me 'a wood butcher' and refused to ever allow me a chisel for fear of injury to myself or others, it never occurred to me that this might be the explanation for my fall. I had the sort of control of my limbs possessed by most people when they're emerging from a coma—capable of jerks and lunges but no finer work.

Billy's dad took us down to London to attend a wargaming conference and to see the multimedia London Experience in the Trocadero in Piccadilly Circus, which I had to be dragged into because I wanted to go to the conference that second, but enjoyed greatly. I had a hot dog, something I'd never tried before, with American mustard on it, which I found disgusting. As I'd naturally finished my packed lunch on the coach on the way down there and had spent all the rest of my money on figures and rule books, I was starving when I got back. However, through Billy, D&D was for once widening my horizons, even if I found the experience not entirely to my liking.

Most of all, though, I remember Billy talking. I'd never met anyone who spoke like that before, and I don't think I have since. When arguing, which was most of the time, he would pull in knowledge from a vast array of areas—history, the law, science, theatre. I'm convinced that half of what I know about anything today I learned from him.

He's the only person I've ever met who could begin an argument about the properties of a resurrection spell with the words 'This is exactly the sort of mistake typical of the thinking of the ancient Medes,' or say something like 'You are confusing, Porter, salt of Alembroth, which is the archaic term for a chloride of mercury and ammonium, with powder of Algaroth, which is a term for antimony oxide. Neither are what you suppose them to be. What you are searching for is the alkahest, a term invented by Paracelus to denote a universal solvent, which is what you say has just squirted all over my character's armour. You, however, said, "Salt of Alembroth, the universal solvent antimony oxide." That, as we say in the union, is bollocks, so his armour can't be dissolving.'

One time I announced that I'd been co-opted into the school play as a stage hand after failing an audition for an acting role. I hadn't wanted to go because of spending time away from D&D, but my drama teacher had been insistent because they were short-handed. It was a musical, and, the music teacher concluded, nothing in the history of the world—including the *Marie Celeste*—has ever been so short-handed it would welcome my singing. Billy said, 'In every stage hand there is an actor. If the stage hand's lucky.' Hardly Oscar Wilde, but totally outside of my experience at that point. I'd often ask Billy where he got his sayings from. I was amazed, and a bit disbelieving, when he told me he just made them up on the spur of the moment. I think it was my first encounter with proper wit.

What I really lost in Billy going was a broader perspective. Without him it was back to boys who shared my exact background, narrower creatures who seemed not interested in anything outside their immediate environment, or even capable of imagining it unless it contained an orc. Andy was more interesting, but he wasn't interested in me. With Billy I felt I had someone whose respect I had won and who cared for me.

Perhaps it was the number of distractions that were appearing to me at that time. I was just coming up for fifteen, and the summer holidays were approaching, when Billy left. We wargamed every day of the holiday and for a while things settled down. When a soccer team loses a manager it traditionally plays well in the next game. I think that, more than me even, Andy was thrown sideways at Billy's sudden departure. Like I said, Andy wasn't a bad kid. He just wanted to be top dog in the group. I think the idea that the rift between him and Billy had been so serious was quite shocking to him.

There were a couple of new members of the group—Sean Gardener and Gary Yardley, and, for a short interlude, the games were refreshed. Sean was a charismatic boy who, for a time, filled the gap Billy left in my social life, although our friendship was of a very different timbre.

The first time I met him set the tone for the rest of our relationship. I'd been given his address by Porter and told there was a game on there. About 100 yards from the house I became aware of heavy rock music banging out from one of its upstairs windows. I rang the bell, and his dad, who in the twenty-five years I was to go round there never once remembered my name, answered the door. I said who I was, and he said he'd get Sean.

'Sean!' he screamed, going light purple in an attempt to make himself heard above the Deep Purple.

Sean came down the stairs. He had the sartorial elegance of someone who has just been rescued from a siege, about five foot six inches tall and six foot wide, like most people's idea of a dungeonmaster—that is, someone who keeps a real dungeon for actual prisoners.

'Was that you ringing the bell?' he said. God knows how he'd heard me.

'Yes,' I said.

'Too high and mighty to use the knocker are you? It's not free, the electricity in that bell you know.'

'Sorry, I just thought.'

'Yeah, you just thought,' he said, 'just thought you'd come and help yourself to my electricity. Maybe I should run a line up to your house to power my stereo. Cheeky fucker.'

He then went to hit me but at the last minute pulled away as if all he'd been going to do was scratch his head. Sean had a physicality to him that all the other wargamers—up until that point—lacked. People might ridicule you or just be straightforwardly nasty, but no one jabbed you with a compass, as Sean often did for his amusement.

'You'd better come in, I suppose,' he said.

'Are you Sean Gardener?' I said.

'No, I'm his mum,' he said.

I didn't know it at the time, but he was on best behaviour. Even Andy Porter had managed a 'hello' and to stay reasonably polite for the first hour or so of our acquaintance. Sean had gone for me from the minute we met.

Sean's great joy in life was being sarcastic or, as he pronounced it, 'sar-car-stic.' That about sums him up—the word 'sarcastic' wasn't sarcastic enough for Sean. In fact he was sarcastic about the word sarcastic. The torment of others was what he lived for. This wasn't the nasty, snidey, particular torment that Chigger delighted in, just a general madness that struck anyone and everyone at the same time.

I thought he was fantastic and began to copy his sarcasm and linguistic tropes—putting 'Amundosville, Kentucky' after everything I said and attempting to take the piss out of everyone for everything.

I even wrote a story of fantasy figures—basically me and him—set in my normal frozen wasteland. What was it with me and the cold? A school personality assessment we did asked us to describe our favourite weather. I wrote, absolutely honestly, that it was fog. I loved the idea of what sorcery might be going on beneath it. Both of the characters in my story wore flying jackets like Sean's and encountered strange creatures that were the products of an enchanted spirit's dream.

In the original story Sean's character engaged in magic duels of wit with his enemies, slaying them with jokes. I didn't know it at the time, but this isn't far away from the insult contests of the Vikings which, bizarrely, aren't that far away themselves from the rap battles of kids today. Unfortunately I decided this idea wasn't 'high' enough. Even though my actual life was beginning to be ruled by a sort of grotesque sense of humour, I couldn't allow it anywhere near the elf-maidens and Celtic dawns of my imagination. They were a gag-free zone. I crossed out Sean's insult duels and gave his character an Icicle Sword with which to kill the dragons instead. Whereas before he'd stopped the mighty Smaug (there were limits to my originality) by saying, 'Wings and feet? Oh, that's OK for you, isn't it, two modes of locomotion, wings and feet? I hope you know there are children in this world that haven't got either!' now he just smote mightily and brooded through the darkened air. D&D inspired some fantasies, but it limited others.

The only way I could envisage my friendship with Sean was as in a fantasy novel—he was Elric, a fat Elric but Elric nevertheless, I was Moonglum; he was Fafhrd, I was the Gray Mouser. The thing is, these adventurers had things to do, enemies to fight, women to love. We had nothing but each other. I bet if you had sat Elric and Moonglum down in a room for eight hours a day for five years, then Elric would have been holding Moonglum down while he farted in his face and telling him he was 'such a twat' or even, like Andy Porter, taking it out on other people's characters.

When I look back, I think of Andy as lacking a sense of humour about himself, a common enough adolescent trait. I was in a worse position than this. I wanted to lack a sense of humour about myself but struggled against an overwhelming tide of evidence that I could in no way be taken seriously.

Alf the Elf at this point had been renamed as Angarn Ceridwen, a po-faced Celtic warrior reflecting the seriousness with which I wanted to be seen. I just found it impossible to sustain in real life. There were so many people laughing at me that it was a case of 'if you can't beat 'em join 'em.' Even Alf's new name contained an indication of how useless my attempts at being mean, moody and magnificent were. Ceridwen, I found out years later, means 'bent white one.' A name like that would make 'Spaz' seem like a blessing at school.

My story was such a piece of hero worship that I could never show it to Sean. In fact, I could never actually have shown Sean that I liked him. This is the lesson I was learning at that time. Your friends are the ones you are most horrible to. You're only actually polite to people you don't like. The best way I could show Sean that I looked up to him was to mock him. It became gruelling, a relentless round of sarcasm and horseplay.

Without D&D I might have walked away, or others might have. United by our addiction, we stayed together, never really finding out about friendship but just testing the limits of each other's endurance.

The wargames club in town was closed for the school holidays. For the first time, it didn't seem to matter, and, with new blood on board, we played some very good games, Andy virtually surrendering playing and solely dungeonmastering. This meant that, if you kept on his right side, you were guaranteed an interesting and inventive dungeon with lots of twists and turns and only a reasonable chance of your character dying—the game as it was meant to be played. And I was getting better at keeping on his right side—less screaming and more praise for his ideas seemed to be the recipe.

Then it was time to return to school. Under normal circumstances I'd have gone back down to the Sidney Stringer wargames club and hooked up with Billy again, maybe even Chigger. Something, however, intervened.

Girls and Other
Non-human Creatures

My parents were becoming slightly exasperated with my obsession and were understandably sick of hearing about my plans for my latest dungeon or the capabilities of my mighty elf.

'I'm surprised,' said my mum, 'that you don't move into a dungeon yourself.'

And so I did.

My interest in heavy metal had been growing, feeding off the D&D addiction. When I found out about the rock disco on Friday nights at the Lanchester Polytechnic—so called because they thought, if they called it Coventry Polytechnic, no one would go—I was down there like a shot. It's the same reason Warwick University is so called despite being a short walk from my nan's house, which was in Coventry and one of the many rougher bits of Coventry too. Warwick, with its castle and tea shops, is eleven miles away.

At first I hadn't thought I'd get in to the Lanch, but there had been a leather sale at a local hotel, and my mum had bought me, for a small fortune, a very high-quality leather jacket, complete with Ozzy Osbourne-like tassels. This was a size too big for me and had the effect of making me look much stockier. I'd stick my dad's crash helmet under my arm and catch the bus down to the disco. Naturally I had a cover story worked out, and, as I got on to the bus, I'd nod to my fellow passengers and say 'Picking up my bike.' This is, I think, one of the big delusions of adolescence—that everyone is looking at you and that everyone will have an opinion on what you're wearing and that that opinion matters. I did get some abuse along the lines of 'Where's your motorbike?' from passing beer boys as I got off the bus, but they were missing the point. I wasn't trying to make out I had a motorbike. I was using the helmet as a primitive and cumbersome identity card. To have a crash helmet would mean that I was at least seventeen, a year younger than I'd needed to be to get into the disco but no one was really going to turn a seventeen-year-old away. I got in, after a bit of arguing with the bouncer and saying 31/8/61 as my birthday, which would have made me just old enough for admission.

The Lanch was more like playing D&D than playing D&D. In my mind it was exactly like entering the first room of a dungeon, and it crackled with the possibility of adventure. For a start it was underground and seemed to be guarded by bouncers who had a good deal of troll in them. There were dangerous, higher-level areas where the Hells Angels sat, saving throws to be made as the barmaid assessed whether she thought you were eighteen or not, subterfuges as you sent a friend to the bar, potion testing as you ordered a straight Tia Maria because it's cheap and quickly discovered it was poison. Very quickly the wargamers formed into a party to chat away and give the impression they'd been there for years. I was petrified of making a mistake—head-banging to the wrong song or not hard enough, or thinking a guitar solo was over when it wasn't. A rule of thumb is that if the guitar solo is by Led Zep or Lynyrd Skynyrd then it's not over. Ever.

Also the walls were decorated as a Middle Earth forest with ents and elves and trolls, and there were dark nooks where strange people gazed from pools of darkness. Most of all, of course, there were girls.

Girls do appear in dungeons and dragons—as characters. There are even female players, apparently, but I can't comment on what they were like because I never met one. The dungeoneer's view of women means that a female character will never appear without some reference to sex. There is actually a chart in the unofficial D&D supplement, *The Arduin Grimoire*, that lets you determine a woman's vital statistics. Feminists should look away now. Role 100 on a percentage dice and your character will have a sixty-inch bust. If you roll a four on the same dice this can be combined with a sixteen-inch waist. Another 100 gives her sixty-inch hips. Or you could do it the other way around, and roll a sixteen-inch chest, sixty-inch waist and sixteen-inch hips. Any combination is possible in what seems to me a rather ill-considered chart. The *Grimoire* goes on to note that, if a 'lady's' waist is thirty-four inches and she 'only' has a thirty-six-inch bust it's obvious she's fat and so the DM should reduce her charisma score. These things were presented as they were received by us—not opinion or prejudice but unalterable fact.

The character appearance chart for male characters could tell you what colour the hair, eyes and skin were, what birthmark or scar he had, but nowhere did it have a table for length of penis. I wonder if anyone would have been comfortable drawing up such a chart for percentage dice: 'Dice Roll 51–60, average—two inches.'

One of the most embarrassing sights available in the late 1970s was a heterosexual boy playing a character from the houri class—basically a cross between sorcerers and prostitutes—and attempting to act like an alluring woman in front of a group of other heterosexual boys.

This was bad enough when the character was played by the relatively restrained Porter, who, in a move that owed more to imagination than practicality, had his houri's . . . actually I'm not sure I can describe this. He had his houri's . . . No. I'm not going to describe it. Oh God. The character had some intimate piercings of what Porter termed her 'flaps.' These piercings were sharp and poisoned so she could inject the penis of any male with whom she was having sex. Right, that's my last word on the subject; psychoanalysts make of it what you will.

When Steve Boscombe got hold of a houri then it was enough to stop your blood in its course, platelets and corpuscles curling in your veins.

'Come hither, young master,' he'd say, Monty Python Spanish Inquisition-style moustache bristling, 'and I will show you the thousand pleasures of Mistress Dyala-Bei. I will make your flesh sing a song of ecstasy such as will echo through the caverns of your soul. Happily shalt thou spend thy sweet seed.'

'Right, cup of tea?' I'd say, praying to God my mum wasn't going to hear this and get the wrong end of the stick.

This, since junior school, had been virtually my only experience of women—as fantasy figures. Reading about women in fantasy novels had set me an even more unrealistic point of view. The *Lord of the Rings* doesn't help, with its sexless visions of elf maidens who may as well be speaking paintings, and neither does other fantasy literature, where women seem to exist solely to be rescued or slept with. The men they want are sorcerer-kings, doomed warriors or deadly assassins. I think the idea that women might fancy good-looking, well-adjusted men who are nice to them is too much for the average fantasy-head to bear.

Male homosexuality is very firmly excluded from most role-playing games, only appearing as a joke or a curse. If a character was turned gay by drinking a potion or putting on a cursed ring (I'm just telling it like it was here), a smell of perfume would immediately attend him; his clothes would become brighter, and he would dab a handkerchief to his nose and be forced to say things like 'Get you, ducky.' That, to us, was the only way to be gay.

This of course, was a product of our age and immaturity as well as of the time. I can still remember an older male relation of mine who doesn't wish to be named discovering that one of my friends was gay. 'He can't be,' he said. 'Look at the muscles on him.' Other evidence for the defence was that this friend was a good soccer player and fixed his own car.

Male homosexuality wouldn't be much of an omission, but in a world that has bothered to include its own system of distance measurement, its own musical instruments, to provide charts for detailing a character's eye colour, clan organization, trades, microscopically detailed accounts of court etiquette, *the size of a woman's breasts*, it surely can't be an oversight.

Lee Gold, who writes the monthly role-playing game journal *Alarums and Excursions* and has designed several fantasy games herself for some of the biggest publishers in the game, has said she censored herself in excluding any reference to homosexuality in her games, assuming her publishers wouldn't be receptive to the idea. She wondered if she'd been right to do so and approached one of them. They said that they were very glad she hadn't put anything like that into her work because it saved them the trouble of taking it out again.

They know their market. We would have avoided any product that had explicit mentions of male homosexuality in it, and it would have been known as 'the bender game.' Just owning it would have made you gay by implication, a social disaster in our world. Actually I think Empire of the Petal Throne may have had some gay non-player characters, but we conveniently avoided those.

However straight they were, the D&Ders were nevertheless paralysed in front of women, which was largely OK because there weren't a lot of them at the HM disco. I'd say the ratio was about seventy to thirty male to female. Coming from the world of Dungeons and Dragons and the all-boys Woodlands School, however, this had the appearance to me of a harem.

I did briefly, in that first term of the fifth year, talk to one girl, but she was rather plain. Andy said that I'd fallen in love with an orc. I didn't care; she was female, and she would speak to me, so that was all that counted.

However, I made that classic male mistake of believing that women want impressing rather than talking to. I imagined my life as a game of D&D and presented myself to her as a high-level character.

'Yeah, I'm in the top sets at school you know. I'm going to get maximum exam results. I'm going for pure science at university, none of the Mickey Mouse stuff.'

'Yeah?'

'Yeah, I've got all Sabbath's records.'

'Yeah?'

'Ask me about them if you like.'

'Do you have *Greatest Hits*?'

'Yeah. In black vinyl.'

There was a pause while we both digested the idiocy of that remark.

'Do you have *Sin After Sin*?' she said.

'Yeah.'

'That's by Judas Priest.'

'Yeah, I know; I didn't want to show you up.'

'I've got to go and stand over there now.'

'OK, bye.'

I walked back to the boys with the swagger of a sailor coming ashore with six months' wages in his pocket. Even though I knew in my heart that I'd blown it, just speaking to her put me on a level above the rest.

The boys were full of advice about what I should have said and done, most of it designed to make me look an even bigger idiot than I'd managed under my own steam. However, I had a project of my own underway that I thought would make me more desirable to women. Most of my D&D characters had extremely beautiful partners. Become a D&D character, and a suitable girl would definitely appear.

A Short Cut to
Mushrooms

The first problem that hit me in turning myself into a D&D character was deciding which character class I was. I ummmed and ahed and finally decided that I was probably a druid. The advantage of being a druid, of course was that I could use a sword, a scimitar at least. One way that D&D discriminates amongst its character classes is to allow some to use more weapons than others. For instance, a wizard can only use a dagger, a cleric blunt weapons, a thief is restricted to light armour. Picking up a sword, to me, was a confession that I'd never cast a successful spell. The druid class gets round this. They can use scimitars and also summon lightning from the heavens or cause the woods to entangle an enemy.

However, I'd already begun to suspect that the D&D system might not be the *exact* recreation of real life that I'd taken it to be. It had troubled me greatly that Michael Moorcock's heroes seemed to be able to cast spells and use swords and that Gandalf himself was handy with a blade. This put me in a dilemma. Either D&D was wrong (impossible) or Moorcock and Tolkien were wrong (equally impossible). I spent a few nights working this out. In the end I came to the conclusion that *Runequest*—a D&D-like game which didn't use character classes—was more like real life. I had learned to criticize something I loved, which might for some have been an important step on the road to maturity. For me it proved a blind alley.

Convinced that my sword skills wouldn't undermine my potential as a spell-caster, I took up fencing on a Monday night. On my first night at the club I was slightly disappointed to learn that there was no option to fight with sword and dagger and that the uniform was a smart white tunic and breeches rather than a cloak and floppy hat. This isn't as stupid as it sounds. It was only after some last-minute behind-the-scenes jiggery-pokery that the sword and dagger event was dropped from the first Olympics. As a sport fencing has a concern that it's not suited to TV—too fast and the participants are anonymous behind the masks. If it reintroduced the dagger, allowed people to move in a circle rather than a straight line and included some good old-fashioned kicks and trips I think it'd be as popular as boxing before long—especially if you insisted people wore floppy hats which they could use to blind their opponents and that they occasionally sliced through candlesticks.

I had, of course, wanted to learn to fight with a dagger because in D&D magic-users are only allowed a dagger or—in later rules—a staff. This is designed to limit the fighting capability of the wizard, but it's a bit of an anomaly. As someone who's faced a quarterstaff while armed with a sword (well, the obsession wasn't going to just evaporate, was it?), I can tell you, the contest is nowhere near as one-sided as you might imagine. If anything the bloke with the staff has a great advantage—it's longer and, compared to a stabbing weapon like a rapier at least, you bloody well know you've been hit with it. There's no 'Gosh am I bleeding? Run straight through and didn't even notice until the end of the fight' when someone's smacked you over the head with 10 pounds of iron-shod English oak.

Oh dear, I am sounding like a D&Der there, aren't I?

I loved the fencing, even though I was predictably crap at it. However, I wasn't as crap as I was at other physical endeavours. It's a highly technical sport, and application can make up for a host of natural inadequacies.

My new interest led to extended sword fights with Porter in his back garden using his English Civil War recreation swords. These had fencing blades mounted in period handles and we duelled without masks or any sort of protection. I deserve to be writing this using only one eye.

Druids are, of course, masters of herb lore. I was a druid, therefore I was exactly such a master. In D&D the druids have a spell known as 'Commune With Nature.' This enables them to speak to spirits in trees and plants. I'd pondered on my lack of success with the holly tree, studied a few library books and come to the conclusion that my mistake in trying to get hold of the spirits of the wood was in omitting to marinate my mind in magic mushrooms first.

Mushrooms were the key to the magic kingdom. I teamed up with my friend Mick Barnes, and, as so often in my teenage collaborations, we made a spirited attempt at suicide. The best way to find magic mushrooms, should any reader be considering it, is to get someone who knows about them to show you one and go from there. The worst way, the one I chose, is to imagine roughly what you think a magic mushroom might look like and then describe it to an excited friend who in every way is a stranger to caution.

Mick was a year older than me and on the dole at the time, so I left the gathering to him. The container that Mick had chosen for his expedition would have given any seasoned mushroom consumer some pause. It was a large rubble sack in tough blue plastic, and he returned with it full to overflowing. Had I known it, there probably weren't enough real magic mushrooms in Coventry to fill that sack, let alone on the golf course where Mick had been picking.

I looked inside. Even I, who so wanted to be on a trip that second, off with the wizards, the girls with kaleidoscope eyes and the magic teapots from outer space, was forced to admit that not everything in there could be a magic mushroom. I think the real clue to that fact wasn't the several pieces of bark that Mick had in the bag, nor the short length of rope. It was the two golf balls. Clearly Mick was even less versed in druidic lore than I was.

'What are these for?' I said.

'I wasn't sure what they were,' said Mick.

'They've got "Dunlop" written on the side,' I said, 'and are clearly golf balls.'

'Oh yeah,' said Mick. 'They looked a bit like mushrooms in the grass so I got 'em just in case.'

There was a metaphor there for my entire adolescence— wishing something to be something else so very hard that it almost is but, crucially, isn't.

It wasn't Mick who was being stupid here, however. It was me. Given these clear and unambiguous warning signals that we did not have the tiniest scintilla of an idea of what we were doing, not even a suggestion of the beginning of the corner of an idea, I delved further into the bag.

'This is one,' I said, pulling out what I now know to be a Death Cap mushroom.

'Right,' said Mick, 'I think you're meant to eat about thirty, shall we nip back up the park and get some more?'

'Right ho,' I said.

Luckily, on the way to the park we met up with Chips Murphy, so called because of his mother's habit of standing at the top of the playing fields at tea time and shouting 'Chips!' to bring him in to eat. Chips actually knew what a magic mushroom looked like and so guided us to what we were looking for. I don't think it's melodramatic to say that he saved our lives.

The mushrooms did enable me to do magic—walking through the woods near my home at dawn I could see faces in the trees and change the colour of the mist—but I'd been totally unprepared for the emotional torrent they unleashed. If I'd just hallucinated I think I'd have been all right, but they seemed to trigger off virtually every feeling I'd ever had all at once with the emphasis on the bad ones. Later on I found out that another unpleasant effect of the drug is to force you to hang around with people who call them 'shrooms' and try to talk pop philosophy, which was more than I could bear. I knew magic mushrooms weren't for me right from that first trip. It didn't stop me taking them for a few months in the hope that I'd suddenly start to enjoy them, though.

I began to question whether I was really cut out to be a druid. As I reconsidered my character class I began to see a new route opening up for me when I took up the martial art Tae Kwon Do. The D&Ders had all descended on this en masse, with the exception of Andy Porter.

'The problem is,' he said, 'that you spend all this time practising fighting, and when it comes to it, then you're too knackered to defend yourself. On top of that, you become a slave to your body. If you want to stop you'll instantly turn to flab.'

The idea of Andy turning to flab was like that of a pencil turning to flab. It wasn't going to happen.

By week four at the class I was convinced that I was an expert and was probably ready to start my training in the deeper arts. Soon, I thought, I would be able to kill a man with a single blow or even learn D&D's 'quivering palm'—a skill of the more experienced 'monk' character class that allows you to set up vibrations within a person's body that will eventually kill them.

All my Tae Kwon Do teacher promised was he would teach you to kick and punch someone really hard. However, Tae Kwon Do was an eastern art, and therefore I felt sure that if I stuck with it I'd eventually be taught secrets such as walking over a paper screen without breaking it, being able to run 100 miles a day without tiring and how to catch arrows in flight.

The inspiration for this, of course, was the ninja character class—published in *The Dragon* magazine and simultaneously in a couple of lower-production-value fanzines. Ninjas have now reached the level of icons in western society, but back then very few people had heard of them. The ninja held particular appeal for me because I suspected that in a previous life I had been Japanese, killed by the Hiroshima A bomb. At a very early age I'd seen a John Wayne film in which he'd fought the Japanese. I took an immediate and violent dislike to the Duke, who seemed to represent all those qualities of swaggering self-assurance I most hated in men. Every time he appeared on the TV I'd shout, 'Naganaganaa!' as if machine-gunning him, much to the annoyance of my dad, who enjoyed his films.

John Wayne fans say that he desperately tried to enlist in World War II but couldn't because of a 'bad shoulder.' The English WWII fighter pilot Douglas Bader didn't have a bad shoulder, but he did have two tin legs. It didn't stop him enlisting and recording 22.5 kills in air combat or making numerous escape attempts when he was captured after colliding with an enemy over France. When the Germans confiscated his legs to forestall further escape bids he attempted to crawl his way out of Colditz. Still, he never had to wince through the pain of a poorly arm to apply grease paint in anger.

In contrast to John Wayne, the Japanese seemed very brave in the film and admirably selfless. Accordingly, all my 1/32-scale plastic soldiers were Japanese. So when the ninja popped into my consciousness, bearing the virtues of being Japanese, rock hard and associated with D&D, it's safe to say I was ready to give him a good reception.

Once again my father's motorcycle equipment came in for adaptation. He had a silk balaclava that was worn under his helmet in cold weather. This, to me, very much resembled the ninja's mask. One of the key ninja skills is to be able to hide himself in small containers—baskets, chests and the like. Lying in bed one night and studying the Ali Baba wicker laundry basket my mum had placed in my room in an effort to confine my dirty laundry, I came to the logical conclusion that it was very likely I should have latent ninja powers. A ninja is a nimble Japanese person of maybe five foot two with the flexibility of an octopus, capable of dislocating his limbs in order to pack himself into impossibly tight spaces. I was a galumphing fifteen-year-old of nearly six feet tall, who had discovered through his Tae Kwon Do class that he was relatively flexible.

I stole down to the cupboard under the stairs and retrieved my dad's balaclava. Back in my room, I opened *The Dragon* magazine. I didn't have any mummy-like robes to swaddle myself in. 'Sod it,' I thought, 'I'll make do with my briefs.'

I have never lacked ambition when it comes to things like this. Another boy might have thought it enough to test his powers by merely getting into the basket. This wasn't enough for me. I decided that I would position the basket on my bed, hide inside it, place myself into a trance, awake just before my mum came in to make the beds and wink out of the basket at her to surprise her when she came to move it.

As with the fireball episode, what surprises me is not that I should dare to do it but that I simply couldn't envisage the possibility of failure. I was a ninja; of course I'd be able to get into the basket. With my sword. I had to be ready for combat when I came out, like a proper ninja. It's a historical fact that the favoured weapon of the ninja was the ninja-to, a short sword. The European training foil never caught on, and for good reason, as I was about to find out. Entering a basket is difficult enough at the best of times, without taking in a three-foot length of eye-poking-out metal with you.

I was going to say that I was undaunted as I positioned the basket on the bed. That's not quite right. Undaunted implies that I'd recognized a source of danger but hadn't been put off by it. I was more dauntless, completely oblivious that anything could go wrong as I tried to work out how to get me—in mask and briefs—and my fencing foil into the basket. I dare say that if you'd asked an angel if he fancied fitting himself into it he might have said, 'No thank you, I fear to tread there.' Me, I rushed in.

This is, by the way, what I was doing while others were lying dreaming of girls and tricked out Ford Escorts.

The task I'd set myself would have been difficult enough on a steady surface. Balanced on a mattress, of course, it was a complete non-starter. Those who, like me, have tried to secrete themselves in a washing basket will know that the first decision to be made is by which end to enter. It did occur to me to go in head-first and then attempt to wriggle about until I could see out of the top. Luckily my wisdom prevailed and I got in feet first, planning to wedge in the sword after the hips but before the shoulders.

I must have been much thinner back then than I am now because I managed to get in up to my hips quite easily. Emboldened by this early success I reached down onto the bed for the sword, gaining it at a totter. The difficulty with basket hiding, I came to realize, is the knees. As they fold, so they widen. As I crouched I realized that there was no way I was going to get in any further than the belly button. Still, the fantasy-consumed adolescent views the laws of physics more in the spirit of guidelines. The problem was, I decided, a lack of force. What I needed, was a good jump at it. That would slam my knees down, and I'd magically pop inside.

With a one, two and a jolly good three I leaped into the air, gaining added zoom from the spring of the mattress. The ascent went very well.

I'd managed to jump high enough to get my knees over the lip of the basket. Unfortunately I was so keen to bend my legs that on my way down I bent them before I'd actually got into it. There was no way I was going to land properly. The basket caught around my ankles, and I was projected forward in a dive towards the chest of drawers. I remember being quite impressed by the distance I'd achieved, and the last thought, before I knocked myself unconscious, was that I wondered what D&D character class was the best at diving.

'Thieves, probably,' I thought as my head hit the corner of the unit.

My mum and dad were, naturally, woken by the crash. To their credit, as they took me to casualty, neither asked me what I'd been doing diving off the bed semi-naked with a basket round my feet, sword in my hand and a balaclava on my head.

In future my mum and dad never placed a great deal of confidence in my ability to sort out problems for myself. They had, I think, come to the opinion that I was incapable of masturbating without knocking myself cold.

The
Worlds Collide

I was attending the Lanch on Fridays, so I couldn't go to the wargames club, and our games at the weekend had degenerated into festivals of sarcasm. This meant that I wasn't really getting my D&D fix. In an attempt to pack in more quality gaming I entered a wandering mariachi phase, haunting the night, character book in bag, looking to play with whoever, wherever. In the years I'd been playing the D&D I must have sat down at a table with over 100 other boys. Now I started using my little black book to good effect.

On a Tuesday night with nothing to do—and a 1970s adolescent nothing at that—all three channels dead on the TV and the weather doing a Wuthering Heights outside, the sort of nothing that, unless something happens, will force you to do your homework, I'd go a-wandering.

'Ah, Steve Matlock,' I'd think, 'he only lives seven miles away. I'll cycle over through this filthy night and see if he wants a game. If he doesn't, I'll bike on up to Gaz Dawes on the other side of the city and see what he's doing.'

I'd strap on my bag and emerge on the unfortunate Matlock's doorstep forty minutes later.

'Hi.'

'Oh, hi. It's Sp . . . Mark isn't it?'

'Please, call me Spaz,' I said. 'I was wondering if you fancied a game of Runequest. I've got the new Apple Lane scenario I'd like to run.'

This was the maddening thing about Runequest. It was derived from a game that mentioned white bears, red moons and vast lunar armies, but the pre-prepared dungeons you could buy for it, rather than having names like Glory of the North or The Snows of Ilmirith, were called Apple Lane and Snake Pipe Hollow, which were too hobbity and cutesy for my liking.

'I haven't played D&D for a year,' he said.

'Why not?' I said. This was utterly incomprehensible to me. I think I expected him to tell me he'd been in a coma or tied to a radiator. Part of me felt like calling the police there and then. Skulduggery, I thought, must be afoot. On the other hand, unless he'd just woken up that second, what was he doing not playing a game right then; why didn't he have a book in his hand?

'I've just grown out of it,' he said.

I simply didn't understand this concept. How could you grow out of D&D? It was like growing out of breathing. To me he had given up, accepted he was a dull person and that his life would never contain anything interesting. Years later I'd feel like this when I heard friends had taken jobs.

'Well,' I said, 'I play with blokes of twenty-six, and they haven't grown out of it, so who's right, you or them?'

This wasn't exactly true. We'd seen less of Frank Warner and Steve Boscombe since Sean had joined, and I think the incredibly irritating atmosphere of the games might have had something to do with that. Steve just shrugged and said he wanted to get back to his homework. I said I'd grown out of homework and went on to Gaz Dawes, but he was out. I did often get games or was roped into playing table football or Pong. I rarely returned to the boys' houses I visited; mostly I was received with a kind of baffled politeness, a game was played, or figures were produced and discussed, and then I went home.

This was the other thing about that period—even though we had a party-line phone (cheaper because you share the line with another house, so you can't use it when they're on) I wasn't really allowed to use it. My parents seemed to think that any conversation of longer than thirty seconds was in danger of bankrupting them, and most of my friend's mums and dads felt the same. We very rarely communicated by phone, and the idea of making five or six ludicrously expensive calls in one evening was simply out of the question. Even receiving a call in the evening was a big deal for some boys—their parents were unused to the phone ringing, and, when you said who you were, they would become quite angry, passing it over with words such as 'I thought your grandmother had taken a turn.'

Mum and Dad didn't like me talking for long even if we were receiving the call. As it was a party line, my mother reasoned, the other house might be waiting to call. 'Come on, Mark, be fair,' she'd say, tapping at an imaginary watch. There seemed to be something of this attitude surrounding any luxury at the time, that it had to be handled so circumspectly that it ceased to be a luxury at all.

In the fifth form my schoolbooks lay unmolested as D&D became virtually my whole life—I read about fantasy, played fantasy games and listened to music that sang about wizards and trolls. I have a sick collection of tapes at home. When I was ten I'd received a load of David Bowie's albums that had been taped for me by some students at the college where my mum worked. By the time I was sixteen *Aladdin Sane* had been taped over and erased, replaced with Rainbow's *Rising*. *Ziggy Stardust* was gone, and in its place was Judas Priest. *Germ Free Adolescents* by the X-Ray Spex was sold, and I bought a live bootleg of local HM band Chainsaw. I had gone mad.

Gaming reached a fever pitch. My gnome Foghat was doing very well, and I had a marine in Traveller who I really liked called Slleh Legna—Hells Angel backwards. This, I was sure, was my destiny, to join a mystical band of brothers myself, despite the fact that I was still physically scared of ten-year-olds if they were in a gang. Two's a gang, isn't it? Then, just as I began to think that I'd finally gone over to the fantasy world for good, I got a girlfriend.

Girlfriends are generally poison to a committed life in D&D, particularly ones who don't live on your doorstep. I met her at the Lanch disco, somewhere that had been playing a bigger and bigger part in my imaginative life. I could be who I wanted to be there. I could pass for older; I could be a biker among bikers, and I could feel safe from the world. Coventry felt a threatening place at that time of my life.

Just walking from the bus stop to the Lanch felt like going through some radiation wasteland—concrete and grime and threatening strangers. This was what it was like *before* a nuclear strike. It felt like the sort of area that might have its tone raised by the addition of a few flesh-hungry mutants. And this, on the way up to the cathedral, was the nice bit.

I'd danced with Jane for about five weeks before anything happened, but I knew I was falling for her when I found myself deliberately smearing oil on my jeans before going down to the disco one Friday night. Girls love bikers, I thought. The toughest bikers are the most dirty; therefore I would be the dirtiest biker ever. Believe me, that's a stiff competition to enter.

I ground oil into my fingernails to make it look as if I'd come from working on my bike, and I casually put a wrench so it protruded from the top pocket of my denim jacket. I had no idea that this left me looking like a fake. My life had been about role-playing, and I saw no reason why I shouldn't continue that outside of the game.

My problem with Jane was that I didn't know what to say to her. I tried a few lines like 'hello' and she said 'hello' and winked at me, which had about the effect of a right hook from a decent middleweight, but I couldn't take it any further. I was, for the first time in my life, tongue-tied.

I can't really remember now that clearly what she looked like—small and pretty but quite boyish with mousy straight hair flicked over one eye, I think. She could have looked like anything and I would have been pleased, though.

Week to week, as my exams loomed, I became progressively more oil-stained and battery-acid corroded (cut-off denim only, you never willingly mark your leather) and week to week she danced with me more, leading me to conclude that I was doing something right. As it was, she made a move just in time, before I could come in with a pot of axle grease on my head or start stripping a carburettor on the bar.

I was about to go to get the last bus one night when she just grabbed me by the arm and changed my life. Fairy tales are full of enchantments being broken with a kiss. That was what happened to me. It was over in a second, but it was my first full, proper snog. I had to go because otherwise I'd miss the bus. It's not an exaggeration to say I could feel her kiss all the way down to my boots; it seemed like I'd wired my central nervous system up to some sort of booster pack.

'Give me a call,' she said.

'I will!' I said.

'You'll need my number,' she said.

'I'll get a pen!' I said, desperately searching for one.

Then there was Porter, in his Hawkwind lab coat and pocket full of pens.

'Can I have a pen?' I said.

'What for?' said Porter. Adults don't ask these questions, do they? You either give it or you don't.

'I've got a girl's number!' I said.

Porter looked a little more wan than usual, wan enough for me to see his wanness under the flashing disco lights.

'I haven't got one that works,' he said. He had about twenty in his top pocket.

'One of them must,' I said.

'They're all used up,' he said. 'I wouldn't risk a new pen in here.'

Then I did something that marked the beginning of a total change in my relationship with Andy. I just put forward my hand and took one. I'd never touched him before, apart from one half-hearted attempt he'd made to give me a thumping at Dave's house a year or so before. In his lab coat he had a look of surprise like Dr Jekyll must have had as the effects of his potion began to be felt for the first time. Up until that point Andy had been utterly in command in our relationship. It was the first step towards more equal terms.

I got Jane's number on my hand, gave Porter back his pen, kissed Jane again and set off towards the bus station. Her kiss hadn't turned me from a D&Ding frog into a ladies' man prince, but it had at least given me the idea that there was a world outside my lily pad that was more than boredom and drudgery.

It was difficult for the others to accommodate the fact I had a girlfriend. Most of them were two years older than me and had come no nearer to women than mumbling into their hands at their sisters' mates.

I think some of them presumed I had done it to spite them. The teasing became more physical now, and I had to fight off pulls, pokes and stabs on a regular basis. I'd always come in for more of this than most, but now it seemed to focus exclusively on me. Porter was the only one who didn't actually lay hands on me, but he became more testy than usual and a succession of my characters died in his dungeons.

My exams came and went in a blur. In my English exam I tried to write a story about a killer Dalmatian that was in fact a robot with a chainsaw in its mouth. The story was awful. I didn't mind too much if I passed or failed anyway. Arts subjects were the province of losers to us D&Ders. We wanted to learn about physics, the universe, metaphysics even (surely just physics but *really* hard). Arts students were thick, we thought, and left-wing, which made them doubly thick.

I chose maths, physics and chemistry to study in the two years of preparation for university—subjects I like the look of but that bore me when it comes down to it. It's the equivalent of walking into an airport lounge and thinking, 'Shall I buy the latest page turner to keep me company on the beach, or shall I have a crack at the Hawking?' You take a look to your right, see someone who you want to impress and think, '*A Brief History of Time* it is for me!' But when you're lying on your back in the sun reading an ice-cream wrapper while the Prof's book languishes in your bag you end up wishing you'd gone for *Deadly Games* instead.

Over the summer while I was waiting for my exam results, I was spending more time with Jane and less with the D&Ders. I hadn't given up D&D or fantasy, but I had taken up heavy petting.

I did still play, and we all arranged to go to the Reading rock festival together. What I didn't know was that discussions had taken place behind my back to 'get me' at the festival. They wanted to attack my tent while I was in there with Jane. It all became apparent under the questioning of the practical-joke-mad Glebe.

'Are you going to Reading, Spaz?' he asked one night at the heavy rock disco.

'Yeah, more than likely,' I said.

'You should, er,' he said, 'you should take Jane.'

'She might not have enough money,' I said.

'Well get her to save up,' he said, 'you could . . . you know.'

'What?'

'You know!'

'What?'

He looked left and right and said under his breath in an urgent tone, 'Have sex!'

'Oh, we already do that,' I said, matter of factly.

Glebe took on a far-away look, as if a little bit of him had died. Then he said, 'No you don't.'

'Yes we do,' I said.

'When?'

'Saturdays during the day when you're wargaming,' I said.

Glebe made a noise like an old horse who's quite content in his stable and doesn't want pulling out to take a fat lass on a hack.

He thumped me on the arm hard.

'Liar,' he said.

He was disappointed that he wasn't going to have the chance to ruin losing my virginity for me and very annoyed that I had entered that happy kingdom before him.

The next time I went wargaming I had to account for myself.

'OK,' said Glebe, who'd clearly been giving it some thought, 'if you've been doing it, what's it like then?'

'It's difficult to say,' I said.

'No it's not,' said Porter. 'Frenchy at school has done it, and he says it's like putting your knob between two pillows. If you'd done it then you'd know.'

I reminded myself to be careful where I put my hand next time I sat on the bed at Andy's house.

Having a girlfriend and being a D&Der at the same time was becoming difficult. I sparked outrage when I cancelled a game at my house at the last minute so I could go round to see Jane. It did occur to me to invite her round to play with us, but that would have been out of the question. Even if she'd wanted to come, I wouldn't have exposed her to the ridicule and ribbing she'd have encountered.

So D&D was coming into serious conflict with the rest of my life. Something would have to give.

The Breaking
of the Fellowship

I had died around 200 times by the time I was sixteen—caught in traps, hacked by orcs, fried by evil wizards. I was once gang raped to death by 1,000 kobolds when Andy had become intensely irritated with my houri character and decided to kill her in as gruesome a way as possible.

A couple of these deaths hurt me very badly. What the non-D&Der doesn't see is just how strongly you can identify with one of your characters, much more so than with a Monopoly piece or a figure in a conventional wargame. By the time a character dies you may have spent hundreds of hours in his company. If you compare that to the snatched hellos and goodbyes adolescents exchange with their parents you can see it's possible to feel closer to Samuel Lightenpurse the hobbit thief than to your family.

These characters' only existence outside of your mind is as a list of statistics and notes on a sheet. This means the sheets become labours of love. As they become full or scruffy they're often copied out again in fresh exercise books stolen from school expressly for the purpose. It's cooler to have the characters in an exercise book as it shows the casual disdain for authority and possible criminal tendencies so admired by young boys.

By the end of the summer Jane had gone, which hurt me less than when Effilc Worrab the Elf copped it. She left me for some biker. I knew him, and he was dirtier than me. I wouldn't make the mistake of washing again for a long time. I might have slipped back into playing D&D as an obsession again, but through her influence, and to an extent that of her older sister, Ann, who would sit chatting to us for hours, I'd seen a different life. For instance, when I'd produced a flick knife to show Ann how grown up I was, I was amazed when she said, 'And exactly what are you going to do with that, you little twat?'

'Comb my hair,' I said.

The flick knife was really a flick comb designed to look like a knife. I'd borrowed it from one of the D&Ders for whom the joke had worn thin. Ann laughed, more in relief than amusement. I realized that she wouldn't have been impressed by me having a knife, despite being ancient at twenty-two and having a really old tough biker boyfriend. It sounds a small thing, but it made me see life from a slightly more adult perspective. Still, I wasn't such a changed creature and was still very immature for my age, full of strange ideas about the world.

Around this time I became briefly successful with girls. I had three girlfriends at one point—Jane, although that was drawing to a close, a girl from Scotland I'd met on a trip to Switzerland with the school and Sue, a beautiful biker girl I had picked up by headbanging next to her, proving that there is no accounting for taste. I knew that I was the ugliest person who ever drew breath, so I came to the conclusion it must be my winning personality that was drawing them in, my ability to talk endlessly about Black Sabbath, my outlandish style of dress and my uncanny skill for naming the armour class and hit dice of any creature you pulled out of *The Monster Manual*.

However, I was wrong there. The other day, looking through the few photos I have of my youth—my parents weren't ones for photography, and my dad earned the nickname 'Henry VIII' for his ability to slice the heads off the subjects of his snaps—I realized that I was in fact quite good-looking. Before twenty years of pub and club took their toll, before work had ground its way into my skin, I was what might be termed 'not bad.' I was certainly no Brad Pitt but neither was I the orc I saw when I looked in the mirror. This was a chilling conclusion. Far from going out with me for my personality, these women had clearly been with me despite it.

All my relationships seemed to end after about two months. I think this was the amount of time it took for your average woman to realize she was with a tit. When, at the end of the summer of 1980, I found myself without a girlfriend I went back to D&D and headed for an all-night game at Gary Yardley's.

His house was in the Hillfields area of Coventry, a rough spot renowned, fairly or not, for its lawlessness, drug-taking and pros-titution. (Years later a friend's band were practising at a Hillfields pub. They got a request to turn the music down in the form of someone shooting out the windows with a shotgun. That's very unusual, even in the roughest parts of the UK.) There wasn't a bus that went directly to his door, so I'd walked up, rather nerv-ously, from the Pool Meadow bus station.

I'd got there slightly late, which was unusual for me and per-haps indicative of some growing reluctance to attend the game. We began. I think Gary was running the dungeon, and it was some sort of town adventure. We weren't five minutes in when the tricks started. Actually 'tricks' does them too much credit. Throwing things at people and repeating the last half of whatever they said about covered it.

'Do you think I could get a glass of water.'

'A glass of water,' said Sean.

'You're not just going to start repeating everything I say are you?'

'Everything I say are you.'

'Can we just get on with the game?'

'On with the game.'

'Oh, for fuck's sake.'

'Fuck's sake.'

'Shut up.'

'Up.'

After about half an hour the dread moment arrived when I needed to go to the loo. I looked at my bag. It suddenly struck me as ridiculous that I should have to take a night's worth of D&D books, a load of sandwiches, two cans of Coke, an apple and my coat to the toilet just to be able to urinate. So I left them there.

Predictably, when I got back, the room was all sniggers, and my character book was gone.

'Give it back to me now, or I'm going,' I said.

The room erupted in 'ooohs!' and 'hark at hims.'

I said I'd count to ten, and if it wasn't produced by the time I finished, I was off. A couple of the D&Ders joined in as I counted.

'Right, goodbye,' I said.

I packed up my remaining stuff and made for the door.

'I don't know why you're going through with this charade,' said Sean. 'You know you won't go.'

'I'll give you £10 you're back in five minutes,' said Gary Yardley as I went through the door.

'You might never see your character book again,' said Glebe.

That was a point. There was nearly five years of my life in that book, five kid years too—the long ones, not these flashing mere afternoons of things that pass for years in adulthood. I'd had more meaningful interactions with those characters than most human beings. Poly Styrene was in there, Alf the Elf, Effilc Worrab, my nameless half-orc assassin, Foghat the Gnome, Drizzle the Illusionist, all the companions of my youth. I desperately wanted the book back, which was why they'd taken it. Whoever had it would hope that I'd spend the next twelve hours searching for it, irritating Porter by trying to look in his bag, having to come too close to Gardener and getting tripped or stabbed, wandering in range of whatever Glebe wanted to throw.

I looked into the room and saw clearly for the first time that as much as I'd mythologized myself, I'd mythologized them. Suddenly I didn't see Porter, demi-god of the upper sixth, on his way to one of England's very least prestigious universities thanks to rather mediocre exam results; I didn't see Gardener, chaotic and irrepressible wit, beacon of ungovernable humour, brave rejecter of homework, destined for the next ten years on the dole—though he can't be faulted for his efforts to stay out of work for longer—I didn't see Gary Yardley, physics genius, whose shining intellect had been rewarded by a place at a coastal poly; I didn't see Dave and I didn't see Glebe—who was all right but was mildly distinguished as the only older boy I hadn't hero worshipped. Individually they were fine, but together I finally saw them for what they were—farting, silly boys who had no idea of the world outside their own limited company.

So I left, and I didn't come back. I'd broken the spell, stepped back through the wardrobe from Narnia, and I was free. In a manner of speaking.

Dabbling with Reality

A cloak is an apt garment for an adolescent, though that's not the way I saw mine at the time. To me it was the first step in a new magical life and went well with the belt with thirteen skull studs that I wore at my waist and the medieval-style jug purse that dangled from it. The cloak had been stitched together for me by my girlfriend Caroline, who I'd met at a sixth-form disco. She'd made it just long enough for it to hover above the floor when I wore my square-toed cowboy boots. When I wore my Green Flash sneakers I had to be careful not to trip over it as I attempted to sweep majestically along the A45 on my way to my nan's with the dog or to swoop like a descending vampire onto the bus downtown.

The cloak was, had I known it, a symbol of my manful struggle against reality. I'd envisaged the full sorcerer job, velvet with a high collar, when I'd described it to Caroline, but she'd come up with what was basically a large black polyester curtain tied at the top with a bow. Ironically, this material was a bugger for static electricity, and, rubbing up against the wool of my mum's home-made sweater, I often ended up virtually throwing lightning bolts as I moved about.

I'd decided I was a hippy, largely because there were no other hippies in the sixth form and because it made a virtue out of my extreme physical cowardice. I finally got a motorbike, a lumbering Honda commuter which I attempted to drive everywhere at its top speed of 70 mph. The cloak couldn't be worn on the bike—even I could see that the pleasure of looking like a black rider running on the wings of a storm over Weathertop was likely to be offset by being strangled as the cloak was snarled in the back wheel. I carried it tucked up my leather. When I stopped I'd unpack it and wear it over the top of the jacket in a manner not unlike, I thought, Darth Vader.

My problem was that the abrupt withdrawal of D&D had left me with an orc-shaped hole at the centre of my life. My lust for fantasy was undimmed. In fact I think my lust for D&D was undimmed. What was dimmed was my lust for sitting about in a room with eight other adolescent boys summoning up a storm-head of irritation between us. I still played occasionally, but never in the full group any more. In smaller numbers it was just about possible to prevent the games evolving the atmosphere more normally generated amongst nine-year-olds in an eight-hour trip in a car. Still, one game a month is scarce rations for someone who has done nothing else and thought of little else for five years.

Fantasy, which had more or less been confined to the gaming table, began to spill into my ordinary life. I began role-playing all the time, in the supermarket, at school, with my girlfriend, on the bike. I'd stride the Whoberley Estate clad in motley trying to look like a sorcerer king while Caroline at my side, clad in Top Shop, would try to look nice. I was going to say that I was burning for something to come along and define my existence, but it was a bit simpler than that. I was burning for just something to do.

Disconnected from D&D, I felt connected to nothing but with a massive need to experience those highs the game had brought me. D&D had given me a deep dissatisfaction with the ordinary world and the strong conviction that the magical life I'd been born to—that of an artist, entertainer or wizard—simply had to start at any moment.

As Gandalf was showing a marked unwillingness to hop up on my doorstep asking me to get it sorted in Middle Earth, I decided to embark on a magical quest all of my own.

We had a fair few séances, which I found pleasing, not least because it involves ten people round a table, and I was extremely comfortable with that situation. American Evangelists would have people believe that D&D leads inevitably to the occult, but I don't think that's true. The idea of our first séance came from a kid who had never picked up a twenty-sided dice in his life; he was a keen golfer. Perhaps golf leads to Satanism, I don't know. Maybe those plus fours are to cover up goaty back legs.

Although we managed a few interesting effects through the séances—one possession, one Grand National horse race prediction and a weird stoned feeling when we tried to summon the spirit of Marc Bolan, it wasn't enough for me.

Accordingly I was drawn to the works of Aleister Crowley, the Edwardian occultist and self-styled 'wickedest man in the world.' Through the library I took out a book setting out the rituals of the Golden Dawn. At first I experimented with ceremonies on my own, but I lacked the dedication to see them through. I'd always end up smoking on my bed and listening to records half-way through invoking Horus. This did cause my mum something of a surprise when she came in to berate me for having the music too loud, to discover me wearing a pair of her red slingbacks I'd dug out from under the stairs. The magician, you see, needs red shoes to show his warrior status, and I didn't have any of my own. That's my story anyway.

Really, I think, I wanted to bring the social aspect of D&D to my idolatry, to have someone to go for a pint with after I'd summoned the powers infernal and discuss highlights of the ceremony as if it was a game of squash. Accordingly I found a Golden Dawn ceremony that required at least three celebrants. Celebrant is the occultist's word for 'gullible idiot who would be better employed doing his homework.' The noble aim of our practice was to get magic mushrooms to grow next to the school sixth-form room so we could all get off our nuts during lessons.

For this I engaged an occasional D&Der—Rat. He was called Rat because some wit had noticed he looked like a rat. Imagine how much more friendly the name 'Ratty' would have been. He wasn't called Ratty, he was called Rat.

I met Craig and Rat at Craig's house, and we made our way down Allesley Park towards Allesley Village graveyard. There's been a church there for nearly 1,000 years, but it was extensively rebuilt in the early Victorian period, so it has that spooky Gothic feel to it.

On the way down Rat started telling us about his attempts to summon the god Cthulhu, he who lies dreaming in his tower at Rleyh beneath the sea, and Hastur the Unspeakable, he who is not to be named (not to be confused with Voldemort, who is not to be named, off *Harry Potter*). The thing is that these were fictional gods. Summoning Cthulhu is roughly the same as trying to summon Peter Pan. Even if you accept the existence of demons and spirits you can't say that *all* demons and spirits ever mentioned exist. For Rat, though, like me, the boundaries between reality and fantasy were slim.

I went along with him discussing the use of Elder Signs to keep the god at bay once he materialized and talking about what we should get him to do. This is the equivalent of deciding to take up tennis and, rather than buying a racquet, making your first priority clearing space on your shelf for the Wimbledon trophy.

We descended through the park. What Craig was doing with us, God only knows. He was fashionable in a gypsy rover way, sporty, good-looking, tall, dark and handsome with a line in easy, relaxed humour that the ladies loved. The occult is the preserve of socially ostracized, power-hungry nerds with superiority complexes. He shouldn't have been allowed to muscle in on our turf. He had cricket.

As we neared the graveyard, the reality of the situation hit us— we were going to have to stand in the churchyard on top of piles of dead bodies, buried but still a 1,000-year stack of them, using incantations we'd nicked out of a book the day before. If it worked we could be in similar trouble to Mickey Mouse in *Fantasia,* maybe worse.

We looked out over the dual carriageway towards the church.

'Do you think,' I said, 'it would be better if we performed our first ceremony actually in the park?'

'Isn't that a bit of a shit out?' said Craig, with some penetration into the realities of the situation.

'I don't know the ceremony yet,' I said. 'I have to read it out of the book. It'll be too dark in the graveyard.'

There were 'ahs' of understanding, and we settled for a spot just off the path behind a high hedge, under the light of a lamp post. I opened my bag and took out my equipment. For my Athame (sacred knife) I had an ornate paper opener I'd pinched from my mum; I had some incense for the element of air, salt for earth, water in a saucer for water (or for a cat) and a candle for fire. We laid all this out according to the instructions. I didn't need to put on my cloak, I was already wearing it.

The ceremony began, me declaring the temple open and passing the book around so we could get a few replies off the other two. There was a lot of stuff about opening the gates of the east, as I seem to remember, and circumnavigating counter-clockwise. We were making a bit of a hash of it, like once-a-year church attenders during the Christmas mass. Then, though, the one thing that none of us had been prepared for happened. The ceremony began to work.

'Rik, ri, rik, ri.' It was a voice, but we couldn't tell from where.

'Fucking hell,' said Craig, looking a bit scared. Rat gulped, and I, far from welcoming at last my entry into the magical world, felt like I wanted to run.

I'd reached a bit in the ceremony that required me to stand with my arms spread wide, dagger in one hand, chalice in the other. I'd bought the chalice at a visit to a National Trust property with the school, I think. It's surprising what happens when your adrenaline begins to rise. All I could focus on was that chalice and the fear I might drop the water inside it and what that would mean for the ritual. My hands began to shake, and I tried to relax, to keep the chalice still. A wind rose up—the night had been entirely still up until then—and I thought I was going to be sick. Something, we knew, was coming. I suddenly felt very silly and stupid and afraid with the realization that I'd dabbled in forces well outside my control.

Under the wind the voice continued. 'Rik, rik, ri, ri, rik.' There was a low whistle, exactly the sort of thing I'd expected from the appearance of a demon or an angel. Only in pantomime do they appear with a thunderclap. In the literature of the occult they arrive to the sound of bells, or a mad flute or, for all I knew, low whistles.

'What shall we do?' said Rat.

'We can't back out now, we have to complete the ceremony,' I said.

'You need to send it back,' said Craig.

Bracing myself, I went on. I can't remember the exact words, but they were something like: 'Na, Ngarda, Ptah, Magrada Klom!' I screamed them into the growing wind, putting body and soul into them with the hope that whatever was on its way from wherever would heed them and do my bidding, as the book had said that it would. I lifted the dagger and the chalice up high and cast my arms out, the wind pushing at my cloak so it almost enveloped me.

A small white dog pootled around the corner of the hedge and came towards us. It sniffed at the water in the bowl on the floor but didn't drink and then walked across our pentagram towards me to take a look at my leg. I still stood with the chalice and dagger out, wondering what the angel would make of the dog. I liked dogs and hoped it wouldn't think it was a sacrifice.

'Nahm Ptah, Haranda!' or something like it, I shouted, hoping it would make the dog and the demon/angel go away.

'Rikki!' said a voice. 'Will you bloody well stay on the path!'

At that moment a man in a tracksuit came around the corner, smoking. He looked at me with my arms outstretched and dagger raised, looked at Craig and the pale-eyed Rat, his face twitching in fear, looked at his dog gearing up to foul my cloak and just ran for it with a great scream, throwing his fag to the floor as he went.

The dog went bolting after him.

We looked at each other and began to laugh. For the first time in my life I had to concede that fantasy had fought reality in a major battle, and reality had won.

Strangely, this didn't halt my occult pretensions, nor inspire self-knowledge. I joined bands, did performance poetry, took drugs and practised magic, oblivious to the far more interesting things that I could have been doing had I seen myself clearly. I wasn't a druggie or an artist or a poet or a rock star but just an unhappy and directionless boy who didn't even recognize that he was unhappy.

When I say I was directionless, this isn't quite true. I did have a direction, but I couldn't bring myself to accept that it was the way I was going. I was doing the classic march of the bright-ish working-class lad of the period—university, a job, marriage, kids. As a band I liked would say a few years later—Birth, School, Work, Death.

For a time I opted off that conveyor belt, setting up in a house that had all the disadvantages of a squat (slugs in the kitchen, ice on the inside of the windows, no heating) but none of the advantages (we still had to pay rent). I played in a band and wrote execrable poetry, but by the time I was twenty I'd had enough. Two years of scratching by on the dole and waking up with dew on my hair were all I could stand. I was back on the treadmill and heading for the radical hotbed of eighties student politics—Sussex University, spell books in my suitcase.

The Shadow of the Past

It's sometimes when people are gone that you feel their influence most acutely.

I said at the start of the book that my D&D years are still etched onto my personality. My experience playing the game certainly made things difficult for me throughout my twenties. When you've been brought up to believe that the way to show you'd like to get to know someone better is by identifying some mental sore point and giving it a sharp prod, then making friends can be hard.

I'd grown up only with boys, learning how to impress boys and compete with them, freebasing masculinity over the twenty-sided dice. Boys, as opposed to men, are impressed when you take acid during your exams; they think you're 'mental'—meaning good—for trying to summon dark forces and going to the edge of sanity; they like to talk about who is harder than who and whether Lemmy from Motörhead would beat Lynval Golding from The Specials in a fight. Music is, after all, a competition, and it's important to know who's best. Most of all, they delight in being cruel to each other. So I grew up in this world, this furnace of maleness, learning to kill or be killed with humour and sarcasm. Then, at the age of twenty, I went to university and was set upon the sons and daughters of middle England.

I can't think what it must have been like for the shy and the diffident and the unconfident, finding their feet away from home for the first time and having to encounter me. The pattern was set in my very first seminar. A fine-boned convent girl had been allowed to get well off the subject of English literature and was discussing her passion—alternative nutrition.

'There are people,' she said, 'who don't have to eat at all. They take their sustenance from the air and are known as airetarians.'

'Yes,' I said, nodding away at her, 'my father was one.'

'Was he?' she said, in a lovely innocent trill.

'Yes,' I said, 'he went completely without food for weeks, but just as he perfected it, he died.' I inflected the 'he died' with Gardener's characteristic sarcastic tone.

This got a cheap laugh and made her hate me. Not that I noticed. Years of being attacked quite openly over a D&D table had left me entirely insensitive to mild slights, meaningful silences or just the look in someone's eyes.

In the first term in halls we'd all come back to the common room and sit around a large table, drinking, smoking dope and chatting. Fifteen people around a table was a familiar situation to me, and I'd set about making friends the best way I knew how, by picking on them one by one and systematically psychologically annihilating them.

Really, I think that I was searching for a runt and some revenge for years of being on the receiving end. I didn't want a runt like Rat or like me. I wanted some fashionable, pretentious sort who thought he was cool going on about the Socialist Workers Party. Someone like Sebastian, who was a hardcore punk rocker with 'Icons of Filth' written on his back and who wore a sort of wilted Mohawk that made me label him the Spaniel of Filth. I told him that he did a very bad impression of a working-class person and that his whole life was a pathetic attempt to salvage some street cred from his impossibly privileged upbringing and that no amount of glue sniffing or rolling about with a bottle of cider was going to fool anyone. It was true, but, you know, everyone's allowed a mistake.

Then there was Henry, a public-school boy with a Velvet

Underground fixation who used to walk around in a top hat. I took a photo of him and printed it up into a poster bearing the caption 'This clown is available for Weddings, Bar Mitzvahs and Parties' and put it in the common room I knew he used. The next time I saw him I asked him if I could hire him. I'm sure a shrink might make a lot out of my sudden dislike for strangely dressed people.

My cloak was long gone—discarded after I'd been thrown into a fountain in Coventry city centre by soccer hooligans. When I say 'soccer hooligans,' I mean 'right-thinking people.' I don't remember much about the incident—one minute I was standing there looking magisterial, the next I was in the fountain. The hooligans didn't pause, they just ran off laughing. I do recall the looks on the faces of the Saturday shoppers—barely repressed smiles. They were, I concluded, idiots and deserved their lives of Kwik Save and Woolworths. Still, something had penetrated. The dunking stopped me wearing the cloak and more outlandish clothes, but, in the short term, it did nothing to change the ideas that had made me dress like that in the first place. I was different, I was better than others.

I was uniformly sarcastic and unpleasant to everyone, especially my friends. I'd learned by playing D&D that this was the way to get on with people. My friend Sara had responded to an advertisement outside a trendy hairdressers offering 'experimental styles.' She emerged looking awful, as if she'd intended to have a military buzz cut, but a fire alarm had gone off half-way through the clipping, forcing it to be abandoned. Everyone was telling her it looked OK, but she asked me.

'What do you think, Mark? I know you'll tell the truth.'

'I think,' I said, 'you would look better had you placed a turd on your head.'

She burst into tears. I was a bit shocked at this—I thought everyone essentially regarded themselves as figures of fun—but I was pleased. I thought it would make everyone else like me more that I'd managed to say something so cutting and that Sara herself would be impressed by my barbed wit, once she had stopped weeping.

Having done my time as someone who was bullied I was enjoying spending time as a bully. Not that that's how I would have seen it; I'd have just said I was speaking the truth in a vaguely amusing way. Of course it's possible to bully someone by speaking the truth, as someone called Spaz should have known. In fact, speaking the truth in an amusing way is perhaps the most effective way of bullying someone. The way we get on is to tell ourselves that the ugly, the artless, the untalented and the dull are all special in their own way and to help them sustain the illusion that they are valued and interesting. The best of us may even value them and find them interesting.

At the end of the first year my friend Brendan took me aside and pointed out that I was the most obnoxious person he'd ever met. To me 'obnoxious' had been a compliment. It took some explaining to see he was using it in its more usual pejorative sense.

'If you continue like this,' he said, 'you're going to have no friends.'

The thing was, I'd grown up to put as much value on the fantasy world as I did on the real one. In my mind I was a new Oscar Wilde, king of wit and liked by all. I didn't see that others might have viewed me as an oafish bully.

I did start to modify my behaviour, but, under the influence of drink or just carried away in company, my old self would emerge, snarling and looking for blood. I was a teenage werewolf. No, really I was.

Unhappy and deservedly rejected again, I took refuge in the university D&D society and a social situation whose rules I understood. I had thought that I'd grown out of the game, but it seemed I hadn't. Some of the scenarios the students were running seemed fascinating to me—dead gods being summoned at the time of the Russian Revolution, werewolves battling vampires.

Just as it looked as though I might get sucked back in for life, a way out presented itself in the form of live-action role-play. This is where grown men dress up as knights and trolls and hit each other with rubber swords. In public woods, where normal people go. There was plenty of time for this sort of thing at Sussex, as I only had four hours a week teaching. This low tutor input was justified by saying that the staff didn't want a 'hegemony of knowledge.' Didn't want to do any work, more like, was my view.

I really don't know what I was thinking by venturing into live-action role-play. Never mind the embarrassment, it was the danger that should have driven me away. The danger to others, that is. If any of my friends and family saw me grasping a sword made out of curtain rail and camping roll they'd say the same thing: 'You'll have someone's eye out with that.'

They were right. At the age of twenty-one I went into Falmer Woods near Brighton with a bunch of other student idiots and some fourteen-year-olds who had been recruited as goblins. The main dungeonmaster from the wargames club had organized it all, and he kept popping up as a cross between Billy Connolly and a wizard to give us riddles and directions. We encountered the goblins after about an hour, and battle commenced. The battle took about ten minutes, with breaks to allow dog walkers to pass. I had someone's eye out. One of the fourteen-year-old goblins came leaping towards me with claws represented by a couple of sponges dripping paint. Having trained as a fencer I'm quite good with a sword against a child with a sponge, and I lunged as he dived in, catching him straight in the eye. He fell to the floor with a scream and lay there crying. I tried to console him, but there was nothing for it; he'd have to go to hospital. He was developing a shiner, even as he shrieked. The DM said he'd take him to casualty in his car.

I suppose I should have gone, but, as I stood there with the weeping goblin at my feet, I was alarmed to see Karine, a good-looking Moroccan girl I knew, strolling into view with her friend Mary. They'd decided to choose the one day I'd gone goblin-bashing for a walk in the woods and a talk about political theory. I'd been trying to flirt with Karine for weeks, discovering an enthusiasm for radical left politics to match hers. At Sussex at that time it was death to admit to being middle-class. My background,

then, was gold dust, and I became more working-class than I'd
been when I was actually working-class. I'd spent years feeling
like a misfit among the car workers and brickies; suddenly I was
their best mate, a noble scion of the class struggle. This wasn't a
cynical move. I actually believed it and had milked it for all its
earthy glamour in the hope of getting into bed with Karine. I saw
all my chances evaporating right there in the woods.

'Hello,' I said, casually dropping the sword onto the writhing
child.

'What are you doing?' she said. 'And what are you wearing?'

'A tabard,' I said, like she'd asked me what my jeans were.
There was a low mewling from the floor as I tried to look as if I'd
just been disturbed reading a slim volume of Sartre on the left
bank of the Seine. That's not easy in a wool sweater that's been
spray-painted grey to resemble chain mail.

'What's it for?' she said. I knew she was into film and hoped she
might think it was related to that. The goblin continued wailing,
and I felt like leaning down with a dagger and finishing him off.

I didn't know how to reply to her. I suddenly saw myself as I
was. I wasn't Eric Bloodaxe, berserker of the Wolf Clan, caressing
his legendary sword Helmsplitter. I was me, Mark Barrowcliffe, a
normal man wanting to do a normal thing—that is, chat up a
girl—and being hampered by looking like a kid who'd gone mad
in the dressing-up box. I thought back to the humiliation of
being dumped in that fountain for wearing my cloak and realized,
far from being forced into the water, I should have leaped in myself to wash away my sins.

'You don't want to know what it's for,' I said. 'Look, there's a
tea room up there, do you fancy a cuppa?'

'OK,' she said.

'Aren't you going to see him to hospital?' said the DM.

'Not really,' I said.

'That's mean,' he said.

'Oh well,' I said, 'real life's a shit.'

And that was it for me and fantasy.

The Lost Boys

So what became of us D&Ders?

After university, I spent about a decade being deeply dissatisfied with my life and drinking heavily. All the time I'd been growing up I'd never felt bored, not even once. The trouble is that boredom is a fairly major component of most jobs. I had never learned to cope with it. After all those years in the fantasy kingdoms, life as a nine-to-five commuter felt like the worst sort of curse.

On one occasion, returning from a two-week break in the sun, I actually found myself crying on the way in to work. D&D had prepared me for a life of excitement. Now, it seemed, I was sentenced to crushing ennui for the rest of my days. I couldn't even pretend to be interested in my job and poured all my energies into my social life. If the work was dull on its own, then it became torture with a hangover. My attitude was ungrateful—I had good jobs, starting on a sought-after journalist training scheme and working up to be editor of a magazine—but you can't help the way you feel.

Eventually I really couldn't stand work any longer and decided it was better to be a pauper in a fantasy world than relatively well off in the real one. Without D&D I don't think I'd have been so unhappy and would not have left to become a writer. That might have been a good thing. At the very least I'd be driving a better car.

For Porter the flame of D&D never died while I knew him. He came back from university at the holidays, and some weekends, and we played his latest obsession—Call of Cthulhu, set in a 1920s haunted by ancient horrors and, you guessed it, stalking madness. The Porter who came back and played with me in my sixth-form years, though, wasn't the one who'd been away. The defensive, angry character who could never let a slight go unpunished that I'd known in my early youth had been replaced by someone who was, if anything, something of a softy. Whereas before we'd joked that we should take a photo whenever he made a cup of coffee, now he provided beer whenever we met.

The reason was easy to see. He'd got a girlfriend. Unbelievably she was a wargamer too, but quite a jolly sort who brought out the best in Andy. Those games were very enjoyable—the presence of women calms the excesses of male behaviour and Andy's generally benevolent air actually freed his creativity and allowed him to come up with some memorable scenarios.

I suspect he'd had some sort of falling out with Sean Gardener, although nothing was said, because Sean never showed up at these games in later years. Sean said the problem was that you no longer had to just keep on the right side of Porter, you had to keep on the right side of his girlfriend too.

'He was trailing about on the end of her string and ended up dancing off into the sunset like Pinocchio,' said Sean, with characteristic generosity.

Andy sort of lionized Sean when he first met him and started to copy his unrelenting sarcasm. When he first described Sean to me it was in very complimentary terms, saying how funny he was in lessons and how, due to lack of work in physics, Sean had scored less on the multiple choice than a monkey with a pin would have. We knew this because the physics teacher had said so.

'You, Gardener, have scored less than a monkey with a pin. It's a shame we can't have you replaced by a monkey, pin or no, as it would smell less, and it would certainly be tidier.'

'I can't be expected to compete on those terms,' said Gardener. 'I haven't got a pin.'

I think Andy was living a sort of vicarious defiance of authority through Sean for a time. As much as we fantasized in the game, we fantasized about each other. Boys look up to other boys when they see someone like them, but winning. Sean wasn't winning, but he revelled so much in his bad results and his weirdness that it sort of seemed that way. Eventually, though, I think Gardener's chaotic nature got too much for Andy. He was looking for someone to team up with, a relationship of mutual admiration, which no one was ever going to get from Sean.

Under Julie's influence, Andy's transformation was amazing. Whereas his dungeons had been lengthy exercises in revenge against enemies real and perceived it now became virtually impossible to die in them. His girlfriend did gain the nickname 'The Immortal Julie' because she was particularly invulnerable to death in the game and particularly handsomely rewarded, but there were benefits for us all. The games moved away from the 'bash and grab' dice-rolling fests of our earlier years and became more like storytelling.

He'd also dropped the heavy metal and started extolling to me the virtues of the music I'd been extolling to him when we first met. I still must have looked up to him quite a lot because his embrace of the Talking Heads and New Order allowed me to discover my interest in Joy Division, The Smiths and Half Man Half Biscuit.

The fact that most people turned out to be decent human beings away from the group and under the influence of women leads me to conclude that it wasn't really D&D that had caused us to behave so vilely to each other but masculinity itself. Shutting ourselves away in male-only company for our entire youth was like distilling that maleness, taking all other influences away and just leaving us with our dark selves. The only way that D&D was to blame is that it gave us a reason to be in those rooms, face to face for all those years, like an extended reality TV show that you couldn't be voted off.

I suspect that some of the reason for our more unpleasant behaviour was that we were bored and didn't know it. I don't mean bored by the game, just bored by each other and the limits of our world. In the end Andy and I realized a fundamental truth of our relationship—we weren't that similar—and we simply drifted apart. I know through mutual acquaintances he played for many years after I did, but I have no idea if he's still doing it today.

Most of us grew up. I bumped into Kev Gerling when I was about twenty, and he was embarrassed about his childish Nazism. He too was with a girl, who seemed light-hearted and very good fun.

'I could still never vote for the reds,' he said, 'but all that's behind me.'

His girlfriend listened to the story of when he proposed raising money for the school by raffling for the right to wear his German World War II helmet about the place for a week with absolute amazement. She clearly didn't recognize the person he'd been, and I guessed that, when they spent their evenings in together, he reached for the Barry White rather than the Horst Wessel song.

Hatherley did the best in his exams and became a lawyer and, from what I hear, a credit to his profession. The last I heard he was some key figure in an international human rights charity and politically solidly in the middle ground, so he changed his point of view with maturity too. His childish worship of posh people was only likely to last until he met a few of them. Or perhaps *Brideshead Revisited* came out on the TV and made him fashionable, something he couldn't stand to be.

I don't know what happened to Dennis Walters at all, although I think it inevitable that he grew up too. You can't spend your whole life barking 'niggers and coons!' as your only conversation. Well, not and keep your teeth.

Sean Gardener, despite once weaving his dead gerbil's tail into his hair and wearing its back legs *as a love charm*, eventually married and settled down. His sarcasm, thank God, abated, and now it is quite possible to have a conversation with him.

Chigger dropped out of university because, to quote him, 'I was so far ahead of the others they'd asked me to wait a year to allow them to catch up.' He waited a year and was, the last time I heard, still waiting. All I can say is that the others must have been a long way behind. I know he married and went on to work in computers, but beyond that I am in the dark.

One of the D&Ders who stuck at it into his twenties had a D&D wedding—every guest dressed up as a cleric, magic-user, wizard or monster. This is the sort of thing that's so embarrassing I'm almost ducking beneath the desk as I type. Still, it was his special day and up to him and his bride how they approached it. As an abstract point, though, I can't imagine many mothers being too happy to watch their daughters walk up the aisle accompanied by the horror that is the undead wizard The Lich, particularly if they themselves had been forced to dress as a mummy.

I did meet Billy again. I saw him for the first time in twenty-five years, just after my first book came out. He got hold of my email via my publishers and contacted me out of the blue. We met at Victoria station.

When you see someone after such a gap of time you think that their reality will disappoint your memory, the larger-than-life figures of youth will seem pale in the harsh light of the present. I was nervous, as I saw Billy's train pull in, as to whether I'd recognize him or not. I needn't have worried. From the end of the platform I saw a large red mass moving behind the commuters. It was Billy, bigger than I'd ever known him, clad in a scarlet shirt and leather waistcoat, thumping his way down the platform. It was as if he was the living embodiment of the past looming towards me, diminishing and shrinking the feeble present. I actually felt that I might fall over as the thought struck me: 'He hasn't changed a bit.' Weirdly, I found this a very unwelcome sensation. In fact he'd done something more than not change. From a distance he seemed more like himself than he'd been when he was fifteen.

I'd thought that we rely on people from the past not to alter. In fact, I think it's the other way around. After such a long period apart you kind of expect people to have moved on and to be laughing indulgently at the folly of youth. In Billy's case, just from the look of him, I had the strong feeling he'd not yet started what he was meant to be doing. When we parted he'd been heavily into rock music. Coming towards me down the platform he looked still like the sort of person who was heavily into rock music and, more than that, wanted to be seen to be into rock music.

On top of this, I supposed he'd be thinner. I am a shallow person when it comes to weight, and, even though I tend to the chubby side myself, I can't regard anyone fat as truly happy. I know that position is indefensible. In fact, it's not even a position. My position is that someone's body is independent of their soul, and that it's ludicrous and discriminatory to be censorious. My prejudice is that fatties are miserable and, in some way, failures. Winston Churchill, take note.

I think I'd expected that Billy would have thrown off his puppy fat and would now be dressed for the left bank of the Seine, slim and handsome, with a Gauloise in his hand and a picture of the French actress he was dating in his wallet—in short, still me as I would want to be. I didn't want him to represent an attainable ideal, just to be this source of burning light, some of which would fall on me and that I could reflect, just like when we were kids.

He saw me and came forward to shake my hand. I think I'd expected his normal 'Hail to thee, blithe spirit, thank heavens the sun has gone in so we can proceed directly to the pub without having to go out and enjoy it,' or some quote about railway stations always carrying a little flavour of their trains' eventual destinations. Instead he just shook my hand and said, 'Hello.' I felt odd, as if all the sins of my youth, all that bullshit I'd believed, all the weird ways of thinking and stupid ideas I'd had were going to come crashing down on me, or as if he might deposit their broken remains at my feet and say, 'I'm afraid I'm going to have to ask you to pay for these.' It was so strange, as if he was some magician with the capability of turning me back into my teenage self, and I imagined the crowds of Victoria looking at me now as people looked at me then, but this time I could feel their derision. I knew I cared what people thought, and I had long lost the mechanisms for hiding that fact from myself. I wasn't wearing a cut-off jacket with Black Sabbath written on the back or, God help us, the eagle of the band Saxon acrylized by Andy Porter, but I felt like I was. I wanted to run around shouting 'he's still him, but I'm not still me! Don't think that! I'm Mark Barrowcliffe, Spaz is dead! Look, I got this jacket in Gap like a normal person.' Naturally, I restrained the urge.

'How have you been?' I said, which is a somewhat daunting question after a break of twenty-five years.

'Well,' said Billy, although he seemed slightly nervous. I'd never noticed that in him before. I'm not saying he'd never been nervous, just that I'd never noticed it. I was nervous too. When we'd last known each other our relationship had been clearly defined—teacher and pupil. Between fifteen and seventeen, two years are an eon; between forty and forty-two, a doze in the sun, you scarcely notice them pass. It was as if we'd learned a dance together years before, and now we were trying to perform it again, but this time I was expected to take my share in leading. It was familiar but different and difficult.

Victoria swirled around us, and I realized that Billy, at three hundred sixty pounds in a shirt the colour of a stop light topped by the familiar blond mop, had achieved the impossible. He was standing out, *in London*. I've seen that about two times in nearly twenty years of living in the city, and one of them was bumping into the performance artist Leigh Bowery. Then I had the most terrible feeling, one that I never thought I'd associate with Billy at all, at once patronizing, presumptuous and unasked for—I felt that I wanted to look after him. I could never, ever, have thought that would happen. Billy looked after me, not the other way around.

We went for a drink in the Coach and Horses, the pub popular with the staff of the humour magazine *Private Eye,* because that's where we would have loved to have gone as kids. Billy had introduced me to *Private Eye,* and we'd spent a good deal of effort aping that wit.

I'd been wrong, though. Billy had changed. Not only was he much quieter in manner, but he'd given up smoking. Somehow fags just seemed so much part of him, his irreverence and sod-authority attitude, that I almost wanted to start smoking again to encourage him. That Billy, it appeared, was gone. I was struck by how cowed he was compared to the mad figure I'd known as a kid. What I didn't know was that he was having a truly terrible time at work under a bullying boss and was also quite ill. I was alarmed, though, to see that his former fearlessness seemed to have left him.

It was shocking to discover, as well, that he hadn't done well in his final university exams and was doing the work of a jobbing scientist rather than one of the leaders in the field. I think I'd imagined that he would have gone through what I went through but that he'd have done it better, that he'd be a successful actor or a politician or a top scientist.

I'd arrogantly presumed that he wanted to contact me partly because I'd achieved a sort of very low-ebb fame, beyond the Z list. You'd have needed the Russian alphabet to chart my level of celebrity, but my name had appeared in the national papers a few times. Within three pints I had the hubris knocked out of me.

'Shall we have one more or shall we go to the restaurant now?' I said. I know four pints is few people's idea of an aperitif, but you can take the lads out of Coventry and all that.

'The Bible tells us that drinking is acceptable but drunkenness isn't,' said Billy.

I looked left and right.

'Er, why are we worried about what the Bible tells us?' I said.

'Prepare to suspend your disbelief,' said Billy, with a hint of his old theatricality. 'I have been born again.'

He wasn't winding me up. I would have been less surprised if he'd told me he'd been selected as the next Dalai Lama.

'You didn't get in contact with me to convert me, did you?' I said.

'Well, you might want to think about it,' said Billy.

I had that sensation where the upper body remains perfectly still, but the legs feel as though they are straining to get to the door. Then something strange happened. I'd spent years trying to civilize myself, to restrain the impulses I'd learned in the slaughterhouses of D&D's suburban living rooms. I really had made the effort to be nicer. All that suddenly fell away.

'Have you gone fucking mad?' I enquired.

He, raised in the same slaughterhouses, didn't take offence at all but leaped straight into an argument with a lot of his old verve. And there we were, him on the Bible, me on Darwin, my knowledge of whom comes almost solely from what he told me as a youth. It was great, just like old times. We could have been chewing lumps out of each other over how deeply sleeps the Chimera or the effectiveness of chainmail against needles.

Five hours later we'd actually forgotten to eat, though not to drink, and were continuing the argument back at my house. It could have been 1979. I was almost tempted to break out the Empire of the Petal Throne.

How had Billy come to get God of all things? I have my own ideas that disagree with his. Billy, like me, wanted to believe in the fantasy world, that things were going to be special and amazing and fun and found real life a bit mundane. Like me, he had been drawn to drugs, though not to the occult. The one thing you could say about Billy was that he was never a dilettante. If he went for something he went for it, and it was the same with narcotics. His precocious ability at chemistry meant that he was able to synthesize a personal supply of some fairly potent drugs. I think it's fair to call that a mixed blessing. He told me that he dropped a tab of acid before walking in to his final chemistry exam, one of many he was to drop in the subsequent years. Needless to say, this did not enhance his performance.

He'd gone through that awful hippy demi-monde of late-night hot-knife sessions, and cheap speed in flats with fading Pink Floyd posters covering up the damp, and acid taken beneath thirty-year-old wallpaper. His tragedy was that, at twenty-five, he'd become the sort of person he admired at fifteen, a druggy, a rock DJ, the one who would always take more than anyone else and hold it together better. By forty he was someone he'd never even dreamed of.

'I know what people think, that I've fried my brains on acid and got God,' he said. 'It's not like that; it's a rational decision. If I hadn't taken acid I'd probably be less paranoid and a lot more successful, but that's about it,' he said.

'Well, when you put it like that, I regret not doing a load myself,' I said.

I'm not sure I do think it was the LSD that flipped Billy over to religion. Maybe religion is just another fantasy kingdom, another place where magic is true, or maybe he's right. He said he's looked at his church's interpretation of the Bible and found that it fits reality at every point. I wouldn't know, I haven't read it.

The thing about Billy is that he was always a believer, in some sense. He threw himself wholeheartedly into anything he did, D&D, LSD or religion. I've written some things in this book that I thought he might find uncomfortable or difficult—particularly about his drug-taking and my reactions to him when I first saw him again.

'How could I object to it?' he said. 'It's true.'

I found this a strange viewpoint. The truth about themselves is the one thing the majority of people find the most objectionable. It's certainly a central reason some boys spend every waking hour playing D&D.

This honesty characterized Billy's approach to the game. He was a purist. Even today he's still working on a game. We still see each other occasionally, and he's said to me that he can't quite believe that I don't have the obsession I once did or that I don't want to play any more.

'I really thought we'd be doing it for the rest of our lives,' he said. 'I keep expecting you to tell me about a new dungeon you've designed or a game you've bought. I ask myself was it just me that it meant so much to?'

Earlier on, I said that, in one reading of our personal history the ending of our friendship was a disaster for both of us. Perhaps that's overstating the case, but I think that, had we remained friends, I might have been less rudderless until early middle age and, putting it bluntly, he might not have done all that acid.

I think both Billy and I were looking for a true friendship— people who gave us self-respect—and for a time we had it. Out of each other's company we went, in our different ways, to where unhappy people always go—the extremes.

Still, who knows, and maybe what we had was the best we could have hoped for. When I go for a drink with him today he doesn't think that, without wargaming, I'm quite me, and I don't think that, with religion, it's quite him. We get by well enough, nevertheless.

Homeward Bound

As research for this book I did play a couple of games of D&D again. I was interested to see how the game had changed since my day. Though the rules were more complex and immeasurably better thought out and presented, I had to conclude that it hadn't.

They were all there—the sneaks, the silent, the megalomaniacs and the plain weird. This may have had something to do with the fact that I had to seek out an adult gaming group because, well, how would you feel about a forty-year-old pitching up out of the blue to play with your adolescent son? If you're still playing into your twenties and beyond then you're an addict. Maybe there's a whole load of normal adult gamers out there, but I just have bad luck. So there I was again, at the extreme edge.

As the first game began I could have almost been back twenty-five years before; all the buzz words were there. We were playing a system that didn't involve dice, as that was more 'sophisticated' and 'superior.' The dungeonmaster's voice crackled with emotion as he described the mighty power of the overlord of his game; he became slightly annoyed when someone mentioned a sort of sword he hadn't heard of. One of the players could have almost been turned out from a D&D nerd mould—he was small, weedy and obsessed with martial arts. He also worked as a computer programmer.

'What do you do?' he said.

'I'm a writer,' I said.

'Ah, what format do you find best?' he said. 'Is it the . . .' and he went into some stuff about computers that I didn't understand.

'No,' I said, 'I don't write ebooks; I write real books, like those on the shelf.'

'You have a publisher?' he said.

'Yes.'

'You can buy your books in shops?'

'Some of them, yeah.'

He sniffed and sat upright.

'Well,' he said, 'I think you will find that *I* am a consummate storyteller.'

Somehow, it seemed, I'd managed to offend him, so I clearly haven't completely lost the old magic.

Later there was even a little knowledge competition over casualty rates in combat. Yes, I did get drawn in, and yes, I was quite pleased to point out to the bloodthirsty crew that most soldiers throughout history have actually aimed to miss when it comes to battle and that . . . I stopped there.

I was getting drawn back in. I surveyed the room. It was like that bit in *The Lord of the Rings* on the way to Rivendell when Frodo puts on the ring and suddenly enters the wraith world of the Black Riders with them all chanting 'Come to Mordor' at him. I looked at the character sheet in my hand. If I didn't put it down I was headed back, back into proving how smart I was to a group of nerds who any sane person should run from like a vampire from a twelfth-level cleric.

'Actually,' I said, 'I'm feeling rather ill. I think I'm going to have to go.'

I got out into the cool air of the street and made my way to my car. It was as if I was slightly disembodied as I moved. I could hear a noise I couldn't place. Then I looked down and realized it was coming from my feet; I was running. Something in my subconscious was rushing me back to my wife, the dog, the TV, away from the lands of fantasy and towards reality, the place I can now call home.